NATIONAL GEOGRAPHIC

T R A V E L E R

dominican
republic

Date: 5/22/17

NATIONAL GEOGRAPHIC

TRAVELER

dominican republic

Christopher P. Baker
Photography by Gilles Mingasson

National Geographic
Washington, D.C.

CONTENTS

Pages 2–3: Fishermen on Playa Rincón haul in their nets at the end of the day.
Opposite: Dusk descends upon the Zona Colonial, Santo Domingo

TRAVELING WITH EYES OPEN

Alert travelers go with a purpose and leave with a benefit. If you travel responsibly, you can help support wildlife conservation, historic preservation, and cultural enrichment in the places you visit. You can enrich your own travel experience as well.

To be a geo-savvy traveler:

- Recognize that your presence has an impact on the places you visit.

- Spend your time and money in ways that sustain local character. (Besides, it's more interesting that way.)

- Value the destination's natural and cultural heritage.

- Respect the local customs and traditions.

- Express appreciation to local people about things you find interesting and unique to the place: its nature and scenery, music and food, historic villages and buildings.

- Vote with your wallet: Support the people who support the place, patronizing businesses that make an effort to celebrate and protect what's special there. Seek out local shops, restaurants, and inns. Use tour operators who love their home—who love taking care of it and showing it off. Avoid businesses that detract from the character of the place.

- Enrich yourself, taking home memories and stories to tell, knowing that you have contributed to the preservation and enhancement of the destination.

That is the type of travel now called geotourism, defined as "tourism that sustains or enhances the geographical character of a place—its environment, culture, aesthetics, heritage, and the well-being of its residents." To learn more, visit National Geographic's Center for Sustainable Destinations at *travel.nationalgeographic.com/travel/geotourism.*

TRAVELER

dominican republic

ABOUT THE AUTHOR & THE PHOTOGRAPHER

After earning degrees in geography at the University of London and Latin American studies at the University of Liverpool, **Christopher P. Baker** *(christopherbaker.com)* settled in California and established a career as a travel writer, photographer, lecturer, and tour leader. In addition to *National Geographic Traveler: Dominican Republic,* he has also authored and photographed guidebooks to Colombia, Costa Rica, Cuba, and Panama in the National Geographic Traveler series, plus *Mi Moto Fidel: Motorcycling Through Castro's Cuba* (a two-time National Book Award winner) for National Geographic Adventure Press. The Lowell Thomas Award 2008 Travel Journalist of the Year, Christopher has also written and photographed for publications from *National Geographic Traveler* to *Newsweek.* He has spoken on Cuba at National Geographic headquarters, the National Press Club, and the World Affairs Council, and has appeared on CNN, Fox News, MSNBC, the National Geographic Channel, NPR, and numerous other radio and TV outlets. Baker is a National Geographic Resident Expert and escorts tours of Costa Rica and Panama, plus Colombia and Cuba, for National Geographic Expeditions.

Photographer **Gilles Mingasson** grew up in Grenoble, France, before moving to Paris to pursue photojournalism. After being sent to the United States on assignment, he made Los Angeles his base. In 1990 Mingasson spent six months bicycling 7,500 miles (more than 12,000 km) across the Soviet Union with two cameras (and a serious saddle rash). On the eve of profound changes that few had yet grasped, he photographed ordinary people who had lived their entire lives under the Soviet state. Today, Mingasson works on feature and travel stories for clients including *Newsweek, Fortune, Reader's Digest, Scholastic, Sky, Le Nouvel Observateur, L'Equipe* magazine, *Reppublica Delle Donne, Espresso, Elle,* and *Le Figaro.* Some of his projects have included NASCAR dads, global warming in a northern village, and a documentary on Latinos in the United States. Assignments have taken him to Asia, Australia, Latin America, Europe, India, and North Africa.

Charting Your Trip

Taking up two-thirds of the island of Hispaniola, the Dominican Republic packs all that's best about the Caribbean into one country. Many visitors are drawn to its talcum white sands fringing warm turquoise waters. Beyond the beaches, you'll be captivated by gorgeous countryside rising to forested mountains, by a wealth of wildlife, and by the ancient convents, fortresses, and cobbled streets of Santo Domingo—the capital, and the Caribbean's original colonial city.

Getting Around

The Dominican Republic, or "D.R." as it is colloquially known, is by Caribbean standards a large country at 18,816 square miles (48,734 sq km). Large enough, in fact, that flying is a viable way of getting between distant cities and resorts. Three domestic airlines—Aeronaves Dominicana *(fly-dominicana.com)*, AirCentury *(air century.com)*, and Dominican Shuttles *(dominicanshuttles.com)*—offer commuter flights; and private planes can be chartered through Dominican Shuttles.

Caribe Tours *(caribetours.com.do)* and Metro Expreso *(metroserviciosturisticos.com)* provide frequent service between most towns aboard comfortable air-conditioned buses, and Expreso Bávaro *(expresobavaro.com)* offers similar service between Santo Domingo and Punta Cana. *Colectivos* (shared minivans), which can be waved down on the street, are the staple of intra-town travel and within cities. Remote rural regions are served by pickup trucks known as *gua-guas* (pronounced WAH-wahs): unsafe, but great fun if you don't mind sharing with chickens. In towns and resort areas, stick to tourist taxis. *Carros públicos* (shared taxis) and *motoconchos* (small motorcycle taxis) offer a hair-raising ride. Santo Domingo is served by an efficient subway rail system.

Renting a car is a viable option for exploring, especially off the beaten track. The main highways are well paved, although secondary roads are often badly potholed or even unpaved. You'll need a four-wheel-drive vehicle for venturing away from main roads. Two major highways crisscross the nation. One links Santo Domingo eastward to the main resort of Punta Cana and west to the

Palm trees shade the streets and beaches of the Dominican Republic.

remote Barahona region—an evolving center of ecotourism. A second highway runs north–south, connecting Santo Domingo and Santiago de los Cabelleros (the republic's second largest city), gateway to the northern resort town of Puerto Plata and, beyond, to the town of Monte Cristi. A highway also links the capital city with the Samaná Peninsula.

If You Have One Week

The D.R. is small enough that it is possible to visit two or three distinct regions on a short trip. It makes sense to plan an ideal one-week itinerary around either Santo Domingo (rich in colonial heritage) and Punta Cana (boasting superb beaches and activities), or Puerto Plata (combining a historic core, fine beaches, and nearby mountains) and the north coast. Both are served by direct flights from North America and Europe.

For a Santo Domingo–based trip, depending on your arrival, **Day 1** could be spent exploring the historic Zona Colonial, centered on Parque Colón. On **Day 2** you'll want to continue strolling the Zona Colonial, being sure to include Fortaleza Ozama, a fortress dating back to 1502. At night, you'll want to dine alfresco in Plaza de España.

Day 3 can include a visit to Plaza de la Cultura, hosting a trio of museums that are dedicated to art, history, and natural sciences. Nature lovers should also visit the Jardín Botánico Nacional—a botanic garden whose highlight is the orchid house. Round out the day with the Faro a Colón, a mausoleum supposedly containing Christopher Columbus's remains.

Take a taxi or rent a car (three hours) to transfer to Punta Cana for **Days 4, 5,** and **6.** En route, call in at Cueva de las Maravillas to marvel at this spectacular underground cavern; at Alto de Chavón (a 30-minute drive farther east), outside La Romana, for lunch in a stupendous setting; and at the Basilica de Nuestra Señora de la Altagracia, a magnificent modernist cathedral in Higüey, a 45-minute drive from La Romana. No doubt you'll also want a full day relaxing on the gorgeous white-sand beaches at Punta Cana, while another day can be spent enjoying excursions,

---

NOT TO BE MISSED:

Strolling the cobbled streets of Santo Domingo's Zona Colonial 60–68

A visit to the Catedral Primada de América 61–63

Sunning and swimming at Punta Cana 104–105

Whale-watching in Bahía de Samaná 115

Carnaval in La Vega 147

White-water rafting on the Río Yaque del Norte 166–167

Viewing crocodiles at Lago Enriquillo 189

Tourism Bureaus

General tourism information is provided by the Dominican Republic's **Ministry of Tourism** (*Calle Cayetano Germosen & Ave. Gregorio Luperón, Santo Domingo, tel 809/221-4660, godominicanrepublic .com*). Offices abroad include: **United States** (*136 E. 57th St., Ste. 803, New York, NY 10022, tel 212/588-1012 or 888/374-6361*) **Canada** (*2055 Peel Street, Suite 550, Montreal, Quebec H3A 1V4, tel 514/499-1918 or 800/563-1611*) **United Kingdom** (*18–21 Hand Court, High Holbon, London WC1V6JF, tel 020/7242-7778*) Regional information bureaus can also be found around the country. (See p. 201 for addresses.)

Wet or Dry?

The nation has distinct wet (May–Oct.) and dry (Nov.–April) seasons and weather is fairly predictable throughout the year. Dry season is considered the best time for touring, as sunny skies and lack of rain are the norm. It's also high season, when many hotels are full, rental cars book up, and rates for both are raised.

Wet season sees a fall in visitors and in hotel and car rental rates. This season has its benefits, as the country is lush from all the rains. In most areas, rainfall is typically an afternoon affair, often limited to short-lived downpours. However, heavy, prolonged rain is possible anywhere, even in dry season. Hurricanes are a remote possibility from July through October.

The Dominican Republic also has microclimates and regional variations. While temperatures throughout the country vary little year-round, the relatively dry southwest region can broil in summer. Elsewhere the lowlands are humid year-round. The North Coast receives its heaviest rainfall November to January. And the Cordillera Central offers mild temperatures year-round, with a cool alpine climate at highest elevations.

---

such as paragliding, swimming with dolphins, ATV tours, and horseback rides. On **Day 7,** transfer to Santo Domingo for your flight home, or sun and swim before a flight home from Punta Cana.

Puerto Plata Base: If you choose Puerto Plata, begin **Day 1** with a horse-drawn coach ride around the old city and along the seafront. Then spend the rest of the day on foot, including a visit to the Amber Museum. On **Day 2,** spend half a day at the Ocean World Adventure Park, then cool off in the afternoon with an excursion to 27 Charco de Damajagua Natural Monument, where you can use natural water slides. On **Day 3** take an excursion boat to Cayo Paraíso and Punta Rica to enjoy the beaches. For **Day 4,** hire a car or taxi and transfer to Cabarete, arriving in time to go windsurfing or kitesurfing. Spend **Day 5** relaxing on the beach and **Day 6** exploring Parque Nacional El Choco; scuba divers should head to nearby Sosúa. Next day return to Puerto Plata for your homebound flight.

EXPERIENCE: Renting a Car

Renting a car is a great way to get around the Dominican Republic, but it comes with some warnings. Although roads throughout most of the country are in good condition, a four-wheel-drive vehicle is essential for tackling minor roads. Stray cattle, pedestrians, and potholes are hazards. And local drivers can be reckless. Drive the speed limit and be watchful.

Don't leave anything in your car for fear of theft. Don't pay tickets on the spot; take care of them later with your rental company.

Insurance is mandatory. Check in advance if the rental company will honor insurance issued abroad and if your insurance will cover the Dominican Republic.

Rental companies operating in the D.R. include **Avis** *(tel 809/826-4600 or 800/331-1084, avis.com)* and **Europcar** *(tel 809/688-2121 or 809/686-2861, europcar.com).*

Baseball is a Dominican passion. Many youngsters hope for a big-league future.

If You Have More Time

For a second week in the country, focus on the mountain towns **(Day 1),** such as Jarabacoa (allow two hours driving from Santo Domingo) and Constanza (one hour farther), in the Cordillera Central, where adventure seekers can find thrills white-water rafting **(Day 2)** and hiking to the summit of Pico Duarte **(Days 3–5).** A tour of this region can be combined with exploring the lowland valley of El Cibao **(Days 6–7),** east of the Cordillera: The vale is studded with intriguing colonial towns, such as La Vega, and with tobacco plantations.

Birders will want to head to the republic's southwest, around **Barahona** (a three-hour drive from Santo Domingo), where the Sierra de Neiba **(Day 1)** and Sierra de Baoruco mountains **(Days 2–3)** and nearby Lago Enriquillo and Laguna de Oviedo **(Days 4–5)** offer dozens of endemic species. The region offers plenty of options for hiking, as well as for camping at remote and lovely Bahía de las Águilas **(Day 6).** Return to Santo Domingo from Barahona via **Las Salinas (Day 7)** to hike giant sand dunes; and visit the caves at **El Pomier** to admire pre-Columbian pictographs. ■

Tipping Tips

In the Dominican Republic, tipping is used to reward good service, rather than given automatically. Most restaurants add a 10 percent service charge to the bill; there's no obligation to pay extra. On group tours, tip guides $1 per person per day; $5 daily per person is an appropriate fee for private tour guides (U.S. dollars are accepted everywhere). Tip bellboys 50 cents per bag. Chambermaids are often overlooked—$1 per day is plenty. Note that taxi drivers don't normally expect tips, and should never receive a tip if they display aggressive or disrespectful driving.

History & Culture

Statues of Spanish monarchs at
Quinta Dominicana, Zona Colonial,
Santo Domingo
Opposite: Tumbling 285 feet (87 m),
the Salto de Agua Blanca, near
Constanza, feeds a jade-colored pool.

Dominican Republic Today

Taking up the eastern two-thirds of the island of Hispaniola, which the republic shares with Haiti, this stunningly beautiful country ranges from desert-dry basins to sky-high cloud forests.

No wonder that the Caribbean's most visited isle is currently riding a tourism wave. An all-inclusive resort juggernaut has swept over the north coast and the so-called Costa del Coco, transforming the region into the Caribbean's value-priced leader in mass-market chic. Meanwhile, ever higher levels of luxury are attracting a hip celebrity clientele.

A land with a lively Latin spirit and a gracious people, the second largest country in the Caribbean is affectionately known as the soulful "D.R." True, urban wealth contrasts sharply with poverty. Notoriously bad roads and even worse drivers, a dysfunctional electricity grid, and a dubious water system have helped boost the success of all-inclusive hotels. These and other problems are usually a footnote for tourists, who thrill to sugar-fine sands, a glittering nightlife, a generous people, and a fascinating history dating back to Christopher Columbus's first voyage in 1492.

The ruins of La Isabela and La Vega Vieja (sites of two of the first Spanish settlements in the New World) provide mute testimony to the arrival of Columbus. Santo Domingo boasts the Western Hemisphere's first cathedral and fortress. And the gingerbread structures of Puerto Plata and Santiago de los Caballeros recall the 19th-century wealth of the sugar and tobacco booms. While the cobbled plazas of Santo Domingo still echo with the boot steps of conquistadores, the capital city is also a modern metropolis. It has high-rise banks, hotels, and casinos, plus trendy restaurants and bars serving superb rums and cigars.

> **While the cobbled plazas of Santo Domingo still echo with the boot steps of conquistadores, the capital city is also a modern metropolis.**

Landscapes span the spectrum in this sultry island country. The southeast—the center of beach-focused *turismo*—is lined by seamless white sands and waters in crayon blue colors. Humpback whales pay seasonal visits to the warm waters of the Bahía de Samaná (Samaná Bay). In the Valle del Cibao, the tapestry changes to lush green *vegas* (fields) where some of the world's finest tobacco and coffee is grown. The sierras and cordilleras are rugged mountains shaded by mist-shrouded forests that shelter endangered mammals and a profusion of endemic bird species. The cactus-studded southwest is home to crocodiles, iguanas, and flamingos. Marine turtles crawl ashore to lay their eggs in talcum sands. Manatees thrive amid coastal lagoons.

All that diversity makes for some fabulous recreation. Cabarete, on the north coast, is the extreme–water-sports epicenter of the West Indies, while inland, hikers can take to the trails that lead to the summit of Pico Duarte, the highest point in the Caribbean. Other activities range from world-class golfing to white-water rafting and scuba diving.

The Dominicans

Hispaniola's original inhabitants may have numbered as many as 500,000 indigenous peoples on the eve of Columbus's arrival. Predominant were the Taíno, relatives of the Arawakan people of South America. Most of these aborigines rapidly succumbed to disease and the ruthlessness of 16th-century Spanish conquistadores. As the early Spanish colonists cleared the forests and planted sugarcane, they imported African slaves. The

Santo Domingo's Zona Colonial boasts the first cathedral built in the Americas.

colonists were joined by merchants, seafarers, and entrepreneurs who came to the island from Europe throughout the 17th, 18th, and 19th centuries.

During the 19th century, many Spaniards arrived from the Canary Islands, followed at the close of the century by a wave of Syrian and Palestinian traders and by migrants from Anguilla and Tortola, imported to cut cane—their English-speaking descendants are known as *cocolos.* The 1930s witnessed the arrival of a small community of Japanese farmers and of Jewish settlers fleeing Nazi persecution; both groups were welcomed by dictator Rafael Trujillo as an effort to dilute Dominicans' African blood.

In modern times, European and North American immigrants have added their singular ingredients to the bouillabaisse. Thousands of Haitian immigrants have also poured over the border. Facing extreme discrimination, many of them live in *bateyes*—shantytowns near the fields where they perform backbreaking labor cutting cane. Meanwhile, the island has also experienced a massive exodus of Dominicans seeking brighter horizons in the United States.

Class & Color

Dominicans are intensely patriotic, and their communal identity is shaped in part by the quest for freedom from the yoke of Haiti, Spain, and the United States. The Dominicans' sense of self reflects a convoluted concept of race derived from an uneasy relationship with the nation next door. The evolution of *criollo* Dominican society (emphasizing "pure" Spanish bloodlines) differed markedly from that of Haiti, characterized by its repressive slave system and minority white population. In the Dominican Republic slavery was relatively weak and the population was mainly mulatto—mixed black, white, and Taíno.

> **The friendly Dominican people are gracious to a fault. Family life is the all-important center of social interaction.**

Although Dominican society appears well integrated, it is in fact hierarchical, with a white *(blanco)* elite at the top, blacks at the bottom, and all manner of shades in between: *trigueno* (olive-skinned), *lavado* (washed), *canelo* (cinnamon), *quemado* (burnt), and *oscuro* (dark). Although some 84 percent of the population of 10.5 million is either black or mulatto (officially classified as *indios*), Dominicans downplay their African heritage: Trujillo, for example, used skin-lightening creams to cover up his dark skin. The term *negro* (black) is reserved by Dominicans for Haitians, who are treated with a disdain born of Haiti's historical attempts to conquer the Dominican Republic.

The close-knit *genta primera* (first people) compose an aristocratic elite derived from the colonial gentry. Based in Santiago and the Cibao Valley, the group still dominates the country's political and business life. Down the social ladder, the predominantly mulatto middle class and *nuevos ricos* (nouveaux riches) dominate the civil service, professions, and tourist industry.

Fishing boats rest on a beach in Baoruco, a small village on the Barahona Peninsula.

Dominican Lifestyle

The capital, Santo Domingo, is an urbane city of 2.9 million people; Santiago de los Caballeros (population 575,000) competes. Most other towns are regional market centers. Two-thirds of the population is urban, with many forming an underclass of *marginados* (including *campunos,* rural-urban migrants) living in slum shacks hammered together from scraps. The majority of rural folks are landless and live simply, often in humbling poverty.

The republic's annual per-capita income in 2014 was $10,000, but the country suffers from marked income inequality. Almost one-third of the population lives below the poverty line. Unemployment hovers around 15 percent. The availability and quality of health care are poor. While public schooling is obligatory and free, eight percent of the population is illiterate. Cash sent from relatives abroad brightens many Dominicans' lives (for marginados, the quest for a visa to the United States is a national pastime). By contrast, a sizable and forward-focused middle class lives in comfort, while the wealthiest families send their offspring to private schools and to universities in North America. Entrepreneurship is advanced, and hotels fill on weekends with middle-class families spending their disposable incomes.

The friendly Dominican people are gracious to a fault. Family life is the all-important center of social interaction. In the countryside, *compadrazgo* (godparentage) is a strong cohesive force.

On weekends, families head to riverside *balnearios* (swimming areas) and to the beach to slap dominoes on tables under the *palapas* (thatched shade umbrellas) and palms. They smoke cigars, swig rum, and crank up the radios to dance groin to groin to *bachata* country music and sexy, fast-paced merengue.

Machismo & Feminismo: Dominican males see themselves as conquistadores of women, who are expected to adopt a submissive role. Machismo (an exaggerated exertion of masculinity) is not labeled as such in the country: It is considered the way that men are supposed to behave. The label of machismo is fairly new to the culture, and rare is the Dominican male who stops to reflect about what the behavior implies. Laws meant to protect women against violence or sexual harassment are rarely enforced. Homophobia among men is pronounced.

Tigueres (tigers), macho males who make a living by cunning, often by aggressively hustling tourists, are admired by many in the lower classes. Among them are the *sanky-pankys* (or *sankies),* males who seek relationships with female tourists for pecuniary gain. Cockfighting is the ultimate macho pastime that contributes to a national sense of *dominicanidad* (Dominican-ness).

The old chaperone system that helped assure that young women remained chaste has disappeared, replaced by new freedoms. Women are now prominent in business and even politics, although they are paid far less than men. Common-law or free unions far outnumber marriages among the poorer classes, and many men in this social stratum take little responsibility for fatherhood.

San Juan de la Maguana's patron saint festival is an opportunity for parades and treats.

Government & Politics

The latest (2010) constitution defines the Dominican Republic as a democratic republic run by an elected president who may serve two consecutive four-year terms. Power rests with the bicameral National Congress, made of a 32-member Senate and the Chamber of Deputies with 195 members (*diputados*) representing the country's 31 provinces and its Distrito Nacional, which contains Santo Domingo. Voting is compulsory for citizens aged 18 and older; members of the police and armed forces cannot vote. Elections, overseen by a three-member Central Electoral Board, are held the third Sunday in May every four years for the two congressional chambers. Members are elected by proportional representation. The Congress sits in the Palacio Nacional in downtown Santo Domingo. The country's French legal code is overseen by the independent Supreme Court, whose 16 members are appointed by a National Judicial Council.

Each province is run by a governor appointed by the president, while elected mayors and municipal councils run the day-to-day affairs of the Distrito Nacional and 159 municipal districts.

Fucú

Roman Catholicism, introduced by the Spanish, is an integral part of the deeply religious culture. A significant percentage of the populace follows *vodú dominicana* (spirit worship) introduced by African slaves and merged to include Taíno spirits. Superstitions run deep. Dominicans have a general fear of fucú—bad luck omens. Even Columbus's name is considered fucú and is rarely spoken. Dominicans try to counter fucú by exclaiming *"Zafa!"* while making the sign of the cross.

Parties & Personalities: Danilo Medina Sánchez (1951–) was reelected to a second term as president in 2016. He represents the Dominican Liberation Party (PLD) and replaced three-term president Leonel Antonio Fernández Reyna (1953–), of the same party, founded in 1973 by Juan Emilio Bosch Gaviño. Originally left-leaning, the party now comprises progressive conservatives who support business interests. The main rival is the moderately left-wing Dominican Revolutionary Party (PRD), also founded by Bosch in 1961. A distant third, the Social Christian Reformist Party (PRSC), founded by Joaquín Antonio Balaguer Ricardo, is conservative and nationalistic.

Although Dominican parties are evolving a core set of values, they remain strongly influenced by the personalities of their leaders. Dynasties are still evident in government, where blood connections open doors. And corruption is still found in a country whose politics have historically been dominated by charismatic *caudillos* (powerful patriarchs to whom unquestioning loyalty was due).

Police & Security: The nation's 44,000-strong military serves to defend the nation but is principally involved in internal security, including counternarcotics efforts. It is supported by the Dominican National Police force, known in past decades for often brutally exceeding its legal mandate for maintaining public order. Although police corruption still exists, the force is no longer quite the threatening presence it once was. The Dominican Republic's mainstream media serves as a watchdog; it is robust and spans the political spectrum. The Dominican Republic has undergone a dramatic shift in the last two decades as it moves toward a pluralistic democracy with accountable government. ■

Food & Drink

The native cuisine of the Dominican Republic is country food, relying on simple ingredients. Dominicans are unadventurous diners with a fondness for homey peasant fare, fried but not spicy. Fine dining is concentrated overwhelmingly in Santo Domingo, where the restaurant scene presents a full medley of international flavors. Likewise, tourist venues offer dining options that span the globe.

Colorful and aromatic, local markets are cornucopias of fresh produce.

Fried or roast chicken (*pollo frito* or *pollo asado*) and roast pork (*cerdo asado*) are the ubiquitous dishes of *comida criollo,* Dominican cuisine—usually served with sides of white rice *(arroz)* and black beans. *Chimichurris,* sandwiches filled with slices of pork, and *chicharrones,* deep-fried pork rinds, are also popular, as are *batatas,* baked sweet potatoes fresh from the fire. Plantains (*plátanos*) or root vegetables such as cassava (*yucca*) or sweet potato *(boniato)* play supporting roles. The plantain—a relative of the banana—is served fried in strips when ripe (*maduro*), as fried chips (*fritos maduros,* eaten sprinkled with salt), or in thick fried

rounds called *tostones* before it has ripened. For breakfast, traditionalists opt for *mangú,* mashed plantain drizzled with olive oil and occasionally with cheese. Its relative, *mofongo* (mashed plantain with garlic), is usually served as a side dish or appetizer, and is often stuffed with seafoods.

Many locals consider *bandera dominicana* (Dominican flag) to be the national dish: Resembling *ropa vieja* of Cuba, it features marinated shredded beef with rice, red beans, fried plantain, and salad. Goat (*chivo*) finds its way into many dishes—during holidays, it is marinated with rum and spices and roasted as *chivo asado.* Heavily spiced *sancocho* stew features five different meats (including pork, beef, and chicken) plus vegetables. And *sopa de mondongo,* a tripe-based stew with garlic and tomatoes, is a popular brunch dish for Dominicans, especially those who imbibed too much the night before. Among the more flavorful national dishes is *asopao,* a gumbo made with a choice of chicken or seafood.

There's no shortage of seafoods, as befits an island nation. The fish of choice is sea bass *(mero),* often served with garlic *(ajo).* At resort restaurants you'll also find dolphin fish *(dorado),* swordfish *(emperador),* and snapper *(chillo),* while tourist venues charge top dollar for lobster *(langosta)* and shrimp *(camarones).* The Dominicans adore *lambi,* or conch, either as *escabeche*—marinated in a vinaigrette with red peppers and onions—or served hot in a garlic and tomato stew.

Brugal is one of the Dominican Republic's most popular rums.

Other dishes to try include *pastelitos,* tiny turnover pastries filled with minced beef, chicken, or cheese; *quipes,* small wheat pastries stuffed with meat; and *yaniqueques,* hot round corn breads resembling johnnycakes.

As befits a leading sugar-producing nation, Dominicans have a sweet tooth when it comes to desserts. *Dulce de leche* is sugar stirred with whole milk over heat to make a thick cream-like dessert. It's best followed by espresso, drunk thick and sugared. *Café con leche* is coffee served with hot milk.

Everywhere, roadside stalls and *paradas* (simple restaurants) are showplaces for tropical fruits, such as *chinola* (passion fruit), *guanabana* (soursop), and *lechola* (pawpaw), all of which find their way into *batidos,* delicious fruit shakes made with milk or water.

Sugarcane is the source of the republic's excellent rums, such as the Barceló, Brugal, and Bermúdez labels. In the countryside, the workingman's drink is *aguardiente,* cheap clear cane liquor, and *guarapo,* fresh-squeezed sugarcane juice, sold at roadside *guaraperías.* Dominicans are also beer drinkers, and local brewed, lager-style Presidente (an unlikely source of national

pride) and Quisqueya are perfectly suited to the tropical climate. Everyone's favorite tipple, however, is *mamajuana,* a home-brewed aphrodisiacal liqueur and cure-all made from various sticks, leaves, and roots steeped in rum.

EXPERIENCE:
Learning About Cacao Culture

The Dominican Republic is a major producer of cacao for the chocolate industry. The cacao tree, native to the Americas, grows in tropical zones below 1,000 feet (330 m). Large pods that grow from the trunks and branches contain 30–35 large seeds. After being harvested, the bean's outer pulp ferments, and then the bitter-tasting beans are sun-dried for shipment to chocolate factories in the republic and abroad.

El Sendero del Cacao *(tel 809/547-2166, cacaotour.com)* offers tours of an organic plantation at Las Pajas near San Francisco de Macorís.

ChocoMuseum *(Ave. Barceló-Bávaro, tel 809/466-1022, chocomuseo.com),* in Punta Cana, will teach you all you want to know about the "food of the Gods."

Dominican History

When, on December 6, 1492, Christopher Columbus stepped ashore on the island of Hispaniola—believing all the while that he was somewhere near Cipango (Japan)—he claimed the tropical isle for Spain. Thus began the country's long, brutal colonial history in the hands of one ruling power or another—first Spanish, then Haitian, and later American.

First Peoples

Archaeological excavations on the island have unearthed artifacts dating back about 3,000 years. The first significant culture was that of the pre-ceramic Ciboney, nomadic hunters and gatherers who settled the isle around 500 B.C. These inhabitants were displaced around A.D. 100 by the Ignerí culture, ceramists who were eventually absorbed by the Taíno—a canoe-borne island-hopping tribe of the Arawakan group. The Taíno began to settle the isle they called Quisqueya between

The Taíno, who arrived on Hispaniola circa A.D. 500, daubed thousands of cave pictographs.

A.D. 500 and 1000, during the migration of Arawakans northward from the Orinoco region of today's Venezuela.

Taíno communities were made up of common people and nobles. They lived communally in *bohíos,* thatched circular huts, arranged around an open ceremonial court. As many as 20 families formed each village under the leadership of a *cacique,* who occupied a larger hut in the center of each village. Taíno societies, however, were matriarchal. The women chose caciques, who were polygamous and married women from other kingdoms to secure political alliances. Quisqueya's Taíno were organized under five caciques to which lesser chiefs owed allegiance.

The peace-loving Taíno were skilled farmers; their flourishing civilization was based on the cultivation of corn and yucca, or manioc, used to make cassava bread. They were also accomplished potters and, though they went about naked, were so adept at weaving wild cotton and hemp into ropes and hammocks that in time, Spanish conquistadores forced them to weave sailcloth for Spanish vessels. They

> **An estimated 500,000 indigenous people, mostly Taíno, inhabited the island when the first Europeans arrived.**

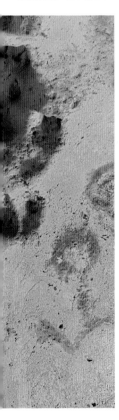

painted their bodies, and flattened foreheads were considered such a height of beauty that infants' heads were pressed between boards to shape their development.

The Taíno also took to the sea in large *canoas* (canoes) hewn from tree trunks, in which they traded with neighboring islands. Though the society wouldn't be considered advanced—they had no written language nor metals, and used neither the wheel nor beasts of burden—they had evolved at least the rudiments of an astrological calendar. Religion played a central role in their lives. They worshiped a pantheon of gods, who were thought to control nature's whimsies and to display their wrath when hurricanes bore down on the isle. During religious ceremonies, the Taíno indulged in alcohol made from corn. They also smoked the dried leaves of a domestic plant called *cohiba,* which they burned in long tubes called *tabacos.* And they buried their dead in a fetal position in anticipation of being reborn.

Around 1100, the Taíno were threatened by the Carib, a warlike race who had moved gradually up the Lesser Antillean chain and who began raiding Taíno settlements on the eve of Christopher Columbus's arrival. An estimated 500,000 indigenous people, mostly Taíno, inhabited the island when the first Europeans arrived. What remains of their cultures is now limited to pottery shards, petroglyphs, elaborate cult objects carved in stone, and words for canoe, hammock, hurricane, tobacco, and bohío, the thatch-roofed hut that still graces the Dominican Republic's lyrical landscapes.

First Europeans

On August 3, 1492, the Genoese explorer Christopher Columbus (1451–1506, known in the Dominican Republic as Cristóbal Colón) set out from Spain on his first voyage to find a western passage to the East Indies. Sailing aboard the *Santa María,* and accompanied by two caravels, *Niña* and *Pinta,* a crew of 90, and about 20 friends of the crown, Columbus made first landfall in the Bahamas before sailing along the north shore of Cuba, where he turned east.

In December 1492, Columbus sighted the island that he named Hispaniola. On Christmas Day, the *Santa María* ran aground and had to be abandoned. Columbus then set sail for Spain, leaving 39 Spaniards behind to found the first settlement in the New World, La Villa de La Navidad. (Believing that he had found Cipango—Japan—by the western route, Columbus named the islands the West Indies; their inhabitants, who had greeted him warmly, he christened "Indians.")

Columbus returned in 1493 to discover La Navidad in ashes and its inhabitants slain, allegedly for abusing the local women. On November 22 he established the settlement of La Isabela 68 miles (110 km) to the east, naming it in honor of the Spanish queen. Then he sailed on after naming his brother, Bartholomew (1461–1515), as governor of the island. The marshy malarial site was unhealthy, however, and in 1498 Bartholomew uprooted the inhabitants and moved them south, where they founded Santo Domingo on the east bank of the Río Ozama near the Caribbean Sea.

The Spaniards considered the Taíno pitiful heathens and quickly put them to work; the conquistadores received land grants and were allotted a specific number of Indian laborers under the *encomienda* (a modified form of feudalism) system. The gentle Indians were no more suited, or inclined, to harsh labor than were the Spaniards, and the indigenous people swiftly began to decline. The Taíno were briefly rallied to resistance in 1495, and again in 1497, by cacique Guarionex. The uprising was crushed, and Guarionex was captured and enslaved. He eventually died en route to Spain.

Treasure Routes: Convinced that beyond Hispaniola lay the palaces of the Great Khan of Cathay, with their gold and precious stones and spices of which Marco Polo had spoken, Columbus returned to the Americas three times, including in 1498. That year in Hispaniola, civil unrest broke out among the Spanish colonists. In 1500, Francisco

Christopher Columbus looks over Santo Domingo's Parque Colón, named in his honor.

Bartolomé de las Casas

Suffering malnutrition, disease, and spiritual sickness, the Indians found a true friend in Bartolomé de Las Casas (1484–1566), a Dominican friar whose job included identifying sites for washing gold and also winning the commitment and loyalty to the crown of the indigenous peoples. Las Casas witnessed the massacre of Indians and soon devoted his energies to their cause. The Apostle of the Indians succeeded: In 1542, the *encomienda* system, ostensibly established with the purpose of converting the heathen to Christianity, was abolished. But by then it was too late. European diseases such as smallpox, measles, and tuberculosis had combined with sword and musket to reap the Indians like a scythe. In less than a century, Hispaniola's aboriginal population was all but wiped out.

de Bobadilla (?–1502) arrived to investigate. He promptly arrested the Columbus brothers, who were sent in chains to Spain but later freed. Columbus died in 1506, dispirited and disillusioned, still believing in his unrealized dream.

Some 2,500 Spanish settlers arrived with a new governor, Nicolás de Ovando (1460–1518), who brutally suppressed Taíno revolts, began importation of African slaves, and established order in the riotous colony. In 1508, Columbus's son Diego (1479–1526) was named governor of the Indies. He built himself a palace in Santo Domingo, which under his tenure evolved its grid pattern and briefly established itself as the Indies' foremost center of power and prestige.

Lust for gold filled the minds of the conquistadores who descended on the New World. The Spanish found traces of the precious metal in Hispaniola, but soon exhausted the primitive mines. The island became a springboard for conquests throughout the New World. On one such foray, in 1519, Hernán Cortés (1485–1547) and his army sailed to Mexico, where they confronted Aztec emperor Moctezuma in his capital and defeated him. Then, in 1532, Francisco Pizarro (1471–1541) conquered the Andean empire of the Incas. Soon thereafter, Hispaniola sank into a period of decline as Havana, with its strategically advantageous position, grew in importance as the assembly point for twice-yearly treasure fleets—*flotas*—creaking with bullion en route to Spain.

The island's real wealth lay in its rich soils. Native forests were felled and hardwoods shipped to Spain, and tobacco—along with sugar and other crops—was planted to feed the new smoking craze then sweeping Europe. Cattle ranching also became widespread in the lowlands. The Spanish monarchy, however, made little effort to develop the colony. It enforced a crown monopoly: Colonists were forbidden to manufacture, and even the most mundane item had to be imported from Spain. Exports of raw materials to the mother country were heavily taxed.

Hispaniola's climate and fertile soils proved propitious for sugarcane, which Christopher Columbus had introduced to the isle. Fostered by Europe's insatiable demand for sugar, cane fields soon came to dominate the economy. With the rapid demise of the Taíno population, alternate labor was needed. Thus, the Spanish crown allotted *asientos*—contracts—granting rights to import and trade African slaves, the first of whom arrived in 1505. The trade rapidly flourished. The island's first slave revolt occurred as early as 1522, on a plantation owned by Diego Colón; like future revolts, it was brutally suppressed. By 1540, the slave population surpassed 30,000, twice that of the island's Spanish settlers.

Unjust laws promoted lawlessness, and many colonists took advantage of the crown's restrictions to smuggle in goods and slaves. By the mid-16th century, sugarcane plantations were developing rapidly, and with them the slave trade. English sea captains such as John Hawkins (1532–1595) and his kinsman, Sir Francis Drake (1540–1596), began their illustrious seafaring careers by bringing in slaves for Spanish planters and slipping away with sugar, hides, and silver under the compliant noses of mostly corrupt Spanish officials. When the Spanish Armada sent to invade England was defeated in 1588, breaking the back of Spanish sea power, the flow of ships packed with African slaves crossed the ocean unchecked.

> By the mid-16th century, sugarcane plantations were developing rapidly, and with them the slave trade.

The Age of Pirates

The increased slave trade in the West Indies and the constant warring between Spain and England, France, and Holland during the 16th and 17th centuries brought new enemies to Hispaniola and its neighboring islands—pirates and *corsarios,* or corsairs. While most pirates acted independently in their harassment of Spanish vessels, corsairs were licensed by Spain's rivals and acted with permission and protection as they plundered ships, cities, and plantations.

Santo Domingo was enclosed by a fortified wall under a far-sighted Alonso de Fuenmayor (ca 1518–1604), who governed the island from 1533 to 1556 and even established a defensive militia and navy. Nonetheless, in 1586 Sir Francis Drake and a fleet of 18 ships captured Santo Domingo. Drake settled into the cathedral and proceeded to ransack the city. When he eventually departed, one-third of the city lay in ruins. Remarkably, in 1605 the Spanish authorities did their own damage to the island. Determined to wipe out smuggling, they razed the towns of Bayajá, La Yaguana, Monte Cristi, and Puerto Plata to the ground—the devastation, alas, caused the collapse of the colony's economy. Sensing Hispaniola's weakness, in 1655 Oliver Cromwell, England's virulently anti-Catholic Lord Protector, ordered an attack on the isle. The British forces led by William Penn were soundly defeated, however (Penn redeemed himself by sailing on to Jamaica and seizing it from Spain).

Meanwhile, a new threat had emerged in the form of the buccaneers—a motley, predominantly French, band of deserters, refugees, miscreants, and vagabonds who

An engraving of Sir Francis Drake's flotilla arriving at Santo Domingo in 1586, by Baptista Boazio

coalesced on the French-held isle of Tortuga, off the northwest coast of Hispaniola. They hunted wild boar on the mainland (the meat was smoked over barbecue pits), stole cattle, and occasionally harassed passing ships. When the Spanish attempted to suppress them, many buccaneers fled and were eventually given a base at Port Royal, in Jamaica, where they rose to infamy as ruthless pirates under the leadership of a Welshman, Henry Morgan (1635–1688). Most buccaneers, however, resisted the Spanish and settled down to ranch and farm western Hispaniola, where they formed permanent, French-speaking settlements. Spanish *cincuéntenas*—squads of 50 troops— were occasionally sent out to quash the French settlements, resulting in a retaliatory attack on Santiago in 1690.

The 1697 Treaty of Rijswijk put an end to privateering. England agreed to suppress piracy, while France and Spain agreed to divide Hispaniola into French-owned Saint-Domingue and Spanish-owned Santo Domingo.

Slave Revolt & "Silly Spain"

The French government invested heavily in its new territory. While underpopulated Santo Domingo stagnated, Saint-Domingue prospered as land was irrigated and efficient sugar plantations established. By 1725 Saint-Domingue was the wealthiest land in the Caribbean. Within another 50 years, it was exporting more sugar to Europe than all the other Caribbean islands combined. The decadent lifestyle of a wealthy French white class—*les grands blancs*—was founded on the brutal labor of African slaves. By 1789, an estimated half a million slaves toiled beneath the blazing sun of Saint-Domingue.

The whites' fear of a slave rebellion heightened as news of the French Revolution reached the isle. Simmering agitation boiled over on August 22, 1791, when an insurrection was launched in northern Saint-Domingue. The colony descended into civil war as supporters of the revolution clashed with fans of the ancien régime. Meanwhile, an uprising of mulattos (free mixed bloods) broke out in the south. An expeditionary force led by revolutionary commanders arrived but failed to restore order. When France and Spain declared war in 1793, slave leader Toussaint L'Ouverture (ca 1743–1803)—a brilliant strategist—allied with the Spanish, who wished to regain control of the entire isle.

Juan Pablo Duarte and other national heroes of La Trinitaria independence movement (1838–1844) are venerated in Santo Domingo's Altar de la Patria mausoleum.

Meanwhile, in September 1793, British forces invaded Saint-Domingue, captured the capital city of Port-au-Prince, and were welcomed by the colony's counterrevolutionary planters. To win L'Ouverture to his side, in 1794 French commissioner Léger-Félicité Sonthonax (1763–1813) abolished slavery; L'Ouverture then forced out both the British and Spanish. The following year, by the Treaty of Bale, Spain ceded Santo Domingo to France.

In reality, L'Ouverture had taken command of the island for himself. In 1801, he marched on the city of Santo Domingo and proclaimed himself governor-general of Hispaniola. Napoleon Bonaparte (1769–1821), having emerged from France's revolutionary turmoil as first consul, sent a fleet of 22,000 troops to retake the island. Although L'Ouverture was captured, the French forces failed to secure the island. Thus, in 1804, ruthless leader Jean-Jacques Dessalines (1758–1806) declared independence from France and named the world's first black republic Haiti, the Taíno word for the island.

Santo Domingo was returned to Spanish rule in 1809, and slavery was reinstated. Inept colonial governors ushered in an ineffectual period known as España boba (silly Spain). Most criollos (island-born Dominicans) identified with their homeland, not Spain. Heavily taxed and harshly ruled by Spanish-born peninsulares, the island-born population had developed independence fever. Thus, in 1821, a group of anticolonial gentry petitioned Simón Bolívar (1783–1830) to join his Gran Colombia federation of nations newly independent from Spain. Before a reply arrived, however, megalomaniac Haitian president Jean-Pierre Boyer (1776–1850) invaded Santo Domingo. Haitian forces occupied the eastern half of Hispaniola for 22 years, during which estates and church property were seized and distributed to newly freed slaves. The massacres that took place then on Santo Domingo soil are etched in Dominican consciousness.

La Trinitaria

Led by a well-educated merchant, Juan Pablo Duarte (1813–1873), in 1838 Santo Domingo's *independistas* formed La Trinitaria, a secret organization dedicated to freeing the eastern half of Hispaniola from outsiders. In March 1843, they allied with disgruntled Haitian troops under Gen. Charles Hérard and toppled president Jean-Pierre Boyer. However, Hérard's troops then turned on the nationalists. Duarte fled to Venezuela as rebel leaders throughout the island were arrested and shot. Finally, on February 27, 1844, Duarte's fellow conspirators seized Santo Domingo's Fortaleza Ozama and drove the Haitians out.

Independence & the Age of *Caudillos*

In 1844, *independistas* managed to reclaim Santo Domingo from Haitian rule (see sidebar above), and the white, red, and green flag of the Republica Dominicana fluttered over the Fortaleza Ozama. Juan Pablo Duarte, the patriot who led the effort to free his country, returned a hero but was swiftly sidelined as ambitious and powerful caudillos (strongmen)—rural patriarchs with their own peasant armies—wrestled among themselves for power. The infighting evolved into a brutal civil war. Duarte again fled into exile.

Ensuing years witnessed several Haitian invasions of the Dominican Republic. Thus a pattern was established in which powerful rural caudillos would raise armies to expel the invaders, then place themselves in power. The second half of the 19th century was marked by internal strife, as cities were laid waste and fields of sugarcane put to the torch. In the countryside, the majority of the population barely subsisted while rival caudillos

Pedro Santana (1801–1864) and Buenaventura Báez (1810–1884) alternated as leaders, enriching themselves with frauds that effectively bankrupted the whole nation.

In 1861, Santana negotiated with Spain to reannex the republic, with himself as head of state. Spanish bureaucrats had learned little from the loss of the colony and after swiftly deposing Santana, they reinstituted their racist, repressive ways. A cry of revolt went up in Santiago in February 1863, sparking the War of Restoration. Within a year the rebels had defeated the Spanish, who unconditionally departed in July 1865. The republic then descended once again into a dark and dizzying period of coups and countercoups among the caudillos, lasting five decades. Báez seized power again during this period, but after an unpopular attempt to sell off the island (see sidebar opposite), popular sentiment forced him from the country, supposedly with $300,000 of government cash in his suitcase.

> **Billing himself as The Benefactor, Trujillo proceeded to rifle the treasury and take control of much of the nation's economy.**

The country enjoyed a brief period of liberalism under President Gregorio Luperón (1839–1897), a tobacco exporter who twice briefly ruled the island from Puerto Plata. Then it was back to the revolving door of corrupt caudillos, whose depravities reached a nadir under Ulises Heureaux (1845–1899), a general whose three brief spells in power—September 1882 to September 1883, January to February 1887, and April 1889 until his assassination in July 1899—were marked by a reign of terror and massive indebtedness. General Lilís, as Heureaux was known, mortgaged the country's finances by closing the National Bank and granting control of the treasury to the U.S.-owned San Domingo Investment Company. A boom in the southern sugar industry (inaugurated when Cuban estate owners fled the wars of independence in Cuba, establishing cane fields and processing mills in the Dominican Republic) revived the country's chaotic economic fortunes, but the 20th century was ushered in by another decade of political turmoil.

The 20th Century

The United States had viewed events in the Dominican Republic with concern. After a series of U.S. commissions failed to pacify the fractious country, President Woodrow Wilson decided to act. Anarchic Haiti had been occupied by U.S. marines in 1915. In April the following year, a military coup in the Dominican Republic prompted Wilson to order marines to Santo Domingo. When a new government refused U.S. dictates to place the Dominican treasury under U.S. control, Wilson declared a formal military occupation. For the next eight years, the country was administered by the U.S. Navy, which built highways, improved health care and education, and established a functioning local government. The country was also opened to American investment. The millions of dollars that flowed into the Dominican Republic reinvigorated the national economy, notably in sugar, which enjoyed boom years. However, thousands of peasant farmers were forced from the land or forced to sell their lands for bottom dollar. Displaced and embittered, they joined the urban disaffected in guerrilla armies—*gavilleros*—that launched constant raids against U.S. interests. The Dominicans' resistance to foreign occupation was met by brutal repression at the hands of a U.S.-established National Police Force—the Guardia Nacional.

The Trujillo Years: In March 1924, liberal politician Horacio Vásquez Lajara (1860–1936), an unusually scrupulous figure for his time, was elected democratically to a four-year term and American troops departed. His progressive administration built roads, schools, and other public works and tolerated political opposition. After extending his presidential term from four to six years, in February 1930 Vázquez was toppled in a carefully orchestrated revolt ostensibly led by his political opponent, Rafael Estrella Ureña (1899–1945). Behind the scenes, Estrella had struck a deal with National Army commander, Gen. Rafael Leónidas Trujillo Molina (1891–1961). Vásquez fled and Estrella became provisional president pending the outcome of elections in May. Reneging on a promise made to Estrella, Trujillo then placed himself on the ballot and launched a scorched-earth policy to terrorize any opponents; his goon squads killed anyone posing a threat. Unopposed on the ballot, Trujillo "won" the election (ostensibly with 95 percent of the vote), beginning a brutal dictatorship that lasted for 31 years.

Billing himself as The Benefactor, Trujillo proceeded to rifle the treasury and take control of much of the nation's economy for personal gain. Rural estates and urban businesses were seized or manipulated into his hands and merged into his vast corporate fiefdom. Massive public works projects were devised for his own personal profit, while a 10 percent tax on public employees' salaries went directly into his pocket. Supremely vain, the egomaniacal Trujillo renamed the capital Ciudad Trujillo and then gave the island's highest peak his name as well. Trujillo, a mulatto who took to whitening his own skin with powder, also pursued a policy of *blanquismo* intended to "whiten" the mixed-race population by fostering settlement by Europeans.

The free press was banned, every citizen was required to carry an identity card, and thousands of Trujillo's opponents real and suspected "disappeared" and were tortured and murdered. In October 1937 Trujillo sank to new levels of depravity when he ordered the massacre of Haitians living in the Dominican Republic; during the ensuing two months, as many as 20,000 Haitians were murdered by machete. In an attempt to rehabilitate his reputation (and perhaps to help whiten the population), the following year he stated his willingness to accept 100,000 European Jews.

Island for Sale

In 1869, Dominican leader Buenaventura Báez tried to sell the entire island to the United States for $150,000. President Ulysses S. Grant (1822–1885) favored the deal, but the U.S. Senate rejected the treaty. Desperate for cash, Báez then leased the Península de Samaná to the New York–based Samaná Bay Company for 99 years. The company intended to lease the bay to the United States as a naval base, but by 1874 it fell behind in its payments and Báez's reform-minded successor, Ignacio María González (1840–1915), rescinded the contract.

Despite Trujillo's brutal corruption, the U.S. government viewed his anticommunism and pro-U.S. business leanings as sufficient reason to grant him tacit support. (Trujillo also manipulated Washington through largesse and a highly effective public relations campaign.) U.S. President Franklin D. Roosevelt famously said of Trujillo: "He may be a S.O.B., but he's our S.O.B." Nonetheless, the mood in the United States inevitably shifted, prompted not least by Trujillo's ill-concealed support for an assassination attempt on liberal Venezuelan President Rómulo Betancourt (1908–1981); and, on

March 12, 1956, by the kidnapping in New York of Jesús de Galíndez, a prominent anti-Trujillo Dominican exile, who was flown to Santo Domingo and brutally murdered.

Resistance to Trujillo's rule crystallized on June 14, 1959, when rebels trained and supplied by Fidel Castro's (1926–) newly Communist Cuban government landed in the Cordillera Central. The brigade—known as 14J, or *catorce de junio*—failed to gain popular support. Though the invasion was a failure, the torture of captured rebels ignited international condemnation and sparked domestic efforts to oust the dictator. The final straw came on November 25, 1960, when three upper-class sisters who had formed the anti-Trujillo Fourteenth of June movement—María Teresa, Minerva, and Patria Mirabal—were ambushed and murdered by Trujillo's agents. A fourth sister survived (see p. 154). The act was met with public outrage. Finally, on May 30, 1961, CIA-supported assassins gunned down Trujillo on Santo Domingo's Malecón after a dramatic car chase.

Bottlecaps

Rafael Leónidas Trujillo Molina was born in San Cristóbal to a Spanish father and Haitian mother. He was an unremarkable student. He worked briefly as a telegraph operator and security guard before joining the Dominican army in 1918. By 1927 he had risen to commander-in-chief. He adopted flamboyant uniforms adorned with so many medals that locals nicknamed him Chapitas ("bottlecaps"). His vanity was so great that he commanded churches to proclaim *"Dios en cielo, Trujillo en tierra* (God in Heaven, Trujillo on Earth)." After his assassination, his family was forced into exile in Paris, where he was buried at Cimetière du Père Lachaise.

The Marines Return: Following Trujillo's assassination, his bon vivant son Ramfis Trujillo (1929–1969) took power and personally oversaw a six-month period of "counterterror" in which his father's political enemies, real and imagined, were hunted down and put to death. Popular disaffection finally forced Ramfis into exile. The Dominican Republic sank again into a two-year cycle of coup, countercoup, and chaos. An articulate author and social reformer—Juan Emilio Bosch Gaviño (1909–2001)—rose above the fray to win the December 1962 election by a wide margin on behalf of the Dominican Revolutionary Party (PRD), which he founded in 1961.

Barely had Bosch initiated his progressive reforms, however, when he, too, was ousted by conservative forces. Pro- and anti-Bosch military leaders squared off, resulting in a three-month general strike and brief civil war in which it appeared that pro-Bosch forces, the Constitutionalists, would prevail.

U.S. President Lyndon Johnson, seeing Bosch as a socialist and citing fears of "a second Cuba" in the years following the Cuban Missile Crisis, ordered U.S. marines to the island. On April 28, 1965, Operation Powerpack was launched and 42,000 U.S. troops, supported by troops from six other Latin American nations, landed on the island to restore order. Rafael Trujillo's former puppet-president, Joaquín Antonio Balaguer Ricardo (1906–2002), won the ensuing election in June 1966. The wily politician dominated Dominican politics for the next 35 years, winning five terms in a series of electoral frauds.

Rafael Trujillo's giant visage looks out over an array of weaponry at a 1955 fair.

The Balaguer Decades: A classic caudillo, Balaguer applied Trujillo's repressive ways while cleverly portraying himself as a benevolent father figure. All opposition parties except the PRD were banned. Bosch fled into exile, where he founded the left-leaning Dominican Liberation Party, PLD. Balaguer's tenure witnessed massive infrastructure projects (much of it U.S. funded), the establishment of the national park system, and a

Latest port of call: Puerto Plata's Amber Cove cruise terminal

program of industrialization. However, cronyism, corruption, indiscriminate largesse for votes, and the barbarous ways of La Banda—Balaguer's freewheeling secret police— eventually earned the enmity of U.S. President Jimmy Carter, ending a long period of U.S. support. In May 1978, Balaguer refused to acknowledge his electoral loss to political opponent Antonio Guzmán (1911–1982) of the PRD. Eventually, Carter pressured the despotic president to step down.

The republic's economy had expanded considerably. Nonetheless, poverty riddled the countryside, fostering massive rural migration to the cities, where unemployment soared. In the 1980s the United States cut sugar quotas, delivering the Dominican Republic a severe blow. With the national economy again stalled, and facing all manner of problems (including accusations of corruption), Guzmán committed suicide. The International Monetary Fund (IMF) imposed stiff conditions on the new PRD government of moderate lawyer Salvador Jorge Blanco (1926–2010), resulting in fatal riots that cost Blanco popular support, despite policies that placed the nation's tottering economy back on its feet.

Balaguer took power again in the 1986 election and set out to destroy Blanco's career. By constant denunciation, he succeeded. Blanco was even arrested; while undergoing medical treatment in the U.S., he was sentenced in absentia to 23 years in prison for corruption (the Supreme Court later overturned the sentence). Balaguer also reversed the IMF austerity program, and through rampant inflationary policies plunged the Dominican Republic back down the path to economic ruin. In 1989, he reneged on the country's foreign debt, and the international community then cut off credit. The value of the Dominican peso plummeted fivefold while annual inflation soared to 60 percent. A huge exodus of Dominicans gathered pace as the populace sought economic freedom in the United States.

Nonetheless, by slandering his PRD opponent, José Francisco Peña Gómez (1937–1998), as a voodoo priest, Balaguer won the 1990 election. He poured millions of dollars into building the monumental Columbus Lighthouse, Faro a Colón, but his popularity had reached a low point and only outright fraud gained him the 1994 election. Even the Dominican military had lost patience with Balaguer, who under pressure from Washington finally agreed to cut his four-year term short. In 1996, the country's first truly fair elections were held, forcing a nearly blind Joaquín Balaguer into reluctant retirement.

The Era of Tourism

During the preceding two decades, the Dominican Republic had gradually weaned itself from an agricultural economy based largely on sugar exports and had instead diversified into valuable cigar production and manufacturing of exportables, mainly textiles and processed foodstuffs. Meanwhile, construction of an airport on the north coast in the early 1980s spurred tourism development. In 1996, the young incoming PLD president, Leonel Antonio Fernández Reyna (1953–), a 42-year-old lawyer, steered the nation down a new course of economic and judicial reform, including a new constitution. Remarkably, Fernández successfully cleansed the military hierarchy without repercussion (he even fired the defense minister for insubordination). The economy boomed and inflation was tamed. Nonetheless, the newfound wealth was highly concentrated and with rapid development came an increase in crime, drugs, and sex tourism.

Fernández was succeeded in 2000 by the PRD's Rafael Hipólito Mejía (1941–), who went back to discredited financial programs. Spiraling inflation returned as government debt climbed beyond control and the economy slid into recession. In 2004 he lost the presidential election by a landslide and Fernández was sworn in for a second term. Fernández was accused of supporting high-tech projects at the expense of social services for the poor. The Dominican Republic hosted the Pan-American Games in 2003 (at a cost of $175 million); Fernández's government has spent millions on building the Santo Domingo Metro subway system; and foreign companies operating within industrial free-trade zones established throughout the nation are exempt from paying the nation's minimum wage. Voters rewarded Fernández by reelecting him by a landslide in May 2008. In January 2009, the president inaugurated both the Santo Domingo Metro and the city's new Sans Souci cruise terminal.

President Medina has faced an international outcry for his defense of a 2013 court decision stripping as many as 500,000 Dominicans of Haitian descent of birthright citizenship.

Tourism has continued to boom under the tenure of Danilo Medina (2012–present), surpassing 4.8 million visitors in 2015. In April 2015, the Amber Cove cruise terminal opened near Puerto Plata, while Santo Domingo's colonial core is in the midst of a years-long mega-facelift initiated in 2013. President Medina has faced an international outcry for his defense of a 2013 court decision stripping as many as 500,000 Dominicans of Haitian descent of birthright citizenship. In July 2015, the Supreme Court upheld the decision, rendering Haitian-descended Dominicans stateless. ∎

Land & Landscape

Roughly triangular in shape, this 242-mile-wide (390 km) nation tapers eastward from the Haitian border to Cabo Engaño, its easternmost point. With the highest and lowest points in the Caribbean—Pico Duarte (10,417 feet/3,175 m) and Lago Enriquillo (150 feet/46 m below sea level), respectively—it packs a potpourri of terrains and climates into 18,816 square miles (48,734 sq km).

Unlike most of the Lesser Antilles, the island of Hispaniola is of tectonic, not volcanic, origin. The collision of tectonic plates below the Earth's crust began squeezing the Greater Antilles up from the sea around 50 million years ago. Hispaniola sits atop the Caribbean plate at its juncture with its rival, the North American plate. Powered in their jostling movement by currents deep within the Earth's molten core, these plates wrestle with each other, sparking earthquakes that frequently rattle the country—including a catastrophic 7.0 magnitude quake that hit Haiti in January 2010.

Though the country lies wholly within the tropics, the extremes of elevation and relief spawn dramatic differences in landscape—from sunbaked semidesert studded with cacti to montane cloud forests smothered in mists. Throughout the island, the scenery unfolds dramatically, reaching its pinnacle literally and metaphorically in the Cordillera Central, where three peaks—Pico Duarte, La Pelona, and La Rucilla—surpass 10,000 feet (3,048 m) and spectacular waterfalls pour from the mountains. Running roughly east–west, this rugged mountain chain is paralleled to the north by the lower and narrow Cordillera Septentrional, and to the south by the Sierra de Neiba and Sierra de Baoruco. Between them run deep valleys, including the Valle del Yaque and Valle del Río Camú—colloquially known as El Cibao—where the republic's world-renowned tobacco is grown. To the east and south, the nation's vast plains are a gently undulating sea of chartreuse—sugarcane fields, dusted in summer with delicate white blossoms.

> **Relatively few visitors escape the all-inclusive hotels to discover the full physical grandeur of the republic.**

One-fifth of the population lives in Santo Domingo, the nation's capital midway along the south coast. Combining colonial charm with contemporary chic, this ancient city is the second largest in the Caribbean after Havana. Its downside is the horrendous traffic, often crawling bumper to bumper through sprawling suburbs where ritzy shopping malls and high-rise apartments nudge up against sobering slums. Reaching almost to the doorstep of Santo Domingo, the Cordillera Central casts a rain shadow over the southwest quarter: a region of arid flatlands and scrub-covered hills that merge westward into the denuded Massif de la Selle of Haiti. White beaches limn the Atlantic shoreline and the Caribbean coast east of Santo Domingo. Palm-shaded and dissolving into seas that gleam peacock blue, these sands are the hub of the country's recent tourism boom, centered on an astonishing assemblage of all-inclusive resorts.

Several roads have been designated as panoramic routes. However, relatively few

Coconut palms are the ubiquitous symbol of the Costa del Coco.

visitors escape the all-inclusive hotels to discover the full physical grandeur of the repub-lic; it is the only island in the Caribbean, for example, that offers white-water rafting.

The Arid Southwest

The nation's dry quarter is a sharp contrast to the lush greens of rest of the country. The region can go months without rain, while temperatures can soar above 100°F (38°C)—this in the lee of mountains whose sodden eastern slopes soak up the rain. Rivers spill down from the curving slopes and provide irrigation for the Valle de San Juan, a major banana- and rice-growing region clasped between the daunting Cordillera Central and the narrow Sierra de Neiba.

Beyond the Sierra de Neiba and shimmering in a sweltering basin (the Hoya de Enriquillo) is Lago Enriquillo—an extremely saline body of water once connected to the sea. It is studded with thorny islands, including Isla Cabritos, a national park, that serve as sanctuaries for exotic reptiles and birds, among them crocodiles lurking on salty mudbanks and gawky flamingos parading in soupy lagoons. The lake is framed to the south by the Sierra de Baoruco, a rugged and sparsely populated mountain region where mists swirl through moist montane forests festooned with orchids. A panoramic road traces the eastern shore of the Península de Baoruco—a stupendously scenic, wave-beaten coastline offering perhaps the most beautiful drive in the country.

The Sierra de Baoruco blocks the rain from the diamond-shaped southernmost tip of the island. Here, arid thorn forests and cacti sprout atop a razor-sharp limestone plateau. Marine turtles crawl ashore to lay eggs on lonesome beaches and the world's smallest lizard, a dwarf gecko, is relegated to a lonesome life on Isla Beata a short dis-tance offshore. Here, too, the country's largest population of flamingos stomps about in the jade waters of Laguna de Oviedo, part of Parque Nacional Jaragua. Much of this region is pocked by caves that contain the nation's finest collection of pre-Columbian rock art. Economically this is the nation's poorest district.

The Southeast & Península de Samaná

A study in contrasts, the southeast, an oblong region bathed on three sides by sea, is the nation's fastest-growing tourist area. Endless miles of sugary sands shaded by swaying coconut palms are the region's motif, epitomized by the 40 miles (64 km) of

Top Ten Beaches

Visitors to the republic are spoiled for choice when it comes to fine beaches, which range from sugar white to choco-latey brown. The lion's share of white beaches are around Punta Cana, in the southeast, but Samaná and the Amber Coast together have dozens of superla-tive beaches. North-facing beaches get more wave action than south-facing shores. Among the best of the Dominican beaches are:

Bahía de las Águilas, Barahona (see p. 187)
Playa Las Ballenas, Las Terrenas (see p. 119)
Playa Bávaro, Punta Cana (see p. 105)
Playa Bayahibe, Bayahibe (see p. 99)
Playa Cabarete, Cabarete (see p. 130)
Playa El Cortecito, Punta Cana (see p. 105)
Playa Diamante, Cabrera (see p. 129)
Playa Dorado, Puerto Plata (see p. 137)
Playa Lava Cama, La Costa del Coco
(see p. 107)
Playa Macao, Punta Cana (see p. 105)

The Sierra de Baoruco shoulders up to the town of La Ciénaga on the Pedernales Peninsula.

reef-protected white beaches of La Costa del Coco—the Coconut Coast, where dozens of all-inclusive resorts coalesce at Bávaro. The sands are punctuated by rocky headlands rising out of the surf around Cabo Engaño. Immediately south, Punta Cana and Cap Cana are the setting for a vast decade-long development project that features the largest mega-yacht marina in the Caribbean. North of Bávaro, the white sands unfurl into the beaches of the Costa Esmeralda, backed by lagoons sheltering manatees and birdlife.

Inland, most of the southeast region is a pancake-flat plain smothered in sugarcane fields. Graced by gingerbread Victorian-era houses, La Romana and San Pedro de Macorís still function as sugar-processing towns and as training grounds where potential baseball stars hone their skills. Offshore of La Romana, Isla Catalina wears a necklace of fine coral reefs that offer spectacular diving. Farther east, Parque Nacional Cotubanamá dangles off the southern tip. Encompassing Isla Saona, the park protects tropical forest teeming with wildlife, including manatees in coastal waters.

A low yet rugged mountain chain—the Cordillera Oriental—hems the southeast's northern shore, lined with mangroves that fringe the Bahía de Samaná. Much of the region's terrain displays classic karst topography: Parque Nacional Los Haitises is a venue for strange rock formations called *mogotes*—conical, weather-eaten limestone hillocks divided by precipitous ravines and chewed through with labyrinthine caves. Indeed, caves stipple the entire southeast region. Adorned with ancient pictographs, they provide fascinating insights to Taíno culture.

Samaná Bay's warm waters are a playground for humpback whales, which congregate here in early winter to mate and give birth. Framing the bay to the north, the thin Península de Samaná probes into the Atlantic and is a setting for once tiny fishing villages fringing glorious beaches that today act as tourist magnets. The marmoreal mountains that form the peninsula's spine are bedecked with sparkling cascades—notably the Salto de Limón—that are best reached by horseback.

The North Coast & Cordillera Septentrional

A tourist playground, the Costa del Ámbar (Amber Coast), as the north coast is known, is acclaimed for its ribbon of white, gray, and golden sands unspooling along shores backed by a rugged mountain chain—the Cordillera Septentrional. The cordillera is also the main source for amber, the semiprecious gem mined in narrow tunnels around La Cumbre. The coast was the site of the first permanent settlement in the Americas, preserved (barely) within Parque Histórico La Isabela. Puerto Plata, the main town and hub for the region's tourism trade, is still steeped in colonial history. Gingerbread structures recall the city's prominence during the tobacco boom of the mid-1800s. Although the charm quotient of other settlements along the shore is limited (Sosúa's reputation as a center for sex tourism lingers), wind-tossed Cabarete is now well established as the Caribbean mecca for extreme water sports, lending a new hipness to the region.

> **Wind-tossed Cabarete is now well established as the Caribbean mecca for extreme water sports, lending a new hipness to the region.**

Inland, the Cordillera Septentrional rises to 4,098 feet (1,249 m) atop Pico Diego de Ocampo. Waterfalls crash through lush foliage to feed coastal lagoons such as Estero Hondo, sheltering waterfowl and manatees. The mountains are popular for adventure sports such as waterfall cascading and canyoning, and for cable-car rides up mist-shrouded Pico Isabel de Torres.

El Cibao

Framed by the Cordillera Central and Cordillera Septentrional, the fertile flatlands of the rivers Camú (flowing east) and Yaque del Norte (flowing west) form the Cibao, a Taíno word meaning "place where rocks abound." The region, the wealthiest in the nation, is famous for the production of full-flavored tobacco. The enterprise is centered on Santiago, the republic's second largest city and a node for the creation of aromatic cigars. Coffee and cacao are grown in the foothills, and rice and bananas form important crops in the Cibao's eastern extreme, where cattle are also raised. Santiago and the neighboring towns of La Vega and Moca were in colonial days centers of political power. Razed by Haitian armies and those of marauding *caudillos,* all but Santiago have been wiped clean of their colonial buildings. Thronged today with traffic, they reverberate to the thrum of commerce.

At the arid west end of the Valle del Yaque, the river spills into the Atlantic. Here, hugging the Haitian border, Parque Nacional Monte Cristi protects the largest mangrove system in the nation, along with cactus-studded scrub and a vast swath of coral-encrusted isles and ocean flats that together offer important nesting sites for American oystercatchers, boobies, and terns. Spanish galleons lie in shallow graves amid the corals.

Cordillera Central

No mountains in the Caribbean compare in scale to Hispaniola's central mountain range, where hikers can stand on the roof of the Antillean archipelago atop Pico Duarte. Known as the Dominican Alps, the towering Cordillera Central forms the island's backbone and runs northwest–southeast, tapering down to the edge of Santo Domingo and extending northwest to the far tip of Haiti. The mountains hold the headwaters of the island's main rivers, notably the Río Yaque del Norte, which cascades through a deep valley filled with birdsong. At the valley's heart, the agricultural town of Jarabacoa is a popular summer retreat and the departure point for exhilarating white-water rafting, as well as being the gateway for treks up Pico Duarte.

A nature lover's paradise, much of the region is protected within national parks, including Parque Nacional Valle Nuevo—a pine-clad nirvana for birders—and Parques Nacionales José Armando Bermúdez and José del Carmen Ramírez, which together enshrine the highest peaks. The fertile eastern foothills supply the nation with strawberries, fresh vegetables, and flowers, which thrive in the alpine climate around Constanza, at 4,000 feet (1,219 m). Set in an exquisitely beautiful Shangri-la valley, remote Constanza is a gateway to Parque Nacional Valle Nuevo, protecting a remote and rugged alpine wilderness, whose thrilling up-and-down roads can only be accessed with four-wheel drive. ■

The Salto de Agua Blanca, near Constanza, tumbles 285 feet (87 m).

Flora & Fauna

Although it lies strictly within the tropics between 18 and 20 degrees north of the Equator, the Dominican Republic is blessed with diversity, its habitats ranging from tidal mangroves and lush coastal forests to cloud forests and even subalpine grasslands atop the windswept heights of Pico Duarte. In bordering wetlands, manatees swim in coastal lagoons sheltered by coral reefs.

The Dominican Republic is home to more than 300 species of orchids.

Though the island has been heavily deforested, particularly on the Haitian side, commercial logging has been banned since the 1960s and forests still cover 45 percent of the Dominican Republic. Nonetheless, landless peasants continue to take down trees, and José Armando Bermúdez and José del Carmen Ramírez National Parks, in the Cordillera Central, are the only extensive tracts of virgin forest in the republic. Currently the country has 187 registered protected areas (including 60 national parks, 35 wildlife reserves, 26 natural monuments, and 10 marine sanctuaries) composing almost one-quarter of the country's total land area under the direction of the Dirección Nacional de Parques.

A Lush Wilderness

Cloaked in a dozen shades of tropical green, the Dominican Republic boasts a truly stupendous diversity of flora. More than 5,500 separate species have been catalogued, including more than 300 endemic orchids, which grow abundantly around Jarabacoa and Constanza, in the Cordillera Central, and on the misty slopes of Parque Nacional

Sierra de Baoruco. Ferns—light-gap pioneers found from sea level to the highest elevations—are the most abundant flora and particularly thrive in the sodden air of mid-elevation mountains.

Despite devastating deforestation at lower elevations, the mountain ranges still have ecosystems typical of the original Antillean vegetation. Although logged heavily since the Spanish arrival, West Indian *caoba* (mahogany) still flourishes in the moist subtropical forests of low-elevation valleys. Blooming from February to April, the caoba's tiny, inconspicuous white blossom is the national flower. Other archetypal species include the swollen baobab, the ceiba, and silvery yagruma, which shimmers as if frosted and bursts forth with huge lily-like blooms. Vegetation changes with elevation. Broad-leafed trees of the mountain foothills give way above to feathery-leafed *palo de cotorra* (parrot tree) and conifers such as Creolean pine, which scents the alpine air above 6,000 feet (1,829 m). A band of mist-soaked tropical montane rain forest, or "cloud forest," cloaks the mountainsides at elevations around 4,000 feet (1,219 m), where branches drip with mosses and galleries of epiphytes thrive in the humid conditions. At the highest elevations, stunted trees cower before wind-driven rains.

Ubiquitous throughout the lowlands, the stately royal palm—*palma real*—soars more than 100 feet (30 m) like a silver column. Regarded with great affection, the royal palm even finds its way onto the nation's and the national university's coats of arms. The tree provides thatch for roofing, as does the silver thatch, also used for weaving. Along the shore, coconut palms conjure images of a tropical paradise. Adapted to cooler heights, the sierra palm—a 13-foot-tall (4 m) relic from the dinosaur age—features cello-like fiddleheads.

The forests flare dramatically with seasonal color, including that of ornamentals such as frangipani, royal poinciana, purple jacaranda, the almost fluorescent yellow tabebuia, the flame red African tulip tree, and bougainvillea in a rainbow assortment of colors. At any time of year, dozens of species are in bloom. Fruiting trees also abound. Mangoes, guavas, and soursops. Passion fruit and papayas. Coconuts, cacaos, and cashews. Wild avocado is found in montane tropical rain forest above 6,000 feet (1,829 m), while prickly pear thrusts up from the parched earth of the cactus forest of the arid southwest.

Small Is Beautiful

No bigger than a dime when curled up, the world's smallest lizard measures barely two-thirds of an inch long (1.5 cm) nose to tail. In fact, its name—*Sphaerodactylus ariasae*—is longer than this dwarf gecko, which lives only on Isla Beata, where it was discovered in 1998. It's the world's smallest terrestrial invertebrate. The dark brown and white speckled gecko, commonly known as the Jaragua sphaero, occasionally shows up on the mainland in Parque Nacional Jaragua. Like most geckos, it can walk upside down thanks to millions of nanofilaments on its toes that tap into the force that draws adjacent molecules together.

Mangroves & Wetlands: The republic's variegated coastline is rimmed by silted strips colonized by mangroves. These halophytic plants (terrestrial species able to survive with their roots in saltwater) thrive on alluvium scoured from the inland mountains and carried to the coast, where the silt is dropped from the slow-moving rivers to form land. Six species of mangroves grow at the juncture of land and sea. Veined with braided channels, they provide a haven for animal life. Migratory waterfowl, wading birds, and small mammals abound in the shallows and tidal creeks at low tide, while amid the stilt roots juvenile fishes spend their early lives, shielded from the predators in the open sea.

Inland, the prime wetland ecosystem is Lago Enriquillo, in the southwest. This hypersaline lake surrounded by wet meadows and swamp is congenial to at least 65 species of domestic and migratory birds, as well as crocodiles and two species of giant iguana.

Tropical Ark

Of land mammals there are only two endemic ground-dwelling species, plus 18 species of bats. Close to extinction, the solenodon lives on the edge in Parque Nacional Los Haitises and Parque Nacional Cotubanamá. With a nose like Pinocchio's, this shy, nocturnal 2-pound (0.9 kg) mammal grubs around with sharp claws for insects and lizards. Its odoriferous scent glands and venomous saliva have been no match against predation by modern-day dogs, cats, and mongooses, introduced to combat rats (also introduced) during the colonial era. The solenodon's cousin, the hutia—a rabbit-size, ratlike herbivorous rodent—faces similar threats, including the loss of its habitat. It, too, is restricted mainly to Parque Nacional Cotubanamá and Parque Nacional Los Haitises.

More numerous are the frogs and reptiles: The Dominican Republic shares 63 frog species and 114 lizard species with Haiti. Thimble-size tree frogs fill the night with a chirping warble like a two-note piccolo. The country is also home to 26 species of neotropical snakes, including the vine snake and Hispaniolan boa. Several species are threatened with extinction due to mongoose predation. Many reptilians are highly local. The dwarf gecko (see sidebar p. 43) that inhabits Isla Beata is the world's smallest lizard, no bigger than the face of a quarter; it was discovered only in 1998. The arid southwest hosts the rhinoceros iguana, named for the hump on its nose. Growing to 4 feet long (1.2 m), it looks as baked and lifeless as the ground it walks on. The Dominican Republic also boasts the Caribbean's largest population of American crocodiles, which can attain a whopping length of 16 feet (5 m) on a diet of fish. Once numerous throughout coastal waters, today they are relegated to Lago Enriquillo.

Marine Life: Four species of marine turtles—green, leatherback, hawksbill, and loggerhead—consider the Dominican Republic's beaches clean enough for nesting. Manatees, marine mammals, are often seen in sheltered waters off Parque

(see sidebar p. 43)

EXPERIENCE:
Encounters With Dolphins

What fun—slipping into warm waters to swim alongside "Flipper" within a protected lagoon. Kids especially will love swimming with trained bottlenose dolphins, which respond to verbal signals. But adults will grin with delight at a dolphin's "kiss" as well. You can even banish your fear of sharks by swimming with harmless nurse sharks.

At **Ocean World Adventure Park** (tel 809/291-1000, oceanworldadventure park.com), in Puerto Plata, you can splash around with dolphins and snorkel with nurse sharks and rays.

Dolphin Island Park (tel 809/221-9444, dolphinislandpark.com), at Bávaro, lets you swim with nurse sharks and rays. You can also swim with dolphins and sea lions at this offshore lagoon.

Dolphins encounter each other at Ocean World Adventure Park.

Nacional Cotubanamá and Parque Nacional Monte Cristi, as well as the Bahía de Samaná and Estero Hondo. Humpback whales, however, steal the show when it comes to wildlife in the country. Every winter, these giants migrate from colder northern waters to spawn in Bahía de Samaná and the sanctuary for marine mammals off the north coast.

Since 1962 the Dominican Republic has been a pioneer in the Caribbean basin for marine protection, and it was the first Latin American country to apply recommendations from the Convention for Biological Diversity and the International Coral Reef Initiative.

Birds: Wherever you travel in the Dominican Republic, you're sure to be surrounded by the calls and whistles of birds. The nation claims 318 recorded bird species, which include 30 endemics, including an entire endemic family, the bizarre palmchat—the songbird of Hispaniola. This gregarious, palm-dwelling bird wears a greenish brown, pin-striped coat and white sash and prefers living in massive communal nests. The endemic Hispaniolan parakeet is found throughout the country, including in the city of Santo Domingo, although its cousin, the talkative Day-Glo green Hispaniolan parrot, is threatened.

The Sierra de Baoruco astounds for the number of feathered endemics, including the Antillean siskin and narrow-billed tody. Other uniquely Dominican birds include the Hispaniolan lizard-cuckoo and stunningly colorful Hispaniolan trogon. Migratory waterfowl—white-cheeked pintail, Baikal teal, king eiders—flock by their multiple thousands. American oystercatchers scurry along the beaches, while flamingos strut their stuff in briny lakes, forked-tailed frigatebirds hang in the air, and ibises pick among the mudflats and shallow lagoons for small crustaceans and fish. ■

Architecture

Complex and kaleidoscopic, the Dominican Republic's distinctive architecture spans four centuries. While the country lacked the sugar wealth that funded the architectural treasure trove of Cuba, the grandeur and scope of its buildings are impressive, showcasing a dizzying amalgam of styles—from 16th-century asceticism to an impressive array of 20th-century designs.

Throughout the centuries, Dominican architects have shown remarkable creativity while adapting their vision to local conditions. The greatest concentration of buildings is in Santo Domingo, the oldest city in the New World. The regional cities and towns tempt visitors, too, with their colonial structures—Santiago, in the Valle del Cibao, almost rivals the capital for architectural complexity.

Various additions have been made to Santo Domingo's Catedral Primada de América since its original completion in 1540.

Early Colonial Structures

The first rustic settlements, such as La Villa de La Navidad and La Isabela, were built of wood and thatched with palm fronds in indigenous style. These simple *bohíos* are still a staple of rural areas. As towns developed, adobe and later limestone replaced wood. The Law of the Indies (1537) systemized Spanish plans for colonial settlements and formalized the grid-plan layout established by Gov. Nicolás de Ovando when he rebuilt Santo Domingo in 1502 after a hurricane leveled the town. The law called for plazas to be built every four blocks, each one with a church. The first churches were simple and austere, in the Isabelline Gothic, Romanesque, and early Renaissance styles. They are epitomized by the Catedral Primada de América (1510–1540), which shows traces of all three styles plus baroque. The period also saw the construction of forts, such as the Fortaleza Ozama guarding the river mouth of Santo Domingo, which was begun in 1502.

> **The Law of the Indies (1537) systemized Spanish plans for colonial settlements and formalized the grid-plan layout.**

The grid-block pattern decreed by law lent orderliness to city development. The typical 17th-century house was of unadorned Spanish style, with two stories built around an inner courtyard. On the plazas, houses typically boasted a portico and loggia to provide shade and rain protection (see pp. 76–77).

18th & 19th Centuries

During the next two centuries, the colony could not afford grandiose expression. Moreover, a series of earthquakes, as well as destructive fires set by invading Haitian forces, leveled many of the finest structures of the epoch. Nonetheless, those edifices that went up were more ornate than in prior centuries, often embellished in the 19th century in European baroque and Palladian styles. Meanwhile, the *ingenio,* or plantation complex, became a fixture of rural areas and featured a sugar refinery, a distillery, storehouses, living quarters for slaves, and, of course, the plantation owner's house.

The Dominican Republic's stylistic eclecticism revived in the latter decades of the 19th century when the boom in the sugar economy boosted civic and private construction. Santiago and Santo Domingo's *criollo* middle classes and aristocrats built *quintas*—neoclassical villas set in gardens in the suburbs—and grand mansions. Many were in Palladian style, then popular in Europe, while Cuban immigrants fleeing the Cuban wars of independence graced the towns of the Valle del Cibao with town houses in the colonial style of their homeland. Wooden *rejas* (window grills) provided decorative touches, while *vitrales*—stained-glass windows—flooded rooms with tinted light. Provincial 19th-century homes were typically one story and, especially in El Cibao, highly embellished.

The nave of the Basílica de Nuestra Señora de la Altagracia is an avant-garde masterpiece.

Civic buildings reflected the growing influence of European neoclassicism. Corinthian columns and lavishly decorated interiors ruled the day. The theme even found its way into ecclesiastical venues, such as the Catedral de Santiago Apóstol (1868–1895) in Santiago. Elsewhere, the Caribbean gingerbread style that evolved around the close of the century blessed the Dominican Republic with peak-roofed wooden structures in tropical pastels. In provincial towns, particularly, buildings were graced with gingerbread trim and intricate ornamentation, often with wrap-around balconies on upper levels. Many of the best examples can be found in San Pedro de Macorís and Puerto Plata, where fine 19th-century mansions still stand today.

Modernist Influences

In the 20th century, art nouveau, which evolved in Europe from 1905 to 1920, came to the Dominican Republic as highly decorative houses in Belgian, French, and Catalonian styles. Pride of heritage also found expression in a Spanish revival.

The 1920s brought a beaux arts movement, introduced by the École des Beaux-Arts in Paris. Pompeiian frescoes and Corinthian columns appeared, as did elaborate stained-glass appointments by Tiffany's. By the late 1920s, the art deco style—terra-cotta motifs, veneer panels, banded facades—became the rage. The sensual nonchalance that marked the style is superbly expressed in the Casa New Yorker Hotel in Santo Domingo.

The 1930s launched a great architectural outpouring as President Rafael Trujillo set out to establish a bombastic legacy in stone. Santo Domingo gained a monumental look, not least in the Palacio Nacional, inaugurated in 1947 and designed by Italian architect Guido d'Alessandro Lombardi in decadent neoclassical style to evoke the grandeur of the Trujillo dictatorship. Hewn in roseate Samaná marble, its interior drips with Baccarat chandeliers whose light is reflected in a surfeit of gilt mirrors.

The years after World War II ushered in modern rationalism. Austere fascist-inspired structures went up, such as the concrete Columbus Lighthouse (Faro a Colón), a massive white elephant that was begun by Trujillo in 1939 and which took 53 years to complete. Its cruciform design is that of Joseph Lea Gleave (1907–1965), a British architectural student at the time. Meanwhile, in Higüey, French architects André Dunoyer de Segonzac (1884–1974) and Pierre Dupré (1913–unknown) designed the Basílica de Nuestra Señora de la Altagracia in the shape of two hands folded in prayer—a tropical version of Le Corbusier–inspired simplicity, it was completed in 1952. More restrained was Santo Domingo's gracefully modernist city hall (erected in 1955) by Guillermo González (1900–1970). Modernity also spread throughout Santo Domingo as new residential districts emerged. The middle class that evolved during the Trujillo era built lavish single-family residences in eclectic, neoclassical, and revivalist styles all over Santo Domingo. The most notable examples are in Gazcue and the upscale suburb of Villa Francisca. Emerging to pioneer the new style was a generation of gifted avant-garde Dominican architects, including Guillermo González, Humberto Ruiz Castillo (1895–1966), and most significantly Teófilo Carbonell (1924–2001). Meanwhile, Trujillo built the self-designed Castillo del Cerro for himself, a pompous semicircular six-story villa completed in 1947 in the architect's birthplace, San Cristóbal.

Trujillo's assassination in 1961 prefaced a new epoch as foreign capital flooded the Dominican Republic, resulting in a building boom in concrete and glass. Fine examples in Santo Domingo include the impressively modernist Teatro Nacional, erected in 1973 and designed by Carbonell; and the fittingly cubist Galería de Arte Moderno by José Minino (1945–2006), completed in 1976. The same period saw the construction of a new breed of high-rise hotels and office buildings in some cities, with prodigal use of curves and broad cantilevered eaves. Among the most experimental and controversial contemporary structures is the neo-Gothic, multi-towered Catedral de la Concepción de La Vega in La Vega. Designed by a team of architects and fabricated in steel pipe and concrete, this entity built in 1992 is generally considered a monstrous embarrassment. It stands in stark counterpoint to nearby Santiago's graceful, multifaceted, post-modernist Centro León cultural center. Juan Mubarak's (1957–) sensual waveform A Des-Tiempo, a multipurpose futuristic structure built in 1995 in the style of Frank Gehry, is more pleasing to the eye.

The past decade has witnessed a new era of stylish contemporary structures, found in huge resort projects sprouting along the shores of the Costa del Coco and in the nail-thin glass-and-marble condominium towers of chic central Santo Domingo that glitter gold in the evening light. ■

EXPERIENCE: Sugar Mills

You can get an intimate feel for the time when sugar was king by touring the ruins of 17th-century mills—*ingenios*—in the flatlands southwest of Santo Domingo. The four major plantations (Ingenios **Diego Caballero, Engombe, Nigua,** and **Palavé**) compose a UNESCO World Heritage site (*whc.unesco.org/en*). Their designs followed a common theme, with a plantation manor, chapel, boiling rooms, slave barracks, and watchtowers. Time your visit to Nigua, near Boca de Nigua, for the last weekend of October, when a fiesta recalls a slave uprising. To get there, take Carretera 2 toward San Cristóbal; turn north on Calle Ingenios for Nigua, then turn left onto Calle Lemba, which leads to the ruins.

Arts & Culture

From Afro-Caribbean rhythms to classical music and jazz, Dominican music reflects a vibrant culture that has produced a remarkable range of the fine arts. Today the Dominican Republic is an international trendsetter in the visual arts. Theater and dance are fast evolving. And classical and contemporary music are avatars of the nation's lively spirit, recalling rich indigenous traditions.

Visual Arts

The Dominican Republic has an art tradition dating back 3,000 years, to the time when pre-Columbian Taíno peoples adorned their cave walls and ceramics with stylized red, black, and ocher motifs. Artistic expression remains an important part of Dominican life. Much of the island is a magical tour of homespun studios selling primitive Haitian and Dominican paintings, their canvases conveying scenes of island life in exorbitant color. And Santo Domingo is world class in its range of galleries displaying works of great complexity and beauty. Virtually every township has its galleries and museums.

Fine arts evolved fairly late in the day in the Dominican Republic compared to many neighboring islands. Realism, romanticism, neoclassicism, and other schools of European art leapt the Atlantic to infuse the works of such native Dominican artists as Luis "Sisito" Desangles (1861–1940) and Abelardo Rodríguez Urdaneta (1870–1933). However, Dominican art didn't find its own expression until the turn of the 20th century, when Adriana Billini Gautreau (1865–1946) helped establish *indigenismo* and *costumbrismo*—portrayals of traditional Dominican life—as a dominant theme. Following the establishment of Francisco Franco's fascist government in Spain in 1939, such Spanish artists as José Gausachs (1889–1959), Eugenio Fernández Granell (1912–2001), and José Vela Zanetti (1913–1999) settled in Santo Domingo. Under the patronage of President Rafael Trujillo, who had a soft spot for the arts, the trio founded the Escuela Nacional de Bellas Artes (National School of Fine Arts, since renamed the Palacio de Bellas Artes), which melded modernism, neo-impressionism, and other European elements into Dominican costumbrismo. Leading Dominican artists to emerge included Celeste Woss y Gil (1891–1985), who gained attention for paintings of black and mulatto Dominican women, portrayed in a trademark modernist style.

Following Trujillo's assassination in 1961, a period of social and political turmoil inspired Dominican artists, often resulting in wildly imaginative works such as the disquieting magic realism of Tony Capellán (1955–), who deals with issues such as prostitution and the plight of Dominican and Haitian boat people. Although no common school of

Museo Bellapart

With an unlikely setting on the fifth floor of a Honda car showroom in Santo Domingo, this fabulous museum *(Edificio Honda, Ave. John F. Kennedy bet. Ave. Los Framboyanes & Calle Del Carmen, tel 809/541-7721 ext. 296, museobellapart.com, closed Sun.)* boasts a stunning private collection of art by many of the nation's foremost contemporary masters, not least Jaime Colson (1901–1975), Darío Suro (1917–1998), and such former exiles as José Vela Zanetti, a foremost impressionist. The works span the mid-19th century onward, and are arranged chronologically.

Fearsome papier-mâché Carnaval masks are a trademark of the Cibao region.

expression exists, portrayals of sugarcane fields and oxen and roosters still form a focus of much of contemporary Dominican art, which fuses costumbrismo into a more mature artistic expression. African primitivism often merges with modernist, cubist, and other contemporary styles. Latter-day world-famous names include Guillo Pérez (1923–2014) and Cándido Bidó (1936–2011), whose vivid, naive works present Cibao's diverse people with mystical, masklike faces. The island's finest artists today compete on an international level, their works fetching tens of thousands of dollars apiece.

Santo Domingo's Museo de Arte Moderno displays the nation's largest collection of works by Dominican artists in permanent and revolving exhibitions taken from the museum's vast archives.

On the crafts front, the Dominican Republic is famous for wildly colorful and frighteningly grotesque papier-mâché Carnaval masks from the towns of El Cibao. Their makers, once regarded as mere folk hobbyists, are today viewed as master artists. El Cibao is also known for its faceless ceramic dolls, and Salcedo for its crafts made of *higuero* (calabash). Market stalls nationwide are brimful of straw hats, available in a variety of styles.

Painting has long overshadowed the plastic arts in the Dominican Republic. Spanish sculptor Manolo Pascual (1902–1983), a co-founder of the National School of Fine Arts, was an exception during his tenure in the Dominican Republic, from 1939 to 1951, where he adopted ancient Taíno elements to shape his vibrant pieces, crafted in materials from wood to marble. The 1990s witnessed an explosion in a wide variety of fine arts, led by Capellán, Jorge Severino (1935–), and Soucy de Pellerano (1928–2014), whose works range from dramatic paintings to ingenious theatrical stage sets. Most famous of Pellerano's works is her trilevel set, made of a seemingly random pile of automotive junk, for the National Theater of the Dominican Republic's 1989 production of Shakespeare's *A Midsummer Night's Dream.*

Literature

The Dominican Republic was slow to evolve a literary culture, which was eventually spawned by the clenched-fist call for independence. Early literary works leaned toward polemic poetry in the tradition of the romantic verses of Spain. The 19th-century Haitian occupation of the republic fostered the evolution of a nationalist spirit in Dominican literature, notably in the poetry of Félix Maria del Monte (1819–1899), who decried injustice and espoused the cause of independence. The subsequent fight for freedom

Santo Domingo's Museo de Arte Moderno displays a world-class art collection.

EXPERIENCE: Where the Music's At

The Dominican Republic has a nightlife hot enough to cook pork. Whether you're seeking mellow jazz riffs or ice-melting salsa, there's a wide choice of venues. Here are some of the best.

Atarazana 9
Perfectly located for clubbing following dinner on Plaza España in Santo Domingo, this two-level club gets packed on weekends with a young moneyed crowd. Live music upstairs. (*Calle Atarazana 9, tel 809/688-0969*).

La Guacará Taína
Also in Santo Domingo, it combines a unique ambience—inside a cave—with top-notch salsa sounds. It has a choice of dance floors and bars (*Ave. Mirador del Sur, tel 809/533-1051*).

Mangú
The hottest club in Punta Cana. Dance to techno and house upstairs, or opt for mellower top 40, disco, and classics downstairs (*Gran Flamenco Hotel, tel 809/685-9955*).

helped nurture *criollo* expression, epitomized by *Enriquillo: Dominican Historical Legend,* Manuel de Jesús Galván's (1834–1910) classic novel honoring the "noble savage." This work, more than any other, proved a precursor of Dominican *modernismo,* which awakened the island's conscience and gave it an enthusiasm for native culture and language.

The early 20th century inaugurated a move to modernism that cast off prior formalities in favor of free expression, espoused by such writers as essayist Américo Lugo (1870–1952) and Gastón Fernando Deligne (1861–1913). The Trujillo years brought new repression, and the best works of the time were written in exile by literary notables such as politician and polemicist Juan Bosch, known for his short stories. The diaspora has continued to be a source for some of the finest Dominican literature, such as New York–based Julia Álvarez's (1950–) *How the García Girls Lost Their Accents,* a seminal work about the tensions that tug at island-born Dominicans living in an adopted homeland. Contemporary writers have focused primarily on daily life in the Dominican Republic, dominated by parochial themes. Junot Díaz's (1968–) highly original *The Brief Wondrous Life of Oscar Wao,* for example, depicts an island of contradictory poverty and wealth that casts a lasting spell over Dominicans at home and abroad.

Despite Dominicans' love of literature, there is a shortage of bookstores outside the capital city, which hosts an annual international book fair each spring.

Music & Dance

Music, the pulsing undercurrent of Dominican life, plays the pivotal role in island culture, while dance—from the early bolero to the latter-day merengue craze—has always been a potent expression of the islanders' sensuality. Santo Domingo's nightclubs explode on weekends to the *vida loca* vibe. Despite the infectious popularity of contemporary forms, the Dominicans also hold fast to their roots: The seductive rhythms and soulful beats pulsing through the streets owe much to the fusion of Spanish and African sounds. There's no better way to experience traditional *música dominicana* than at a *fiesta patronal*—one of the patron saint festivals hosted by each of the country's municipalities, featuring traditional dancing based on the stylized Spanish *paseo,* with men and women circling each other, accompanied by much yip-yipping and tossing of hats and scarves.

Spaniards introduced rural folk music to Hispaniola, which developed a distinctive criollo form—*guajiras* or *trovas*—using a tradition of poetry in song. The fusion of folk music with African rhythms and instruments, such as claves, maracas, the *güira* (a hollow gourd grater), and drums known as *tamboras,* is the basis for modern Dominican popular music. It began with the *danzón,* which derived from the French contredanse in Saint-Domingue. The music evolved into a Creole song called *mereng,* often laced with lewd lyrics. During the 18th and 19th centuries, Haitian invaders infused the eastern half of the island with their rhythmic music. (Most Dominicans are still reluctant to admit that *merengue* evolved from 18th-century Haiti.) Ever adaptive, the genre took on its classical form when accordions (sold by Cibao's German tobacco exporters) were adopted alongside, or even replaced, string instruments. The resulting countrified *merengue típico cibao,* typically played by a minstrel trio colloquially known as a *perico ripiao* (ripped parrot), is considered the definitive Dominican sound.

Trujillo adopted the music as his own to curry popularity with the Dominican peasantry. Beginning in the 1930s, U.S. jazz bands that toured the island also influenced Dominican music. The formation of brassy big band sets opened the way for the evolution of today's fast-paced Latin-jazz merengue, thanks in part to Trujillo, who was accompanied on his campaign tours by a top-notch band, and who ordered state radio stations to play merengue. Gradually the music found favor throughout the nation and was shipped to New York by émigrés fleeing the Trujillo dictatorship. Here, a more sophisticated, marketable form evolved as *merengueros* packaged their product for the record industry. Key among them was Johnny Ventura (1940–), known for his Elvis-like hip-swiveling histrionics. Danced to an impossibly fast and infectious beat, merengue finally exploded on the New York scene in the 1980s and was popularized throughout Latin America by superstar Wilfrido Radamés Vargas (1949–). Merengue continues to evolve as artists such as Vargas and the multi-platinum international merengue sensation Juan Luis Guerra (1957–) fuse traditional boleros and even hip-hop and reggaeton into their polyrhythmic sound.

> **The fusion of folk music with African rhythms and instruments such as claves, maracas, the *güira* (a hollow gourd grater), and drums known as *tamboras,* is the basis for modern Dominican popular music.**

The Dominican Republic is also the heartland for the melancholy ballads known as *bachata.* Birthed in the countryside and impoverished barrios, the form is full of lament about hardship and betrayed love. Today bachata—the "music of bitterness"—is played with plinkety-plink banjo-style acoustic guitar as the predominant instrument and is the nation's most popular music. One of the most admired proponents is Juan Luis Guerra, renowned for marrying bachata into his jazz-steeped merengue. Even great-grandparents rock in time to the music as the young men whirl the young women around in circles, like twins joined at the hip.

Hip-hop and reggae cultures blend at a reggaeton concert in Santo Domingo.

Jazz has gained popularity in recent years and finds its major outlet in the annual Dominican Republic Jazz Festival each October or November. No national jazz style has evolved, although it has a bravura, macho sound with trumpeters playing the highest notes and pianists going as fast as they can go. Major Dominican jazz proponents include Sandy Gabriel & PP Jazz Ensemble and pianist Michel Camilo (1954–).

On the classical front, the country has been neither an inspirational locale nor a breeding ground for composers and instrumentalists, although the classical genres are popular with urban sophisticates. The Teatro Nacional hosts the National Symphony, formed in 1941, and the National Youth Symphony. The annual Santo Domingo Music Festival, held each March at the Teatro Nacional, focuses exclusively on classical music. The annual Festival of Dominican Song Eduardo Brito is intended to foster composition among Dominicans; it is named for Eduardo Brito (1906–1946), who rose from being a shoeshine boy to become one of the world's great baritones. One of the nation's hottest new classical performers is young composer and guitarist Anthony Ocaña (1980–).

Dance, Cinema, & Performing Arts

On the dance floor, Dominicans swivel as if on a hinge. It's in their blood, and Dominicans are appreciative of all forms of dance, from merengue to modern dance and classical ballet, in which the nation excels. The National Classical Ballet—formed in 1981 by exiled Cuban ballerina Clara Elena Ramírez (1919–2007) and Hungarian ballerina Magda Corbett (1916–2006)—performs through a year-long season. The Dominican Ballet Concierto also raises the curtain to ovations at home as well as abroad.

The Dominican Republic has a lively theater scene, notably in experimental theater performed in tiny parochial venues—such as Santo Domingo's Casa de Teatro—by such avant-garde groups as Teatro Gayumba. The few Dominican-born actors and actresses to gain any sort of stardom include María Montez (1912–1951), who excelled as a camp heroine in almost 30 Hollywood movies; and 21-inch-tall (54 cm) Nelson Aquino de la Rosa (1968–2006), whose role in *The Island of Dr. Moreau* with Marlon Brando was the inspiration for Mini Me in the Austin Powers movies.

The nation's filmmaking industry is virtually nonexistent. Still, Puerto Plata hosts the annual six-day-long Dominican International Film Festival (and the Dominican Film Commission) founded by President Leonel Fernández with the goal of bringing filmmakers and filmmaking to the republic. The nation fares better as a film location. It has been the setting for more than 60 films, from *The Godfather II* and *Apocalypse Now* to *Jurassic Park* and *Fast & Furious*.

Sports

Dominicans of all social strata are fanatical about sports, primarily baseball, in which Dominicans vie with their Cuban neighbors for best in the world. The country has a long history of producing top talent, beginning in the 1960s, when the Alou brothers (Felipe, Matty, and Jésus) and Juan Marichal (1937–) became prominent major league players. The Liga de Béisbol, founded in 1981, has six national teams considered stepping-stones to the U.S. major leagues. At any one time, dozens of Dominicans are pitching, fielding, and swinging their bats for U.S. teams, most famously Sammy Sosa (1968–), who grew up impoverished in San Pedro de Macorís.

Basketball runs a close second to baseball, although Dominican players have had less success on the international scene. The hardscrabble life of many Dominicans has also reaped a remarkable crop of world champion boxers, such as brothers Carlos (1937–1970) and Leo Cruz (1953–), and Joán Guzman (1976–), former lightweight, junior featherweight, and super bantamweight champions, respectively. ■

EXPERIENCE: Festivals Not to Be Missed

The Dominican Republic's calendar is a whirlwind of fiestas. Almost every town has its patron saint's day *(fiesta patronal)*, typically featuring a parade, fireworks, children in traditional costume, and plenty of music and dance. Religious *feriados* (holidays) and processions are held during Holy Week, while more bacchanalian Carnavales take place around Lent. Here are some key fiestas to know:

Carnaval *(Feb.; La Vega, Santiago, Santo Domingo)* is the biggest and most festive event of the year. People dressed in horned devil masks and colorful costumes hit each other with inflated pig bladders.

Merengue Festival *(July; Santo Domingo)*, a two-week marathon on the Malecón, features the republic's top acts.

Fiesta Patronal de la Nuestra Señora de las Mercedes *(Sept. 24; La Vega)*, the most important religious day in the nation, draws thousands of devoted Dominicans to the shrine at La Vega.

Dominican Jazz Festival *(Nov.; Cabarete)* brings world-class Latin jazz performers to this beach venue.

A vibrant, traffic-thronged capital city, both cosmopolitan and historic

Santo Domingo

Detail of a stained-glass window, Catedral Primada de América

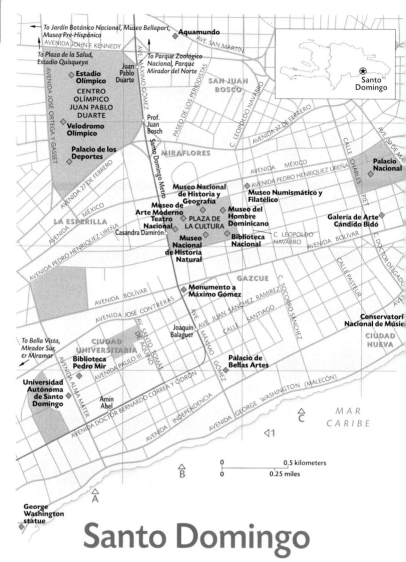

To Jardín Botánico Nacional, Museo Bellapart, Museo Pre-Hispánico
AVENIDA JOHN F KENNEDY
To Plaza de la Salud, Estadio Quisqueya
To Parque Zoológico Nacional, Parque Mirador del Norte
Aquamundo
AVE SAN MARTÍN
AV. MÁXIMO GÓMEZ
Juan Pablo Duarte
Estadio Olímpico
CENTRO OLÍMPICO JUAN PABLO DUARTE
Velodromo Olímpico
Palacio de los Deportes
AVENIDA JOSÉ ORTEGA Y GASSET
AVENIDA 27 DE FEBRERO
MÉXICO
LA ESPERILLA
AVENIDA PEDRO HENRIQUEZ UREÑA
Prof. Juan Bosch
Santo Domingo Metro
MIRAFLORES
Casandra Damirón
Museo Nacional de Historia y Geografía
Museo de Arte Moderno
Teatro Nacional
PLAZA DE LA CULTURA
Museo Nacional de Historia Natural
SAN JUAN BOSCO
PASEO DE LOS PERIODISTAS
C. LEOPOLDO NAVARRO
AVENIDA 27 DE FEBRERO
AVENIDA MÉXICO
AVENIDA PEDRO HENRIQUEZ UREÑA
Museo Numismático y Filatélico
Museo del Hombre Dominicano
Biblioteca Nacional
C. LEOPOLDO NAVARRO
AVENIDA BOLÍVAR
CALLE CHARLES
Palacio Nacional
PIET
Galería de Arte Cándido Bidó
CALLE DOCTOR DELGADO
GAZCUE
Monumento a Máximo Gómez
AVENIDA BOLÍVAR
AVENIDA JOSÉ CONTRERAS
CIUDAD UNIVERSITARIA
Biblioteca Pedro Mir
Universidad Autónoma de Santo Domingo
Amín Abel
AVENIDA ALMA MATER
AVENIDA DOCTOR BERNARDO CORREA Y CIDRÓN
AVENIDA PAULO III
AV SANTO TOMÁS DE AQUINO
Joaquín Balaguer
AVE. JUAN SÁNCHEZ RAMIREZ
CALLE SANTIAGO
SOCORRO SÁNCHEZ
Palacio de Bellas Artes
AV. MÁXIMO GÓMEZ
AVENIDA INDEPENDENCIA
AVENIDA GEORGE WASHINGTON (MALECÓN)
Conservatori Nacional de Músic
CIUDAD NUEVA
CALLE PASTEUR
MAR CARIBE
To Bella Vista, Mirador Sur, & Miramar
George Washington statue
AVE 30 DE M.
CALLE CHARLES
Santo Domingo
0   0.5 kilometers
0   0.25 miles
◁1
△ C
△ B
△ A

Santo Domingo

Built on the west bank of the Río Ozama as the first European city in the Western Hemisphere, Santo Domingo is today a cosmopolitan metropolis of 2.9 million. Radiating inland like a Spanish fan, it combines Old World charm with modern sophistication—reason enough that Santo Domingo was voted Cultural Capital of the Americas 2010.

Founded in 1498 by Bartholomew Columbus, Christopher's brother, the early city established itself as the launch pad for colonizing expeditions throughout the Americas. The city was originally called Nueva Isabela and located on the east bank of the Río Ozama. In 1502 a hurricane leveled the wooden settlement, and Gov. Nicolás de Ovando reestablished it

(in stone) across the river and renamed it Santo Domingo de Guzmán. Laid out in a grid, the colonial city lay within a cordon wall (muralla), still extant, with six entrance gates and 20 baluartes (bulwarks). In 1586 privateer Francis Drake and his fleet of 20 ships raided the city, presaging a month-long orgy of destruction and looting. Though rebuilt, Santo Domingo never

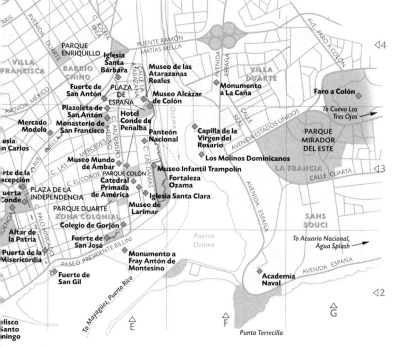

PARQUE ENRIQUILLO

Iglesia Santa Bárbara

PUENTE RAMÓN MATÍAS MELLA

VILLA FRANCISCA

BARRIO CHINO

Museo de las Atarazanas Reales

Fuerte de San Antón

PLAZA DE ESPAÑA

Museo Alcázar de Colón

Monumento a La Caña

VILLA DUARTE

Faro a Colón

Plazoleta de San Antón

Hotel Conde de Peñalba

To Cueva Los Tres Ojos

Mercado Modelo

Monasterio de San Francisco

Panteón Nacional

Capilla de la Virgen del Rosario

PARQUE MIRADOR DEL ESTE

esia n Carlos

Los Molinos Dominicanos

Museo Mundo de Ámbar

PARQUE COLÓN

Museo Infantil Trampolín

LA FRANCIA

CALLE CUARTA

rte de la cepción

Catedral Primada de América

Fortaleza Ozama

uerta Conde

PLAZA DE LA INDEPENDENCIA

Iglesia Santa Clara

SANS SOUCI

PARQUE DUARTE
ZONA COLONIAL

Museo de Larimar

Colegio de Gorjón

To Acuario Nacional, Agua Splash

Altar de la Patria

Fuerte de San José

Puerto Ozama

Puerta de la Misericordia

Monumento a Fray Antón de Montesino

PASEO PRESIDENTE BILLINI

Fuerte de San Gil

To Mayagüez, Puerto Rico

Academia Naval

elisco anto mingo

E

F

G

Punta Torrecilla

regained its importance and in the 19th century fell into the hands of French and British forces before succumbing to Haitian domination (1822–1844). Half a century of strife followed as Dominican *caudillos* fought over the city.

Much of the city was effectively leveled by Hurricane San Zenon in 1930. In 1936, Congress voted to rename the capital Ciudad Trujillo, after Rafael Trujillo. The dictator launched a massive construction program that graced the city with many fine contemporary edifices. Following Trujillo's death, new middle- and upper-class neighborhoods arose, and the city reclaimed its former name. Today Santo Domingo is a fast-paced, modern city, with fashionable shopping, superb dining, and a sizzling nightlife reflecting the Latin mystique.

The modern yang to the colonial yin is found along the Malecón, a faded seafront boulevard lined with casinos and high-rise hotels, and in the modern Naco–Winston Churchill–Piantini business, shopping, and dining districts. The art scene is also enticing, centered on the superb Museo de Arte Moderno in Plaza de la Cultura. The city fans out with parks such as the tendril-thin Parque Mirador del Sur and the Parque Mirador del Este.

The most interesting sites are concentrated around the three main plazas of the Zona Colonial, currently in the midst of renovation. The old city deserves a three-day minimum, and the Ciudad Nueva, Gazcue, and outlying districts a day each. An informal system of *públicos* (minivans), *gua-guas* (buses), and taxis serves the city, and the Metro de Santo Domingo subway system links major sites.

In the Zona Colonial, the presence of tourist police helps keep crime at bay. However, visitors should steer clear of much of the city, not least the districts immediately north of the Zona Colonial, and the Malecón. ■

NOT TO BE MISSED:

Zona Colonial

Declared a UNESCO World Heritage site in 1990, the Zona Colonial is a trove of historic attractions guaranteed to enthrall for days. Spanning a hundred city blocks within the old city walls, its ancient streets and cobbled plazas are graced by an architectural A-list of castles, palaces, and mansions, many turned into restaurants, boutiques, hotels, and eclectic museums.

The Colonial Zone's eclectic architecture reflects colonial and modern influences.

The Zona Colonial brims with architectural gems, including more than 300 buildings of historic import. It is easy to imagine yourself cast back 500 years to when Bartholomew Columbus founded the New World's oldest city. Vibrant with street life, the Colonial Zone is fascinating, too, for the timeworn appeal of life lived in the shadow of a colonial past. Horse-drawn carriages clip-clop through the plazas, and the hurly-burly of the 20th century quickly fades as you stroll the shady courtyards and cobbled alleys.

Calle El Conde—the main east–west artery—is pedestrian only and thronged with locals busy shopping, and sections of Calles Isabel la Católica and Arzobispo Meriño are now also pedestrian only. Beyond this core zone, vehicular traffic clogs the roads. Still, even the poorest streets have a lingering dignity beneath the grime baked in by centuries of tropical heat. Wrought-iron balconies blaze with bougainvillea, while weathered limestone facades and ornate gingerbread in pastels smolder gold in the afternoon sun.

In 2013, the government launched a three-year revitalization project to enhance the colonial zone's appeal, including with more pedestrian-only causeways. Note that although gentrification is ongoing, pockets of poverty remain, and caution is required while walking at night.

Parque Colón

The heart of the Zona Colonial and a center of cultural and political life since early days, this lovely bohemian square is lined with cafés. It's a perfect spot for watching residents drink espresso beneath shade trees while shoeshiners buff their shoes and *chiriperos* (pushcart vendors) hawk their wares.

Originally known as Plaza Mayor, the square is pinned at its core by a statue of Christopher Columbus (known here as Cristóbal Colón), erected in 1887 by French sculptor Ernesto Gilbert, with Taíno queen Anacaona staring up adoringly.

The original plans called for the square to be surrounded by the cathedral, governor's palace, town hall, and court of justice, but pirate attacks precluded the plan's realization. Still, lovely colonial buildings rise to each side.

The South Side: Dominating the plaza, the **Catedral Primada de América**—officially known as the Catedral Santa María de la Encarnación—is the New World's oldest church. Its foundation stone

was laid by Diego Colón, the first-born son of Christopher Columbus, in 1510. After a turbulent construction process (the original architect, Alonso de Rodríguez, sailed for Mexico with the drawings), the church was completed in 1540. The belfry, however, was

INSIDER TIP:

Explore the Zona Colonial on Trikke Colonial's three-wheel electric scooters, or on the Chu Chu Colonial sightseeing train.

—CHRISTOPHER BAKER
National Geographic author

destroyed by Francis Drake and the bell tower remains exposed. Its main (northern) facade with stained-glass windows (reproductions of the originals) combines Gothic, baroque, and classical influences. The western plat
esque facade with twin pointed "battlements" is adorned with fanciful friezes, including cherubs surrounded by sea dragons and impious women. The **Puerta del Perdón** (Portal of Clemency), on the south side, afforded sanctuary to renegades.

Though Drake and his men vandalized the interior in 1586, the church—entered today through plate-glass doors—still contains friezes and a bishop's throne. Beneath the ribbed-vault ceiling, 14 chapels contain murals, stained-glass windows, and vaults, one supposedly the first resting

Parque Colón
A 59 E3
Visitor Information
✉ Calle Arzobispo Meriño 157
☎ 809/687-8217
🕐 Closed Sat.–Sun.
**gosantodomingo
.travel**

Catedral Primada de América
A 59 E3
✉ Parque Colón, Calle Arzobispo Nouel & Calle Arzobispo Meriño
☎ 809/682-3848

Trikke Colonial
✉ Calle Padre Bellini 54
☎ 809/221-8097
💲 $$$$

Chu Chu Colonial
✉ Calle El Conde 60
☎ 809/686-2303
💲 $$$
chuchucolonial.com

place of Christopher Columbus. A dress code applies: no shorts for men, no trousers or short skirts for women.

To the rear of the cathedral, the cobbled **Plazuela de los Curas** (Priests' Square) was the city's original cemetery. A narrow walkway, the **Callejón de los Curas** (Alley of the Priests), connects to Calle Padre Billini; it was once lined with priests' homes, most of which are still private residences. A stone's throw west, **Plazoleta Padre Billini** *(Calle Arzobispo Meriño & Calle Padre Billini)* was a setting for bullfights in ancient times. Today the small plaza is lined with chic boutiques and antique and jewelry stores. Facing the plaza to the south, the beautifully restored, Gothic-style Casa de Tostado dates from 1503 and features a double Gothic

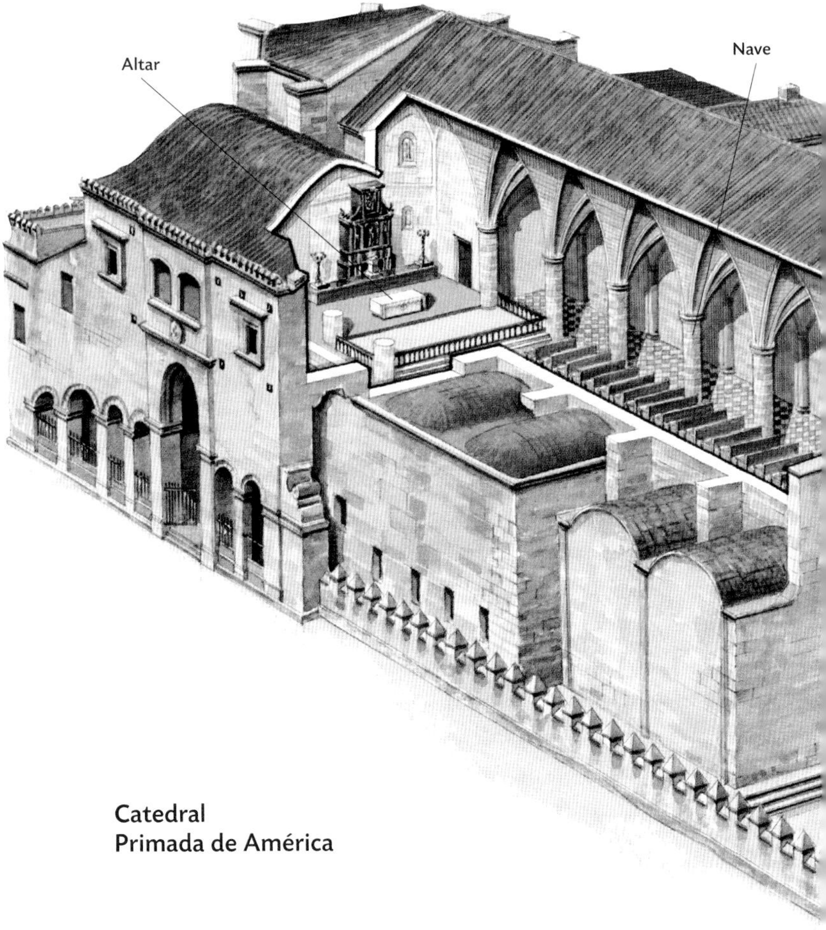

Altar

Nave

**Catedral
Primada de América**

Churchgoers find inspiration in the austere grandeur of the interior of Catedral Primada de América.

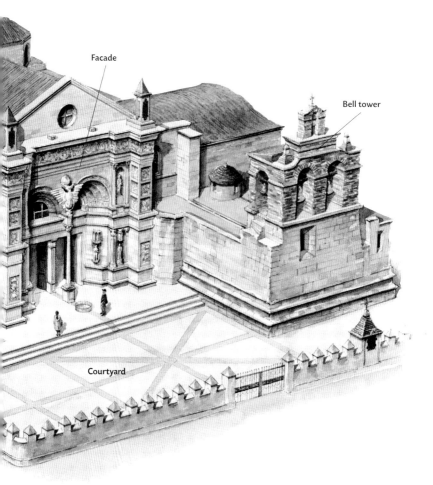

Facade

Bell tower

Courtyard

Museo de la Familia Dominicana del Siglo XIX

- ✉ Calle Padre Billini & Calle Arzobispo Meriño
- ☎ 809/689-5000
- 🕐 Closed Mon.
- 💲 $

Museo de Larimar

- 🅰 59 E3
- ✉ Calle Isabel la Católica 54
- ☎ 809/689-6605

larimarmuseum.com

Museo de Ámbar

- 🅰 59 E3
- ✉ Calle El Conde 107
- ☎ 809/221-1333
- 🕐 Closed Sun.

window, unique in the Americas. It holds the **Museo de la Familia Dominicana del Siglo XIX** (Museum of the 19th-Century Dominican Family), exhibiting the myriad furnishings and personal items of a well-to-do local family. You can ascend the spiral mahogany staircase for a fine view over the city.

The East Side: Standing over the park's east side is the **Palacio**

Columbus's Remains

Christopher Columbus died in Valladolid, Spain, on May 20, 1506. What happened to him afterward is a matter of some controversy. According to the Dominican Republic, he was laid to rest in Seville before being transferred to Santo Domingo, where he was buried in a crypt in the cathedral. In 1795, Spanish authorities sent what they believed to be Columbus's remains to Cuba. In 1877, workers discovered a lead urn in Santo Domingo's Catedral Santa María that was labeled as containing Columbus's bones. These remains were removed to the Faro a Colón for the quincentennial celebrations in 1992. However, Spanish authorities claim that Columbus's true remains were returned to Seville; Italy also claims to possess his remains.

---

de Borgellá, fronted by a gracious two-story loggia. One of the original 15 homes ordered built by Ovando, it was briefly owned by Hernán Cortés, who was then the city clerk. Following independence, it served as the Senate house, then as headquarters for the Haitian occupation, and today hosts the Patronato—the body in charge of restoring the UNESCO World Heritage site.

To its south, the Spanish Revival **Casa del Sacramento** (*Calle Isabel la Católica*) gleams afresh since given a face-lift. Built in 1520 to house Diego de Caballero, secretary of the Real Audiencia (the colony's judges), it is today the archbishop's residence. Across the street in a charmingly restored colonial home, the **Museo de Larimar** has the nation's finest displays of this semiprecious stone.

Diagonally across, to the south, the simple Renaissance **Iglesia y Convento Santa Clara** (*Calle Padre Billini & Calle Isabel la Católica*) was built in 1522 as the first Franciscan nunnery in the New World. Rebuilt after being sacked by Drake, it still serves as a Catholic school run by nuns.

The North Side: Pedestrian-only Calle El Conde runs along the park's north side, linking Parque Colón to Parque Independencia. Named in honor of the Count of Peñalba, this bustling commercial thoroughfare is renowned for its shoe and jewelry stores; on the square's north side, the **Museo de Ámbar** is a private store with splendid upstairs displays of amber and larimar pieces. To its east

Students from nearby schools often meet in verdant Parque Colón.

stands the Antigua Bank of America and to the west, graced by wrought-iron balconies, is the **Hotel Conde de Peñalba.**

On the northwest side is the Antiguo Palacio Consistorial *(Calle El Conde & Calle Arzobispo Meriño),* the former city hall. Originally built in 1504, it was remodeled in 1911 with a neoclassical facade. Today it houses a branch of the Banco de Trabajadores. ∎

A Walk Around the Zona Colonial

↪ This walk explores the heart of the Colonial Zone, taking in a veritable trove of significant buildings dating back many centuries. The past is palpable as you stroll the Zona Colonial, comprising a hundred square blocks within the old city walls, with the most significant structures concentrated around three main plazas.

Children play in the shadow of the Catedral Primada de América.

Walking the main streets of the Zona Colonial is safe by day, especially with a licensed guide. Nonetheless, much of the periphery is down-at-the-heels; at night, especially, you should avoid dark streets away from the main plazas.

Begin your walk at **Fortaleza Ozama ❶** (see p. 70). After exploring the fortress, walk north past the office of the **Sociedad Dominicana de Bibliófilos** (*Calle Las Damas 106, tel 809/687-6644*), which restores ancient documents; and the **Academia de Ciencias** (*Calle Las Damas 112, tel 809/687-6315*). Across the street, the **Museo Infantil Trampolín** (see p. 70) is worth exploring.

Continuing north to Calle El Conde, you'll pass on your right the broad **Escalinata de la Victoria** (Victoria Stairway), which leads down

> **NOT TO BE MISSED:**
>
> Museo de las Casas Reales • Museo Alcázar de Colón • Catedral Primada de América • Museo Mundo de Ámbar

to Avenida del Puerto and the port. Passing the **Casa de Francia** (see p. 71) and Hostal Nicolás de Ovando, visit the **Panteón Nacional ❷** (see p. 71) before ambling north to explore the **Museo de las Casas Reales** (see p. 73). Exiting, step north across **Plaza de España ❸** (see pp. 72–73) to visit the **Museo Alcázar de Colón** (see p. 72) before taking the steps down to the **Museo de las Atarazanas Reales** (see p. 73).

Turn left onto Calle Vicente Celestino Duarte and walk one block to Calle Isabel la Católica; turn left. Two blocks south, stop to admire the **Casa del Cordón** (see p. 73) and, on the left, the **Banco de Reservas** (*Calle Isabel la Católica 201, tel 809/682-6438*). Step inside to see the lobby, featuring a socialist-realistic mural, "Moneda," by Spanish artist José Vela Zanetti. At Calle Las Mercedes, turn left and detour 20 yards (18 m) to the **Casa de las Gárgolas** (*Calle Las Mercedes 2*), guarded by several gargoyles.

Continue south three blocks to **Parque Colón ❹** (see p. 61). After exploring the **Catedral Primada de América ❺** (see pp. 61–62), continue past the **Casa del Sacramento** (see p. 64) and call in at the **Museo de Larimar** (see p. 64) to admire the semiprecious stones. Turn right onto Calle Padre Billini; the **Iglesia Santa Clara**

(see p. 64) will be diagonally across. Passing **La Casa de Codia** (*Calle Padre Billini 58*), once the home of Gov. Buenaventura Báez (1810–1884), stop at the **Museo de la Familia Dominicana del Siglo XIX** (see p. 64), facing **Plazoleta Padre Billini.**

Westward you'll pass **Parque Fray Bartolomé de las Casas** (*bet. Calle Hostos & Calle Arzobispo Meriño*), a dour plaza with a contemporary statue of the benevolent Brother Bartolomé looking to heaven in anguish. At the junction with Calle Hostos, note the **Iglesia y Convento Dominico** (see p. 69) on the

🅰	See also area map p. 59
►	Fortaleza Ozama
🕐	6 hours
↔	3 miles (5 km)
►	Plaza de España

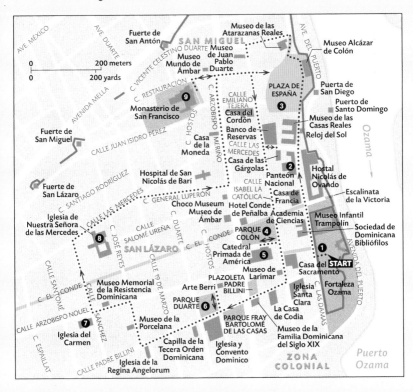

southeast corner, then nip north 75 yards (69 m) to **Arte Berri** *(Calle Hostos 105, tel 829/343-4514, arteberri.com, closed Sun.)*, a gallery selling contemporary art. Retrace your steps to **Parque Duarte** ❻ (see opposite) to admire the **Capilla de la Tercera Orden Dominicana** (see opposite) before continuing west. Boasting an imposing facade and baroque altar, the **Iglesia de la Regina Angelorum** *(Calle Padre Billini)*, Queen of the Angels Church, was built in 1537.

Turn north at Calle José Reyes. Walk 50 yards (46 m) to the **Museo de la Porcelana** *(Calle José Reyes 6, tel 809/688-4759, closed Mon., $)*, the Porcelain Museum, on your left. This exquisite Moorish structure is inspired by the Alhambra in Grenada, Spain. Continue half a block to Calle Arzobispo Nouel. Turn left and walk one block to **Iglesia del Carmen** ❼ *(Calle Sánchez & Calle Arzobispo Nouel)*, rebuilt in brick in 1590 following Francis Drake's depredations.

One block farther, stop at the somber **Museo Memorial de la Resistencia Dominicana** *(Calle Arzobispo Nouel 210, tel 809/688-4444, museodelaresistencia.com)*, which opened in 2010. It details oppression under U.S. occupation and the Trujillo dictatorship. Heading

north, cross Calle El Conde and walk one block to Calle Las Mercedes. Turning right, you'll pass the **Iglesia de Nuestra Señora de las Mercedes** ❽ *(at Calle José Reyes)*, dating from 1555 and worth a peek for its baroque altar and distinctive mahogany pulpit on a serpent-demon base. At the triangular plaza beyond Calle José Reyes, follow Calle General Luperón east two blocks to Calle Hostos and the ruins of the **Hospital de San Nicolás de Barí,** the first hospital in the New World, built in 1503.

At Calle Arzobispo Meriño, head half a block south to the **Choco Museum** *(Calle Arzobispo Meriño 254, tel 809/221-8222, chocomuseo.com)* to learn about cacao and chocolate. Then turn north for 150 yards (137 m) to admire the **Casa de la Moneda** *(Calle Arzobispo Meriño 358)*, completed around 1540 and named for the medallions that adorn the plateresque entrance. Just north, check out the amber collection in the **Museo Mundo de Ámbar** (see p. 74), then turn west a few yards on Calle Emiliano Tejera to view the ruined **Monasterio de San Francisco** ❾ (see p. 74). Finally, retrace your steps along Tejera to Plaza de España for a meal at one of its restaurants.

Nuns are a frequent sight in the Zona Colonial, where convents were established in colonial times.

Parque Duarte

Perhaps the city's most intimate plaza, this redbrick rectangle is graced with elegant buildings and iron benches shaded by flame red flamboyants. It is lively at night when locals gather to play dominoes beside a floodlit statue of the national hero atop a marble plinth.

On the park's southeast side stands **Iglesia y Convento Dominico** *(Calle Padre Billini & Calle Hostos),* begun in 1510 as the first convent of the Dominican Order in the Americas. Here, the priest (later friar) Bartolomé de Las Casas chronicled Spanish atrocities against indigenous peoples. An earthquake toppled the first building; visitors now view a 1649 remake featuring a stone facade with decorative pilasters, plus windows adorned with Isabelline ornamentation. Inside, the **Chapel of the Rosary** contains frescoes of religious figures and a zodiac guarded by pagan gods—a remarkable survival of the Counter-Reformation.

To the west of the chapel is the lovely, coral pink **Capilla de la Tercera Orden Dominicana** *(Calle Duarte & Calle Padre Billini),* the Chapel of the Third Order of Dominicans. Built in 1729, it is the only church in the city to remain unchanged. Although it is closed to the public, its simple and somber baroque facade is to be admired. A lovely bougainvillea-framed garden to its rear features busts of poet Salomé Ureña (1850–1897) and writer Eugenio María de Hostos (1839–1903). With its wrought-iron benches, the chapel's shady courtyard is a delightful spot to relax.

Dominican Friars

Only 18 years after Columbus reached Hispaniola, the first four Dominican friars arrived. Shocked by the Spanish oppression of the island's indigenous people, the community wrote a formal protest in 1511, saying "With what right and by which justice do you hold these Indians in such horrible servitude?" The young priest Bartolomé de las Casas was present and later became a friar and fighter for indigenous rights.

Garlanded in bougainvillea, the block to the west of the chapel is one of the most exquisite in the Zona Colonial. The finest of the several colonial homes there, **Quinta Dominicana** *(Calle Padre Billini 202 bet. Calle Duarte & Calle 19 de Marzo)* hosts revolving art exhibitions.

One block southeast, the whitewashed **Colegio de Gorjón** *(Calle Arzobispo Meriño & Calle José Gabriel García)* housed the continent's first university. Inaugurated in 1538 and named for its founder, Hernando Gorjón, it later served as a seminary and eventually Jesuit headquarters. It is now the Instituto de Cultura Hispánica. ■

Parque Duarte

🅰 59 E3

✉ Calle Padre Billini bet. Calle Duarte & Calle Hostos

Fortaleza Ozama

Commanding the rocky point at the mouth of the Río Ozama, the oldest fortification in the Americas still stands sentry over the ancient harbor. Begun in 1502, this compact and austere castle was the early center of power in the New World. From here, conquistadores set out to conquer Cuba, Jamaica, and much of the American mainland.

Fortaleza Ozama
- 59 F3
- Calle Las Damas
- 809/686-0222
- $

Museo Infantil Trampolín
- 59 F3
- Ave. del Puerto
- 809/685-5551
- Closed Mon.
- $

trampolin.org.do

Squatting atop a promontory overlooking the river mouth and Avenida del Puerto, the rectangular fortress—by master military engineer Gómez García Varela—was two centuries in the making and served a military function into the 1970s. Knowledgeable, multilingual tour guides are available for a fee (*$$ per person per hour*).

The neoclassical main gate opens to a well-worn brick courtyard and sprawling grassy esplanade containing a statue of Gonzalo Fernández de Oviedo (1477–1557), the fortress commander from 1533 to 1557 and chronicler of the *General and Natural History of the Indies.* Beyond, the stout, medieval **Torre del**

Looking down from the fort's highest point, Torre del Homenaje

Homenaje was built as a watchtower in 1503 to sight approaching pirates. Its 6-foot-thick (2 m) walls rising 60 feet (18 m) are riddled with embrasures silhouetted against the blue sky. The tower later served as a prison, even through the Trujillo era. Note the hole through which prisoners were lowered into their cell. Climb the stairs for a sentry's view over the Zona Colonial.

To its south, the windowless, mid-18th-century **El Polverín** (Powder House) features on its door lintel a statue of St. Barbara, patron saint of artillery. Twin batteries of cannon run along the riverside wall, pointing their muzzles toward pirates past, while a collection of 20th-century tanks, armored personnel carriers, and artillery occupy the southeast corner of the esplanade.

Built into the fort's northern wall and accessed by its own gate, **Casa Rodrigo de Bastidas,** dating from 1512, is named for a former mayor of Santo Domingo and future conqueror of Colombia. With its cool, quiet courtyard surrounded by Roman arches, the exquisite though squat *casona* (manor) today serves as the magnificent **Museo Infantil Trampolín.** This fascinating children's museum features hands-on exhibits ranging from natural history to social sciences. ∎

Calle Las Damas

Cobbled Calle Las Damas, the oldest existing street in the Americas, links Fortaleza Ozama to Plaza de España. The street, named for the promenade of María de Toledo and her noble ladies in colonial times, is lined with tastefully restored 16th-century mansions and makes a delightful 400-yard-long (366 m) stroll.

Originating as a Jesuit monastery completed in 1796, the **Panteón Nacional** (aka Panteón de la Pátria) was restored in 1958 to serve as a marble-lined mausoleum for the nation's leaders. Its exquisitely frescoed dome shows "The Apocalypse and Resurrection" by Rafael Pellicer Galeot (1906–1963). An eternal flame commemorates La Trinitaria, led by Duarte, Sánchez, and Mella, who fought for independence from Haiti. A dress code applies—no shorts or tank tops.

The four-square **Casa de los Jesuitas,** adjoining to the north, was built in 1508 as a private mansion in Mudejar fashion. In 1701 it became a Jesuit university.

A soldier stands guard at the Panteón Nacional.

INSIDER TIP:

The new Colonial Gate 4D Cinema offers a thrilling multisensory 4D experience about the Zona Colonial.

—JUSTIN KAVANAGH
National Geographic Travel Books editor

On the pantheon's south side, the tiny **Plazoleta de María Toledo** is unremarkable but for its original 16th-century fountain. It links Calle Las Damas and Calle Isabel la Católica through arches that are all that remain of a Jesuit monastery. The plaza hosts a colorful Sunday *pulga* (flea market).

Facing the square to the east is **Casa de Ovando,** former residence of the island's first governor, Nicolás de Ovando. Built in 1509 with a Gothic facade and restored as the Hostal Nicolás de Ovando (see p. 205), it retains its Andalusian fountain. The hotel also incorporates the adjoining Casa de los Dávila, featuring a private chapel—the redbrick **Capilla de Nuestra Señora de los Remedios** (*Calle Las Damas & Calle Las Mercedes*).

The **Casa de Francia** (*Calle Las Damas 42, tel 809/695-4300*), the French Embassy, is in Hernán Cortés's former home. ∎

Calle Las Damas
🅰 59 E3

Panteón Nacional
✉ Calle Las Damas & Plazoleta de María Toledo

Colonial Gate 4D Cinema
✉ Calle Padre Bellini 52
☎ 809/682-4829
thecolonialgate.com

Plaza de España

The largest of the Zona Colonial's stately squares, this open space has received many face-lifts, most recently for the Revitalización Integral initiated in 2013. Highlighted by two splendid museums, it also bustles at night when the restaurants and bars along the north and west sides vibrate with laughter and music. Standing in the plaza, a statue of Nicolás de Ovando features a plaque denoting the colonial city's investiture as a UNESCO World Heritage site.

Plaza de España comes alive at night, when people flock to local restaurants.

Plaza de España

🅰 59 E3 & E4

Museo Alcázar de Colón

🅰 59 E3 & E4

✉ Plaza de España

☎ 809/682-4750

🕐 Closed Mon.

💲 $ (tickets from office on N side of plaza)

Alcázar de Colón

Built in 1511 as a palace for Diego Colón and his wife Doña María de Toledo, King Ferdinand's niece, the stately Palacio Alcázar dominates the plaza on the east. This part-Gothic, part-Moorish fortified palace was the center of power and the seat of the first Spanish court in the New World. Restored and now the **Museo Alcázar de Colón,** its 22 rooms display a knight in armor, plus tapestries, leather

chests, silver pieces, and household items—some said to have belonged to Columbus. Immediately south, the **Puerta de San Diego,** completed in 1555, granted access to the city from the harbor below.

North Side

Along the plaza's northwest side, **Calle La Atarazana** ("the shipyard") comprises a row of former warehouses connected via interior courtyards that once contained taverns and a public market. The complex now hosts sidewalk cafés.

To the northeast, a staircase called Los Escalones del Alcázar leads to the **Museo de las Atarazanas Reales,** depicting maritime life in the colonial era. Glittering under spotlights is salvaged treasure from the *Nuestra Señora de Guadalupe* and *El Conde de Tolosa* galleons, which foundered in 1724 (see p. 94). The museum faces east to the **Puerta de La Atarazana,** the old city gate that opened to the colonial-era port. Tiny **Fortaleza Trujillo,** a fort rising from the middle of Avenida del Puerto, was actually built in 1937 in colonial style.

South Side

The delightfully cool and spacious **Museo de las Casas Reales** (Museum of the Royal Houses), on the south side of the plaza, is housed in a mansion completed in 1520 to serve as the Real Audiencia, or Supreme Court. The two-story limestone building later became the governor's mansion and today gleams with impressive suits of armor and opulent period furnishings. Downstairs features an excellent exhibition on Columbus's voyages. Facing the entrance is the **Reloj del Sol,** a giant sundial erected in 1753 to enable judges to check the time from their windows.

Rising over the southwest corner of the plaza is the recently renovated art deco **Palacio de los Comunicaciones** and, next to it, the modernist **Banco de Reservas** (see p. 67). Calle Emiliano Tejera leads west one block to the simple **Casa del Cordón** (*Calle Isabel la Católica & Calle Emiliano Tejera),* the city's oldest structure, dating from 1503. Its first occupant was Francisco de Garay (died 1523), who arrived with Columbus. Note the chiseled sash-and-cord motif of the Franciscan order above the door—hence the name, House of the Rope.

Stepping north one block along Calle Isabel la Católica, you reach the **Museo de Juan Pablo Duarte,** a modest one-story home where the freedom fighter was born. Its three rooms hold furniture, art, and icons relating to Duarte's independence movement. It was closed for a lengthy renovation at press time. ∎

Museo de las Atarazanas Reales

 59 E4

✉ Calle Colón 4

☎ 809/686-2453

🕐 Closed Mon.

$ $

Museo de las Casas Reales

✉ Calle Las Damas & Calle Las Mercedes

☎ 809/682-4202

🕐 Closed Mon.

$ $

Museo de Juan Pablo Duarte

✉ Calle Isabel la Católica 306

☎ 809/687-1436

🕐 Closed Sun.

$ $

EXPERIENCE: Dine Like a Local

There's no shortage of impressive restaurants in the city serving international cuisines. The recent trend is for globe-spanning menus that have little in common with native traditions. But you'll come to appreciate the country more, and save money, if you adopt local habits when dining.

Roadside *colmados* (see sidebar p. 85) offer filling *criolla* meals, such as *bandera dominicana,* for a pittance. You'll find them throughout the country.

In Santo Domingo, try **Colmado Bodega Colonial** (*Calle Arzobispo Meriño 101, Zona Colonial, tel 809/685-1113*) and **Colmado Los Muchachos** (*Calles Nouel & Sánchez, Zona Colonial, tel 809/688-8406*).

Around Plazoleta de San Antón

The stepped Plazoleta de San Antón rises over a slightly shabby part of the city that in 2013 was included in a revitalization program. Although the northern *muralla* (city wall) lies mostly in ruins, the area boasts a lovely church, a splendid museum of amber, and other sites.

Plazoleta de San Antón

🅰 59 E3

Museo Mundo de Ámbar

🅰 59 E3

✉ Calle Arzobispo Meriño 452

☎ 809/682-3309

💲 $

Occupying a hill next to the remains of the northern perimeter wall, the barrio around Plazoleta de San Antón *(Calle Hostos bet. Calle General Cabral & Calle Restauración)* has long been the Zona Colonial's low-income district. At their base, to the south, the hilltop ruins of the **Monasterio de San Francisco** *(Calle Hostos & Calle Emiliano Tejera)* form a dramatic backdrop for concerts held on the lawns to the west. Built in 1508 as the New World's first monastery, the original structure was destroyed by Francis Drake, and two reconstructions were toppled by earthquakes. The curling belt of the Franciscan Order can still be seen over the entrance. The site is being restored as a Parque Arqueológico—a themed archaeological park. One block east, the **Museo Mundo de Ámbar** displays a vast collection of amber from around the world, including some with fossilized ants and other insects.

Calle Hostos curves south from the monastery, dropping sharply to Calle Las Mercedes. Lined with simple homes, it provides a rare perspective over the colonial city. The **Casa de José Martí**, 50 yards (46 m) west of Calle Hostos, hosted the Cuban nationalist hero in 1892.

The plaza opens north to the paltry ruins of **Fuerte San Antón** and narrow, congested, Avenida Mella outside the city walls. One block northeast, tiny, asymmetrical **Iglesia Santa Bárbara** *(Calle Gabino Puello & Calle Isabel la Católica)* is dedicated to the patron saint of soldiers. The church was completed in 1574 and vandalized by Drake, but has since been restored. North of the church, marking the northernmost point of Zona Colonial, are the ruins of **Fuerte de Santa Bárbara,** built about 1574. ∎

Alert Travel

Although the vast majority of tourists return home without mishap, some are victims of scams large and small. Use a healthy dose of skepticism, especially when dealing with "good Samaritans" and anyone who approaches you with a strange request. Here are some scams to watch out for:

- If you get a flat tire, drive to a secure place where there are other people. Many victims are robbed by "helpful" strangers offering to change a tire.
- Never trust that a plainclothes policeman is who he claims unless he can show identification—study it carefully.
- Arguments are often a ruse to distract your attention. Whether the argument involves you or not, beat a retreat.
- Never accept unsolicited help with your luggage.

Around Plaza de la Independencia

A thrumming, chaotic hub of the modern city at the gateway to the old, Plaza de la Independencia is encircled by a maelstrom of traffic as avenues converge and radiate through the city from here. A 32-point brass star in the ground marks "kilometer zero": the point from which distances in the country are measured.

On the plaza's east side, the **Puerta del Conde** (also called the Bastión de San Genaro) was the main entrance to the old city. Made of two big columns supporting a vaulted arch and a belfry, the gate is named for the Count of Peñalba, who led the defense of the city against English invaders in 1655. Here the Dominican flag was first raised.

INSIDER TIP:

It's worthwhile learning a little Spanish before you visit to enjoy chatting to local people on *gua-guas.*

—ALICE SAMSON
*National Geographic
field researcher*

Commanding the plaza, the **Altar de la Patria** (Altar of the Nation) is an imposing sunken marble mausoleum beneath which slumber the country's three main heroes—Juan Pablo Duarte, Francisco del Rosario Sánchez, and Ramón Matías Mella. No hats or indecorous attire are allowed.

To the north, sealed off from entry, the **Fuerte de la Concepción** (*Ave. Bolívar & Calle Polvorín*),

Cementerio de la Avenida Independencia, catercorner to the Plaza de la Independencia, holds national heroes.

built in 1678, was a battery protecting the Puerta del Conde. Two blocks farther is the pentagonal **Iglesia San Carlos** (*Ave. 16 de Agosto & Calle La Trinitaria*), built in 1715.

Calle Palo Hincado runs south from Puerta del Conde along the remains of the original city wall, ending at **Fuerte de San Gil,** a bulwark rising over the rocky shore. Midway, two blocks south of the park, stands **Puerta de la Misericordia** (Gate of Mercy), where Mella fired the shot proclaiming national independence on February 27, 1844. ∎

Plaza de la Independencia

🅜 59 D3

✉ Calle Palo Hincado bet. Ave. Bolívar & Ave. Independencia

Colonial Architecture

The Dominican Republic's colonizers brought with them a Spanish aesthetic that they adapted to the tropical clime. Glorious buildings from centuries past display the evolution of an architectural heritage influenced by Mudejar style.

Dusk falls gently on Calle Padre Bellini, which retains much of its colonial appearance.

The island's first colonial settlements were of single-story adobe dwellings with palm-fiber roofs. By the 17th century, houses had become more complex. Typically built of local limestone, with two stories and tiled wooden roofs, they followed the Moorish convention of having an inner courtyard that permitted air to circulate through the house—a design that lasted four centuries.

The ground floor was devoted to commerce and the upper stories to private apartments. Relatively austere, their facades were softened by turned wooden balconies and by ornamental *portales,* doors with elaborate baroque moldings that through the years grew large enough to admit a horse and carriage. Typically, these massive doors contained smaller doors—*postigos*—set at face level. Inner arcades provided access to *dependencias*—commercial rooms that opened to the street. The rooms around the patio's perimeter were given over to offices and storage, while those at the rear of the house surrounded a yard and were devoted to stables and domestic activities. Houses that faced the plazas and main boulevards featured facades embellished by galleried walkways with arches supported by columns, providing shelter from sun and rain.

A staircase led to the private quarters—a chapel, kitchen, dining room, and bedrooms. Rooms were divided by *mamparsas,* intricately decorated inner doors something like saloon swing doors, to provide privacy while retaining a sense of communal living. By the 18th century, the typical town house had added a low-ceilinged mezzanine level *(entresuelo),* either below or above the second story and given over to offices and slave quarters. The beamed roofs were often built by shipbuilders and frequently enhanced by *alfarjes*—wooden ceilings featuring angled beams set in exquisite star patterns in Mudejar fashion.

Decorative Elements

The greatest evolution of form was in orna-mentation, notably in windows, which were initially protected by wooden panels and later by the addition of ornate grills or bars of lathe-turned wood. By the 19th century, when neoclassical forms were adopted in town house design, elaborate metal grills

Archways are expressive elements of colonial architecture in Santo Domingo.

INSIDER TIP:

Right off the main highway west from Santo Domingo, visit the New World's first sugar mill in Engombe to appreciate 16th-century Seville architecture.

—BRIAN RUDERT
Retired Foreign Service officer

had replaced wood. Colored glass began to appear within the engraved window panels, which featured slatted blinds. These decora-tive windows evolved into fanciful geometric patterns, with larger windows topped by arches. The arches were typically filled with stained-glass windows in geometric designs. The stained glass filtered the sun and cast diffused colors into household interiors.

Additional artistic touches were lent by bands of decorative plasterwork on interior walls.

Meanwhile, the balconies and upper stories of contiguous homes adopted ornate (and usually spiked) metal grills—*guardavecinos*—to guard against burglars.

Religious Structures

Religious buildings followed the same conven-tions and evolution, being at first relatively small and quite austere. Convents were gener-ally the largest ecclesiastical structures. They, too, adopted the Mudejar style of utilizing shaded inner courtyards and alfarje ceilings. As the 17th century progressed, church facades were adorned with baroque decoration, although usually more restrained than the grandiose cathedrals of the mother country. By the 18th century, ornamental altar panels—known as retables—were adopted for exteriors, too, and often featured full-size figures of saints. The bold baroque faded by the following century, as ecclesiastical architects harked back to Rome for a neoclassical look.

Ciudad Nueva & Gazcue

West of the Zona Colonial lie the leafy residential districts of Ciudad Nueva and, farther west, Gazcue—together, a setting for boutique hotels and bohemian restaurants. Laid out in a grid, they recede inland from the Malecón boulevard that unfurls along the rocky seashore.

A group of boys whiz down the Malecón in a quad-ped, a common sight along the boulevard.

Ciudad Nueva
🄰 58 D2

Gazcue
🄰 58 B2 & C2

Palacio de Bellas Artes
🄰 58 B2
✉ Ave. Máximo Gómez & Ave. Independencia
☎ 809/687-0504

bellasartes.gov.do

Ciudad Nueva, immediately west of the colonial core, is a neighborhood of narrow streets with fine examples of 19th-century architecture, while strip clubs lure the salacious. Worth seeking out is **Galería de Arte Cándido Bidó** *(Calle Dr. Baez 5 & Calle Luise Ozema Pellaramo, tel 809/685-5310, candido.bido@claro.net.do),* in a 1950s-era mansion: This gallery showcases works by one of the country's most acclaimed contemporary artists.

Ciudad Nueva merges west into Gazcue, a slightly decaying middle-class residential district dating from the 1930s. The main draw is the neoclassical **Palacio de Bellas Artes** (Palace of Fine Arts), completed in 1956. Here are the country's National Ballet, National School of Dance, and National Folkloric Ballet, plus the headquarters of the National Symphonic Orchestra. Restored to splendor in 2007, the building also hosts exhibitions and occasional concerts.

Farther west, the sprawling **Universidad Autónoma de Santo Domingo** complex

INSIDER TIP:

On the Malecón, ask locals about the USS *Memphis*, wrecked on the rocky shore in 1916. Her bells now chime in the Mercedes church, Zona Colonial.

—BRIAN RUDERT
Retired Foreign Service officer

(Ave. Juan Sánchez Ramírez & Ave. Santo Tomás de Aquino, tel 809/835-8273, uasd.edu.do) is cut east–west by Avenida Paulo III, lined with busts of national heroes. Note the superb ceramic mural by Amable Sterling (1943–) adorning the **Biblioteca Pedro Mir.**

Linking the regions, the long seafront **Malecón** *(Ave. George Washington)* twines west for several miles from the mouth of the Río Ozama past a series of small, littered beaches. This busy, palm-lined avenue hosts most of the city's high-rise hotels and casinos. On Sunday evenings, the section between Calle Pasteur and Avenida Máximo Gómez is closed to vehicles and the boulevard gets crowded with music-blasting youth; this district is particularly riotous during the annual Carnaval parade, held the closest Sunday to February 27. New recreational piers now frame the littered beaches.

Rising from the Malecón is the **Obelisco de Santo Domingo** *(Ave. George Washington & Calle Vicini Burgos)*, erected in 1937 by Trujillo. Every year a noted artist is invited to paint the obelisk in lively murals. ∎

EXPERIENCE: Learn Spanish in the D.R.

The Dominican Republic is renowned as a center for Spanish language instruction. There are dozens of schools to choose from in Santo Domingo, Cabarete, and Puerto Plata, and others are sprinkled around the country. You can choose from a one-week quick immersion class to month-long (or longer) intensives.

Spanish language courses are also a tremendous way to immerse yourself in local culture, not least because most schools room their students with local families. And many combine instruction with classes in local dance and cultural mores. Some include excursions.

Rarely do classes take up more than 20 hours a week; 4 hours daily, Monday through Friday, is the norm. Check to ensure that classes are small—the more personal attention you can get the better. If you seek one-on-one instruction, make sure it's available before signing up.

Here are a few reputable schools:

CEIC *(809/560-7012, ceic-spanish-school.com)*, in Santo Domingo, offers a choice of beginner, advanced, and special-interest courses.

Hispaniola Language School *(809/689-8350, hispaniola.org)*, in Santo Domingo, has a dozen different courses to choose from, including business and medical language, plus dancing and cooking classes.

Instituto Intercultural del Caribe *(809/571-3185, edase.com)* has schools in Santo Domingo and Sosúa, where it combines Spanish instruction with wind- and kitesurfing lessons.

Plaza de la Cultura

A massive 1970s-era modernist plaza stretching for several blocks, Plaza de la Cultura is a cultural destination holding the nation's preeminent arts institutions. Busts and statues are sprinkled around the plaza, which consists mainly of a series of shady lawns. What it lacks in visual appeal, it more than makes up for in stature, with four first-class museums plus the National Theater.

Modern sculptures rise from the floor of the Museo de Arte Moderno.

Plaza de la Cultura

🅰 58 B3

Visitor Information

✉ Plaza de la Cultura bet. Ave. Máximo Gómez & Ave. Felix María del Monte and Ave. Pedro Henríquez Ureña & Calle Cesar N. Pensón

Teatro Nacional

Rising over the west side of the plaza, and an exquisite statement in modernist taste, the Teatro Nacional *(Ave. Máximo Gómez 35, tel 809/532-6648, teatro.com.do)* opened in 1973. Architect Teófilo Carbonell clad the gracious structure with a travertine facade of three arched tiers. Home to the National Symphonic Orchestra, it is best appreciated during a concert, when the city's elite descend and a chic dress code applies. In front are statues of early Spanish literati, including

Calderón de la Barca (1600–1681), Tirso de Molina (1579–1648), and Félix Lope de Vega (1562–1635).

Museo de Arte Moderno

To the theater's east, the superb four-story Museo de Arte Moderno is the republic's foremost repository of artistic expression, with works by such leading masters as Cándido Bidó, Jorge Severino, Julio Guerra, and Amaya Salazar (1951–). The 1930s *costumbrismo* movement is well represented, as are works by Spanish exile artist José Vela

Zanetti (1913–1999), known for his murals at the United Nations headquarters in New York. The lower floors hold sculpture and temporary exhibits.

Museo Nacional de Historia y Geografía

Diagonally across, to the northeast, exhibits at the slightly musty Museo Nacional de Historia y Geografía span the nation's history from the Taíno era through the Trujillo epoch. Displays are arranged chronologically in three wings devoted to the early 19th-century Haitian-Dominican conflicts (the weapons collection is notable); the late 19th century (focusing on the imperial pomp of various *caudillos*); and the Trujillo era.

On its south side, the building houses the **Cinemateca Dominicana** *(tel 809/689-6102, dgcine .gob.do)*, which promotes, distributes, and screens films.

Museo Nacional de Historia Natural

Less engaging, but worth a perusal on the south side of the plaza, the Museo Nacional de Historia Natural features exhibits on geology, zoology, and astronomy. Notable among them are the three-dimensional dioramas of local fauna in native habitats, an impressive humpback whale exhibit, and a spectacular collection of amber. Labels are in Spanish only.

More Sights

Some 50 yards (46 m) east, the **Biblioteca Nacional** *(Calle Cesar N. Pensón 164, tel 809/688-4086,*

bnrd.gov.do), erected in 1971, boasts an elegant facade.

A stone's throw north from the library, the splendid, albeit dowdy, **Museo del Hombre Dominicano** (Museum of the Dominican Man), on four floors, traces the history of the island's

occupants, principally the Taíno people. Displays range from Paleolithic flint-stones to syncretic religion and Carnaval masks. One exhibit profiles the impact of African slavery on the nation. Signage is in Spanish, but English-speaking guides can be requested.

The modernist Banco Central de la República Dominicana *(Ave. Pedro Henríquez Ureña & Calle Leopoldo Navarro)*, erected in 1947 in an eastern extension to the park, hosts the **Museo Numismático y Filatélico.** The museum, housed in the dramatic neoclassical Superintendencia de Bancos on the north side of Avenida Pedro Henríquez Ureña, will delight coin and stamp lovers with its glittering exhibits, featuring New World coins dating from 1505 and stamps from 1865. ∎

Museo de Arte Moderno

🅰 58 B3
☎ 809/685-2154
🕐 Closed Mon.
💲 $

Museo Nacional de Historia y Geografía

🅰 58 B3
☎ 809/686-6668
🕐 Closed Mon.
💲 $

Museo Nacional de Historia Natural

🅰 58 B3
☎ 809/689-0106
🕐 Closed Mon.
💲 $
mnhn.gov.do

Museo del Hombre Dominicano

🅰 58 B3
☎ 809/687-3622
🕐 Closed Mon.
💲 $

Museo Numismático y Filatélico

🅰 58 C3
✉ Ave. Pedro Henríquez Ureña & Calle Felix María del Monte
☎ 809/221-9111 ext. 3662
🕐 Closed Sat.–Sun.
www.bancentral.gov .do/museo

Bella Vista, Mirador Sur, & Miramar

Lying to the west of Avenida Abraham Lincoln, the middle- and upper-class residential districts of Bella Vista, Mirador Sur, and Miramar went up in the mid-20th century. The seat of government is here, with buildings in modernist style, while a cave-riddled park provides a bucolic escape from the city hubbub.

The region is linked to the colonial city by Avenida George Washington and Avenida Bolívar, the latter boasting **monuments honoring Máximo Gómez** (*Ave. Máximo*

Government buildings and the Pabellón de las Naciones

Gómez) and **Simón Bolívar** (*Ave. Abraham Lincoln*). Paralleling Avenida Bolívar to the north, the gridlocked, commercialized Avenida 27 de Febrero highway runs west to **Plaza de la Bandera** (*Ave. Luperón*), in a vast, deteriorated rotunda. Here, traffic runs rings around the **Monumento a la Patria,** built in 1997 as a triumphal arch. The national flag suspended from the arch flutters over the statue "La Madre Patria" ("The Motherland") by Spanish sculptor Juan de Ávalos (1911–2006).

Spanning 15 miles (24 km) of shoreline between the Río de Haina in the west and Río Ozama in the east, **Parque Nacional Litoral Sur de Santo Domingo** was created in 1968 to protect the city's beaches and offshore waters. It has no facilities for visitors, but swimming is allowed.

Centro de los Héroes

The austere setting for the Free World Fair for Peace and Fraternity, sponsored in the 1950s by Trujillo, is today the nation's seat of government. Rising over its southern end is the **Pabellón de las Naciones** (Pavilion of Nations; *Ave. George Washington & Ave. Enrique Jiménez Moya*), with a huge

Simón Bolívar

Venezuelan Simón Bolívar (1783–1830) trained as a soldier and thereafter was the principal leader in the attempts to gain independence from Spain for the Caribbean and Latin American colonies. After liberating his homeland and adjoining nations, he earned the title El Libertador (The Liberator). Internal dissent among the independence factions forced Bolívar to flee to Haiti in 1815 after attempts were made on his life. Haiti provided aid for Bolívar to continue his fight on condition that he would abolish slavery. His brilliant military tactics were decisive in freeing Colombia, Venezuela, and neighboring countries, and were inspirational to independence movements throughout Latin America. A barrio (district) of Santo Domingo bears his name.

---

arch and globe. To its northeast rises the **Palacio de Justicia,** a seven-story postmodernist structure inaugurated in 2006 to host the Supreme Court; its lobby boasts a profound mural by Amable Sterling. Northward stands the five-story modernist **Palacio del Congreso Nacional,** the National Congress Building. The striking 1955 edifice to the west is the **Palacio Municipal,** designed by Guillermo González in stark Le Corbusier style.

West of the Pabellón, the **Monumento Mausoleo Héroes de Constanza, Maimón y Estero Hondo** is dedicated to the Dominican Liberation Army fighters killed in June 1959 after an illfated attempt to topple Trujillo.

Parque Mirador del Sur

Formed by an uplifted marine terrace, this slender park (also known as Paseo de los Indios) unfurls west from Bella Vista to the outlying industrial zone of Herrera. Although hardly scenic, its lawns draw picnickers for the views south toward the Caribbean. The park is flanked by the serpentine **Avenida Cayetano** Germosen and ruler-straight **Avenida Anacaona,** lined with deluxe high-rise condos, diplomatic missions, and the home of baseball superstar Sammy Sosa *(Ave. Anacaona 21).* Treelined **Avenida Mirador del Sur** runs through the park atop the cliff. The boulevard is closed to traffic daily from 6 a.m. to 9 a.m. and 4 p.m. to 8 p.m., when it floods with joggers and cyclists, while rock climbers tackle the cliffs above **Lago Subterráneo** *($),* an underground lake.

The hangar-size **Cueva del Paseo de los Indios,** the largest of several caves in the park, is home to roosting bats. Another cave is the dramatic setting for the Mesón de la Cava restaurant (see p. 207); a third hosts the pulsating Club Guácara Taina nightclub, with stalagmites overhanging dance floors 100 feet (30 m) underground.

At **Ciudad Ganadera** *(Ave. George Washington & Ave. Nuñez de Caceres),* half a mile (0.8 km) south of the park, a concrete monument commemorates the assassination of Trujillo on May 30, 1961. ∎

Bella Vista, Mirador Sur, & Miramar

- 58 A2
- ✉ Bet. Ave. Winston Churchill & Ave. Luperón and Ave. Anacaona & Ave. Cayetano Germosen

Palacio de Justicia

- ✉ Calle Juan de Dios Ventura Simón & Ave. Enrique Jiménez Moya
- ☎ 809/533-3191

poderjudicial.gob.do

Palacio del Congreso Nacional

- ✉ Ave. Jiménez Moya bet. Calle Paul Harris & Calle 4
- ☎ 809/532-5561 (Senate) or 535-2626 (Chamber of Deputies) Guided tours: 809/535-3031

senado.gob.do

www.camarade diputados.gob.do

Northwest Santo Domingo

The middle-class homes of the Arroyo Hondo and Cristo Rey barrios meld northward into impoverished neighborhoods with an elevated position that catches the afternoon breezes. Plenty of greenery is on hand within three of the city's loveliest parks.

Visitors stroll through the serene Jardín Botánico Nacional.

Northwest Santo Domingo

 58 A4 & B4

Parque Mirador del Norte

🗺 58 A4 & B4

✉ Ave. Máximo Gómez bet. Ave. Hermanas Mirabal & Ave. Jacobo Majluta

☎ 809/926-9022

💲 $

Parque Mirador del Norte

The natural lung for the city, Parque Mirador del Norte, north of the Río Isabela, offers a bucolic escape from the hubbub of Santo Domingo. A fully fledged wildlife refuge and forest environment within city limits, this 15-square-mile (40 sq km) park of wetlands, hilly forest, and artificial lakes teems with wildlife. Hispaniolan boas slither along the branches, squirrels cavort in the treetops, and the more than 200 bird species include the Hispaniolan woodpecker and the endearing palmchat. An early morning visit is best for wildlife viewing. Guides are available for nature hikes; hiking alone isn't advised for safety reasons. Gate Four (one of six entrance gates) grants access to horseback rides, bicycle rental, and a lake—**Lago Artificial Yaguaza**—with paddleboats. Locals flock on weekends, eager for a trip on the river. There's a restaurant, and a natural history visitor center is planned at Gate Six.

North of Parque Mirador del Norte, the suburb of **Villa Mella** is infused with the spirit of ancient African rituals. Shrines dedicated to the syncretic Afro-Dominican pantheon abound, and conga drums vibrate during the **Festival de Espíritu Santo** *(June),* while the **Féria de Chicharrón** *(mid-May)* features traditional fare.

INSIDER TIP:

Ride Santo Domingo's new subway to Villa Mella, famous for its *chicharrones de cerdo—* deep-fried pork rind.

—BRIAN RUDERT
Retired Foreign Service officer

Parque Zoológico Nacional

The huge National Zoo spans 400 acres (161 ha) of hilly terrain, partially landscaped so that many beasts can roam free (other creatures inhabit rather cramped quarters). African animals predominate. Elephants and hippos, tigers and chimpanzees are among the most popular critters. Two of the island's most endangered mammals—the hutia and solenodon—are also to be seen here, as are native American crocodiles. And you can stroll through a massive aviary, where the endemic Hispaniolan parrot is among the many exotic and native species. Hop aboard a free shuttle for an introductory circuit of the facility, which has a petting zoo.

Jardin Botánico Nacional

Covering 450 acres (182 ha) of lush grounds, the city's serene and beautifully maintained botanical garden spans a densely forested canyon lined with wild ginger,

heliconia, and climbing philodendron. Its stream winds through a nature reserve offering spectacular birding. A riot of color and wonderful scents, the garden displays more than 300 native orchid species in its orchid house (an orchid show is held each March). There's a palm garden plus an arboretum and specialty collections of succulents.

Other attractions include aquatic plants, bromeliads, and fern pavilions, as well as a Japanese garden and a lake with rowboats for rent. The **Museo de Ecología** *($)* at the entrance explains Hispaniola's ecology. You can hop aboard an open-air trolley *(every 30 mins., $)* for a half-hour tour of the park narrated in Spanish. Free guided birding walks are offered every first Sunday of the month at 7 a.m.

Orchid lovers on a mission should also head to nearby **Orquideario Arroyo Hondo,** a private orchid garden with more than 30,000 plants. ∎

Colmados

Colmados are small grocery stores, usually located on street corners, that also double as working-class bars and, sometimes, cafeteria-style diners. They're found nationwide, including city centers, and are popular with Dominicans for cheap luncheons. They sell all the basic food necessities. Local men like to sit outside in plastic chairs, drinking beer and rum and talking or playing dominoes.

Parque Zoológico Nacional
  58 B4
✉ Ave. Paseo de los Reyes Católicos
☎ 809/378-2149
🕑 Closed Mon.
$ $$
zoodom.gov.do

Jardín Botánico Nacional
  58 A4
✉ Ave. República de Colombia
☎ 809/385-2611
$ $
jbn.gob.do

Orquideario Arroyo Hondo
✉ Calle Polanco Billini 28
☎ 809/567-1351 or 809/565-1930

Parque Mirador del Este & Around

To the east of the Rió Ozama, the airport *autopista* (tollway) and seafront Avenida España frame the bombastic Faro a Colón (Columbus Lighthouse), gateway to the peaceful counterpoint of Parque Mirador del Este. Athletes and fitness freaks enjoy the park's splendid facilities, and the national aquarium is nearby.

Aquatic life surrounds visitors to the Acuario Nacional.

Parque Mirador del Este

🗺 59 G3

Three bridges span the Río Ozama, granting access to Avenida España, running south to the port and Caribbean shoreline via the low-income quarter of Villa Duarte. Rising from the boulevard is **Monumento a La Caña** *(Ave. España, 600 feet/183 m S of Puente Mella)*, a metal sculpture depicting peasants driving an oxcart laden with sugar.

On the avenue's west side, facing Fortaleza Ozama, is a promontory jutting into the Río Ozama that was the site of the original city—then called Nueva Isabela—established in 1498 by Bartholomew Columbus. All that

remains is the whitewashed **Capilla de la Virgen del Rosario** *(Ave. Olegario Vargas)*, where three brick portals stand atop the site of a wooden chapel, the New World's oldest, erected in 1496. The chapel, restored in 2007, exists under the shadow of Los Molinos Dominicanos, ungainly grain silos; ask at the security gate for entry to the chapel.

Avenida España curls along the Caribbean shore to the **Acuario Nacional** *(bet. Ave. 28 de Febrero & Calle de Cuarto, tel 809/766-1709, acuarionacional.gob.do, closed Mon., $)*, the National Aquarium. Sharks, turtles, and rays glide over visitors' heads in a large plexiglass tunnel. Marine turtles are bred here, and colorful reef fish create a dazzling kaleidoscope. **Agua Splash** *(Ave. España 50, tel 809/766-1927, aguasplashrd.com, closed Mon., $)*, across the road, is a water-based theme park with slides.

Faro a Colón

Criticized as both a vast waste of money and a giant monstrosity, the Columbus Lighthouse— colloquially known as El Faro (The Lighthouse)—is the nation's most imposing monument. Connected to Avenida España by the half-mile-long (0.8 km) Avenida

Mirador del Este, this vast mausoleum in the form of a cross was dedicated in 1992 for the quincentennial celebrations and contains, supposedly, the mortal remains of the Great Discoverer. (Other countries dispute this claim; see sidebar p. 64.)

In 1929, a competition was held for the design. The massive monument that resulted, stepped like a Babylonian ziggurat, was built of reinforced concrete to a design by British architect Joseph Lea Gleave. Trujillo adopted the project in the 1930s; it was eventually abandoned as too costly. In 1966, President Belaguer committed vast sums to complete the project for the 500th anniversary of the explorer's first encounter with the New World. Pope John Paul II celebrated Mass here on October 11, 1992, when the ashes believed to belong to Columbus were transferred from the Catedral Primada de América.

The remains are contained in a bronze urn in the center of a 45-foot-tall (14 m) Gothic marble sepulcher. The urn is guarded by four bronze lions and by a real-life soldier, while a figure representing the Republic presides from above.

El Faro also contains permanent exhibitions on Columbus. The ten-story-high monument measures 680 feet (207 m) east–west and 195 feet (59 m) north–south. High-powered Xenon lasers can project a vertical cross-shaped sheet of light into the sky. They are rarely turned on, however, as a flick of the switch is sufficient to plunge much of Santo Domingo into darkness.

Parque Mirador del Este

Paralleling the road to the airport and flanked by Avenida Boulevard del Faro (north) and Avenida Iberoamerica (south), this tree-shaded park runs east from El Faro and is filled with sports stadiums and arenas. The eastern end of the park contains the **Cueva Los Tres Ojos** *(closed Mon., $)*, a natural attraction named "cave of the three eyes" for the three *cenotes* (sinkholes) in the limestone terrace edging up to the sea. One contains fresh water, a second salt water, and a third sulfurous water.

Centro Olímpico

Occupying a vast area separating the Miraflores and Naco districts, this wooded park *(bet. Ave. John F. Kennedy & Ave. 27 de Febrero and Ave. Máximo Gómez & Ave. José Ortega y Gasset, tel 809/616-1224)* **is an epicenter of sports, with the Palacio de los Deportes Olympic stadium, an Olympic swimming pool, baseball fields, and basketball and tennis courts. One mile (1.6 km) northwest, on the west side of Plaza de la Salud, the Estadio Quisqueya** *(Calle Tiradentes & Ave. San Cristóbal, tel 809/616-1224, estadioquisqueya.com.do)* **is the republic's premier baseball stadium. Nearby, in Centro Comercial Sambil, the modern Aquamundo** *(Ave. John F. Kennedy & Máximo Gómez, tel 809/547-4014, aquamundosambil.com)* **rivals the Acuario Nacional with marine exhibits.**

A steep flight of steps descends to the first cavern, refreshingly cool. The Taíno considered the caves sacred. Access today is far more prosaic as you push your way past hustlers and hawkers. ■

More Places to Visit in Santo Domingo

Mercado Modelo

On the north side of Avenida Mella and taking up an entire block between Calle Del Monte y Tejada and Calle Santomé, this former farmers market is today the nation's largest emporium of arts and crafts. Everything from Haitian paintings, amber (and fake amber) jewelry, and tourist trinkets are for sale amid a whirlwind of motion and color. Hearty bargaining is expected. In the rear of the building, and far more interesting, is a produce and flower market; and tucked into the northwest corner are *botánicas* (herbalists) selling aphrodisiacs as well as potions and icons. The surrounding area is best avoided by night. Leave your valuables in the hotel safe.

🅰 59 E3 ✉ Ave. Mella 50 ☎ 809/686-6772

Shopping With a Conscience

Many craft and souvenir items for sale in the Dominican Republic are made from endangered flora or fauna. Buying such items contributes to their demise. Trade in endangered products is illegal, and such items may be confiscated by customs. Avoid jewelry or anything else made from turtle shell or black coral; stuffed baby sharks; or other souvenir items made from animals. Only buy tropical hardwood products if they are made from fallen trees. Shop with a conscience!

Metro de Santo Domingo

Inaugurated in 2009 and now comprising two lines with 30 stations, the city's modern Metro subway takes the grief out of exploring Santo Domingo. Even if your goal is nothing more than the experience, a ride is well worth it.

metrosantodomingo.com

Palacio Nacional

A 1940s statement of neoclassical pomp, this baroque palace inaugurated in 1947 by dictator Trujillo was designed by Italian architect Guido d'Alessandro Lombardi with a facade of roseate Samaná marble. The sumptuous interior is a mini-Versailles with its gilt mirrors, glistening mahogany furniture, and exorbitant Baccarat crystal chandeliers. Forty-four sculpted women grace the Room of the Caryatids. Today the palace houses government departments and, some believe, Trujillo's troubled ghost. A dress code applies for tours, which are by request; the visitors entrance is on the south side, guarded by bronze lions.

🅰 59 D3 ✉ Calle Dr. Delgado Báez ☎ 809/695-8359, edecanes@presidencia .gob.do 🕐 By appt. Mon. & Fri., 15 days' notice required

Paseo Presidente Billini

This traffic-thronged drive, an easterly extension of the Malecón, runs along the rocky foreshore on the Zona Colonial's ocean side. It is lined with open-air oceanfront restaurants and is thronged at night and on weekends. At the foot of Calle 16 de Marzo, the remains of a tiny fort, **Fuerte de San José,** which once guarded the harbor entrance, point cannon toward a statue of Fray Antón de Montesino, champion of the Taíno cause. Overshadowing the **Fuerte de San Gil** (*Paseo Presidente Billini & Calle Palo Hincado*) is the **Monumento a la Independencia Financiera;** the obelisk was erected in 1941 to celebrate repayment of a long-standing debt to the United States. The avenue is at the center of the Sans Souci port development plan, which includes a massive marina.

🅰 59 E2 ✉ Bet. Calle Arzobispo Meriño & Calle Palo Hincado

A setting for the country's most spectacular beaches, with turquoise waters, glitzy resorts, and rugged national parks

The Southeast

Wooden carvings of macaws from Altos de Chavón

The Southeast

It's not hard to see why the southeast has become the Dominican Republic's most popular area, given that it holds the island's best beaches. The sands of Boca Chica and Juan Dolio begin within a hour's drive of Santo Domingo and are easily accessed along the coast-hugging Carretera 3. Farther east, La Costa del Coco—the Coconut Coast—dazzles with its 40 miles (64 km) of palm-shaded sands lined with all-inclusive resorts.

Development is centered on Punta Cana, the island's easternmost point jutting out into the Pasaje de la Mona. Served by the island's busiest airport and protected by a peninsula from the rougher Atlantic, the region appeals to travelers drawn to village-size resorts. In Punta Cana, the stunning beaches melt into sandy-bottomed shallows the color of melted peridots. Dozens of new hotels have opened in recent years, with many more under construction, including at least three deluxe megaresort developments. An additional terminal opened in 2014 at Punta Cana International Airport. There's no shortage of water sports nor of nonstop activities—from midday merengue dance lessons to exploring the rugged interior by ATV to swimming with dolphins at such theme parks as Manatí Park.

Nearby Bayahibe attempts to cling to its low-key fishing village vibe in the midst of its own blossoming of all-inclusive resorts. Bayahibe is gateway to rugged Parque Nacional Cotubanamá, teeming with exotic birds and subtropical vegetation camouflaging caves full of Taíno art. Day trippers set out for Isla Saona—an island idyll with flamingos and the possibility of seeing manatees, dolphins, and even whales. Scuba diving is superb, notably in the shipwreck-littered, reef-protected cove of Boca Chica and around Isla Catalina. This coral-fringed island is popular with excursions from La Romana, the main coast town—and the setting for Casa de Campo (a superdeluxe resort to the stars) and Altos de Chavón (a Tuscan-themed village).

"King Sugar" still reigns around La Romana and nearby San Pedro de Macorís, center for the nation's baseball and for its *cocolos*—Afro-Dominicans of English extraction—who celebrate their heritage each June. Higüey, gateway to the Costa del Coco, is worth a stop

for its remarkable cathedral. To the north, Parque Nacional Los Haitises is studded with dramatically sculpted limestone hillocks and fringed by mangroves providing a habitat for endangered mammals and countless birds, also to be seen in the remote Lagunas Redonda and Limón. These lagoons fringe the Costa Esmeralda, an as-yet undeveloped stretch of coast lined with stunning white-sand beaches.

Between Parque Nacional Los Haitises and the southern cane fields lies an off-the-beaten-path zone with a long tradition of cattle ranching. Ox-drawn carts still plod down back-country lanes; visitors will need four-wheel-drive vehicles for their explorations. ■

NOT TO BE MISSED:

Diving at Parque Nacional
    Submarino La Caleta   92

A concert at Altos de Chavón
    amphitheater   97

Hiking in Parque Nacional
    Cotubanamá   102–103

Sunning on Playa Bávaro   105

The Basilica de Nuestra Señora
    de la Altagracia   105

Birding at Parque Nacional Los
    Haitises   109

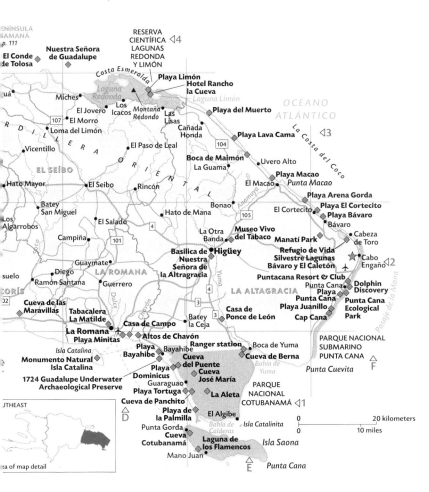

Boca Chica

Curling around the Bahía de Andrés, a mere 19 miles (30 km) east of Santo Domingo, the dense, party-hearty beach town of Boca Chica boasts a wide range of accommodations, restaurants whose cuisines span the globe, and an entire galaxy of bars and noisy nightclubs—many with a salacious edge.

Close to the capital city, Boca Chica's beaches draw families on weekend outings.

Boca Chica

 90 B2

Visitor Information

✉ Oficina de la Secretaría de Turismo, Plaza Boca Chica, Calle San Rafael

☎ 809/523-5106

💲 Closed Sat.–Sun.

Caribbean Divers

✉ Ave. Duarte 28

☎ 809/854-3483

caribbeandivers.de

Tropical Sea Divers

✉ Ave. Duarte 35

☎ 829/697-9522

tropicalseadivers .com

Boca Chica got its start in the 1950s, when Santo Domingo's monied classes built vacation homes in what was then a small fishing village. A decade later the country's first beach resort was established. Today, overdeveloped, budget-oriented, and slightly seedy Boca Chica is crowded on weekends with Santo Domingo's music-loving masses. Traffic-thronged **Avenida Duarte** is closed to vehicles at night, when bars set out their tables; prostitution is noticeable.

Playa Boca Chica

Roads slope down to Playa Boca Chica, where palm-lined sands shelve into calm shallows inside a cove billed as the largest reef-protected lagoon in the Caribbean. The beach bustles with hair braiders, mariachis, and vendors selling coconut water. The nicest stretch fronts the Don Juan Beach Resort (p. 210). To the east, at low tide you can wade out to tiny **Isla La Matica.** Farther east, **Playa Caribe** draws a young crowd for its surf.

Baseball fans might consider heading to **Campo Las Palmas**, the Dominican training camp of the Los Angeles Dodgers, in the town of Guerra *(9 miles/14.5 km NW of Boca Chica).*

Parque Nacional Submarino La Caleta

Acclaimed for its offshore wrecks and fabulous reefs, the nation's smallest national park was created in 1978 to protect more than 25 dive sites accessible from **La Caleta** *(5 miles/8 km W of Boca Chica).* Pre-Columbian skeletons are buried in a fetal position under the meager **Museo Ceremonial La Caleta** *(Carretera Aeropuerto Luperón & Autopista A3),* atop a shore-front Taíno cemetery. The park's signature wreck is the *Hickory,* scuttled in 1984 to create an artificial reef 9 fathoms (18 m) down. ∎

San Pedro de Macorís

Once considered a pearl of the nation, this city prospered during the economic boom known as the "dance of the millions." Known today for its baseball prowess, the chaotic, congested industrial Cradle of Shortstops still spawns major league players.

San Pedro, 40 miles (64 km) east of Santo Domingo, was founded in 1822 on the east bank of the Río Iguamo and grew into a major sugar town. In its heyday, the elite built palatial homes. Today, crumbling Victorian houses speak of better days.

Still, the oceanfront **Malecón** (Ave. Charro) boulevard makes for pleasant strolling or a horse and buggy ride. The neo-Gothic **Iglesia San Pedro Apóstol** (Ave. Independencia & Ave. Charro), built in 1911, has a mahogany altar and exquisite stained-glass windows. Two blocks south, **Centro Cultural Fermoselle** (Ave. Charro & Calle 10 de Septiembre, tel 829/449-2611, closed Sun.) showcases local art. View the Victorian buildings of

---

Cocolos

This region around San Pedro is unique for its cocolos—English-speaking descendants of Afro-Caribbean migrants who were brought in to cut cane in the late 19th century. The cocolos introduced their vernacular architecture and sensual dance forms, such as *momise* and *guloya*, still performed most colorfully during the **Festival de San Pedro** in late June.

INSIDER TIP:

Estadio Tetelo Vargas has some of the most exciting baseball games in the country. The seats are a bargain.

—MAGALY TORIBIO
Vice minister, Dominican Republic Ministry of Tourism

Parque Duarte (Ave. 27 de Febrero & Calle Ramón Duarte), the main square, then climb the staircase of the Victorian **fire station** (Calle Ramón Duarte 46) for city views. **Azucarera Porvenir** (Ave. Independencia & Calle Porvenir, tel 809/339-0019, closed Sat.–Sun.), a sugar mill, offers tours January through August. The new **Centro Histórico Ron Barceló** (Carretera Ingenio Quisqueya Km 6½, tel 809/948-4160, visitron barcelo.com), northwest of town, has tours of the rum company's production facility and historic museum. The town comes alive October through February, when the lights of **Estadio Tetelo Vargas** (Ave. Circunvalación & Carretera Mella) are turned on for the baseball season.

The long, touristy beach resort of **Juan Dolio,** west of San Pedro, has many all-inclusive hotels. The **Guavaberry Golf & Country Club** (tel 809/333-4653, guavaberrygolf .com.do) has an equestrian center. ∎

San Pedro de Macorís

⬛ 90 C2

Shipwrecks

The waters surrounding the Dominican Republic are littered with wrecks of Spanish galleons and the treasures they spilled when they foundered. Latter-day vessels also lie in ocean graves in transparent jade waters a few fathoms down. Scuba divers swim past while archaeologists probe these well-preserved yesteryear icons—lured, perhaps, by the glitter of gold and silver.

Divers survey the *Akwa*, sunk off the Silver Bank.

Diving in Dominican waters provides a truly unique history lesson spanning hundreds of years. Dozens of Spanish galleons sank off the coast, victims of bad navigation, storms, pirates, or war. The nation's most famous wrecks are the Spanish galleons *El Conde de Tolosa* and *Nuestra Señora de Guadalupe*. Laden with mercury (used to refine silver and gold) and cannon, the two vessels were en route from Cadíz to Mexico when they were overtaken by a hurricane while navigating the Pasaje de la Mona. They were blown into the Bahía de Samaná, where they foundered on August 25, 1724. In 1976, fishermen discovered the *Guadalupe* buried in sediment, and the wrecks eventually yielded up cannon, jewelry, and other treasures. Many are displayed in the Museo de las Atarazanas Reales (see p. 73) in Santo Domingo.

Salvagers also raised tons of silver from the wreck of the Spanish galleon *Nuestra Señora de la Pura y Limpia Concepción*, which sank in

INSIDER TIP:

When exploring archaeological sites, such as caves and shipwrecks, respect them by not taking or buying artifacts as souvenirs.

—ALICE SAMSON
National Geographic field researcher

Salvager Tracy Bowden pours out mercury found in *El Conde de Tolosa.*

September 1641 after being thrashed by a hurricane. She foundered on a shallow coral reef 70 miles (112 km) north of Hispaniola, giving the area its name—Silver Bank. In 1686, a New England skipper, William Phipps, successfully raised a king's ransom in silver and gold from the wreck. In 2009, the wreck of Captain William Kidd's *Cara Merchant* was discovered off Isla Catalina—the only pirate ship found in the Caribbean.

In the west, the Pipe Wreck lies 13 feet (4 m) down off Isla Cabra, near Monte Cristi. Named for the vast quantities of Dutch clay tobacco pipes recovered, this English-built merchantman is today overgrown by a reef, where silver coins minted in Peru in 1651 have been found encrusted in coral.

Some wrecks are more recent and tantalizingly close. The *Astron*—a Russian freighter—ran aground in a storm just off the coast of Punta Cana in the 1980s; its rusting remains jut from the waters like a beached whale within fingertip distance of vacationers on the sands.

Some ships have been sunk deliberately. The *St. George,* a Norwegian cargo ship, was laid to rest off Bayahibe in 1999 to enhance local diving. Even *Guadalupe* salvager Tracy Bowden's own vessel, the 128-foot-long (39 m) *Hickory*, was itself sunk in 1984 to form an artificial reef within Parque Nacional Submarino La Caleta (see p. 92).

EXPERIENCE: Dive! Dive! Dive!

The waters off the Dominican Republic give anywhere in the Caribbean a run for the money when it comes to diving. Pristine coral reefs combine with scores of shipwrecks to offer divers a metaphorical rapture of the deep. Many resort hotels have on-site scuba facilities, while independent outfitters have shops at all the key beach destinations.

The best time to dive is June to September, when water clarity is at its best, with visibility typically about 100 feet (30 m). The worst time to dive is October to May (north coast) and May to

October (south coast). Stand-out dive sites include:

Airport Wall, off Sosúa. Lots of elkhorn corals plus swim-through caves and, nearby, the *Zingara* wreck.
Isla Catalina, south of La Romana. It has a spectacular wall dive that begins just 15 feet (4.5 m) down, plus the possibility of spying humpback whales.
Islas Las Ballenas, off Las Terrenas, Samaná. Underwater caves to explore.
Parque Nacional Submarino La Caleta, near Boca Chica. Features four wrecks.

La Romana & Around

A center of sugar production, this sprawling, congested town on the west bank of the Río Romana is the unlikely setting for the nation's most lauded resort and for a Tuscan village conjured atop a ravine. A beautiful island with superb diving awaits visitors offshore.

The Altos de Chavón amphitheater hosts major international performing arts acts.

La Romana

🗺 91 D2

Visitor Information

✉ Oficina de la Secretaría de Turismo, Gobernación, Ave. Libertad

☎ 809/550-6922

explorelaromana .com

La Romana, with its pretty houses, has been dedicated to processing sugar since 1917, when it became the center of the nation's sugar industry. A huge sugar mill—**Central Romana** *(Ave. Libertad & Calle Castillo Márquez)*—still lords it over the town. In the 1960s, the Gulf + Western company bought the mill, invested in the town, and eventually built Casa de Campo as the Caribbean's most deluxe resort.

Downtown, the clock tower of the art deco **town hall** *(Calle Eugenio Miranda & Calle Diego Ávila)* and, adjacent, the steeple of **Iglesia Santa Rosa de Lima** cast shadows over **Parque Central,** the town's large tree-shaded square, studded with wrought-iron sculptures. Painted with murals of

Taíno culture and contemporary Dominican themes, **El Obelisco** *(Ave. Libertad & Calle Francisco del Castillo)* occupies a plaza two blocks southeast of the park; it's a miniature reproduction of the Washington Monument. Also worth a peek is the bustling **Mercado Municipal** *(Calle Frey Juan de Utrera & Calle Dr. Teófilo Ferry),* a colorful market featuring religious trinkets and tokens. To its southeast, the **Estadio Francisco Micheli** *(Ave. Abreu & Ave. Luperón, tel 809/556-6188, lostorosdeleste .com)* baseball stadium hosts La Romana Azucareros team. The **Tabacalera de García** *(Ave. Libertad, tel 809/550-3000, cigarcountry tours.com)* claims to be the largest handmade cigar factory in the world; it offers tours.

The impoverished Haitian cane-cutter community of **Batey La Ceja,** 11 miles (18 km) east of La Romana, is famous for its Semana Santa (Easter) celebrations.

Casa de Campo (see p. 211), immediately east of La Romana, put the town on the map in the 1970s. Sprawling over 12 square miles (30 sq km), the resort is a jet-setter's getaway. Private jets wing into the resort's airport, while other visitors arrive by yacht to a marina evoking Italy's chic village Portofino. The **Teeth of the Dog Golf Course** (see p. 98) features rolling fairways suspended above steep river gorges and the Caribbean. Casa de Campo sometimes grants visitors access by request.

Altos de Chavón

Built in 1976 to resemble a Tuscan village, this coralstone contrivance hangs on a precipice—the Heights of Chavón—overlooking the Chavón river gorge. The village is a cobbled cultural center: Artists can be seen working in galleries and craft workshops at **La Escuela de Diseño** (tel 809/523-8011, altosdechavon.edu.do), offering classes in fine arts and fashion.

On the main plaza, tiny **Iglesia St. Stanislaus** was blessed by Pope John Paul II and is used for weddings. Behind, the excellent **Museo Arqueológico Regional** (tel 809/523-8554) displays more than 3,000 pre-Columbian artifacts, including ancient canoes. An immense 5,000-seat limestone amphitheater features Greek columns. Frank Sinatra performed the inaugural concert, and show-stoppers from Andrea Bocelli to Gloria Estefan perform at all times of the year.

Altos de Chavón is best visited in late afternoon, when the tour buses have departed. A free shuttle departs Casa de Campo every 30 minutes.

Monumento Natural Isla Catalina

This emerald jewel in a jade setting is everything you hope a tropical isle will be—white rimmed, shaded by tousled palms, lapped by ripples washing lazily onto the half-mile-long (0.8 km) beach. A 20-minute boat ride from La Romana marina, the 6-square-mile (15 sq km) idyll draws day trippers who arrive by glass-bottom boat. Snorkelers can marvel at the underwater treasures. **The Wall,** off the north shore, is the pinnacle of Dominican dives. ∎

Altos de Chavón
◪ 91 D1
✉ Casa de Campo
☏ 809/523-8011
casadecampo.com.do

EXPERIENCE: Getting Married in the D.R.

Many visitors find the republic so romantic that they choose to tie the knot during their stay. Although a few do so on a whim, most plan their weddings in advance. Your hotel of choice will make all the arrangements with several weeks' notice; most hotels in the D.R. offer wedding package specials.

If you choose to plan your own wedding, you need to contact the local *oficial del estado civil* (city clerk). Allow three to six months for planning. You'll need to provide copies of your birth certificates and passports, as well as notarized affidavits of your single status, including any divorce or spouse death certificates. These must be translated into Spanish and certified by a Dominican consulate.

The Dominican Ministry of Tourism website (godominicanrepublic.com) provides complete details. Here are a few perfect wedding venues:
Iglesia St. Stanislaus (Altos de Chavón, La Romana, at Casa de Campo, tel 809/523-8171, casadecampo.com.do)
Casa Colonial Beach Spa Resort (Playa Dorado, Puerto Plata, tel 809/320-3232, casacolonialhotel.com)
Puntacana Resort & Club (Punta Cana, tel 809/959-2222, puntacana.com)

EXPERIENCE: A Round of Golf

No other Caribbean island even comes close to claiming the republic's title as the region's undisputed golf capital.

Teeth of the Dog Golf Course forms part of the Casa de Campo resort.

When golf architects Pete and Alice Dye visited and fell in love with the La Romana area four decades ago, they invested and carved out an 18-hole course from dense forest above the shore. They called it Teeth of the Dog for the sharp limestone formations named *diente del perro*. Ever since it opened in 1971 at Casa de Campo, this golf course with a coral-fanged bite has been the only Caribbean course ranked in the world's top 50. Dozens of stunning fairways have since been laid out.

The green revolution has picked up pace in recent years. World-champ golfers turned designers Nick Faldo, Tom Fazio, Pete Dye, Gary Player, and Nick Price have all lent their names and design skills to new courses, including several that are still under construction.

At least one new championship course is added every year. Most are concentrated in the southeast. Overlooking coconut white sands and turquoise ocean, most make use of seashore paspalum—a new hybrid grass that tolerates seawater irrigation.

INSIDER TIP:

Walking 18 holes under a tropical sun without a hat and lots of sunscreen is a recipe for a ruined vacation. Cover up.

—ALED GREVILLE
National Geographic Books

Here are five courses you really *must* play:

La Cana Golf Course *(Punta Cana, tel 809/959-4653, puntacana.com)* has sensational ocean vistas, with four shoreline holes. President Bill Clinton is a regular.

Hard Rock Golf Club *(Cana Bay, tel 809/687-0000 ext. 4444, hardrockhotelpunta cana.com)* was designed by Jack Nicklaus. Meandering through lush terrain, this par 72 course offers a free introductory program with a golf pro.

Playa Dorada Golf Course *(Puerto Plata, tel 809/320-3472, playadorada golf.com)*, in Puerto Plata, is a venerable course laid out in 1976 by master-designer Robert Trent Jones and still considered one of the finest courses in the Caribbean.

Punta Blanca *(Cap Cana, tel 809/486-4734, punta-blanca.com)* was designed by professional golfer Nick Price and opened in 2007 at the Majestic Colonial Beach Resort.

Teeth of the Dog *(La Romana, tel 809/877-3643, casadecampo.com.do)* is considered the republic's top course. Named for the ragged *diente del perro* limestone cliffs on which it's laid out, this spectacular course was revamped in 2005 with new tees, greens, and bunkers.

Playas Bayahibe & Dominicus

With perhaps the finest snorkeling and diving in the entire country, plus gorgeous beaches, the Bayahibe area still clings to bucolic ways in the midst of evolving tourist development. Ancient wrecks lie a few fathoms down.

Until just a few years ago, the beach resort of **Bayahibe** was a sleepy fishing village where dogs snoozed on dusty dirt roads. It retains an agreeably laid-back feeling, although it is fast evolving. Large hotels now nose up to the meticulously maintained main beach—Playa Bayahibe—and the waterfront is marred by tasteless malls that have pushed aside many of the quaint wooden homes in ice-cream pastels. The village bustles briefly morning and afternoon when tour buses arrive with day trippers bound for **Isla Saona** (see p. 103).

For now, though, you can still watch fishermen bring in the daily catch dripping from the sea. And Bayahibe has plenty of small inns for travelers seeking intimacy. The all-inclusives are centered on Playa Dominicus—marked by a black-and-white-striped lighthouse—in the Dominicus Americanus district, farther east; beach access is limited to a track beside the Viva Wyndham Dominicus Beach hotel.

The talcum-powder sands at both beaches dissolve into peacock blue waters famous for their abundance of corals and sponges. The underwater world is a treasure trove of unsurpassed beauty with some 20 easily accessible dive sites. Advanced divers can tackle the wreck of the **St. George,** which occupies a

watery grave 135 feet (44 m) down in front of the Viva Wyndham Dominicus Beach hotel. Inland, divers might visit the **Manantial de Padre Nuestro,** a freshwater *cenote* (sinkhole) dripping with stalagmites—it's 9 miles (14.5 km) east of Bayahibe and 1.5 miles (2.4 km) south of Padre Nuestro community.

Scubafun *(Calle Principal 28, tel 809/833-0003, scubafun.info)* and Casa Daniel *(tel 809/833-0083, casa-daniel.com)* offer dives and snorkeling. Pepe at the **Bayahibe Fishing Center** *(tel 809/401-6346, bayahibefishingcenter@ yahoo.com)* provides boat trips in the bay and to Isla Saona. ∎

Playas Bayahibe & Dominicus

🗺 91 D1

Visitor Information

✉ La Romana–Bayahíbe Hotel Association, Ave. 27 de Febrero, La Romana

☎ 829/520-7391

explorelaromana .com

1724 Guadalupe Underwater Archaeological Preserve

Billed as the "world's first underwater shipwreck museum," this marine reserve *(La Romana–Bayahíbe Hotel Association, Ave. 27 de Febrero, La Romana, tel 829/520-7391, explorelaromana.com)* in front of the Viva Wyndham Dominicus Beach and Viva Dominicus Palace hotels, in Bayahibe, was established by Indiana University in 2002. It has 18th-century cannon, cannonballs, ballast stones, an anchor, and other relics retrieved from the *Guadalupe* shipwreck and repositioned close to shore in 12 to 15 feet (4 to 4.5 m) of water to give easy access to snorkelers and divers.

Reef World

Among the most biologically productive ecosystems on Earth, coral reefs encircle the Dominican Republic's shores—luring scuba divers and snorkelers from afar to explore the colorful array.

Coral reefs are built by tiny organisms called polyps: the coral animals. Each polyp, some no larger than a pinhead, secretes calcium carbonate from its base to form an external skeleton, a protective chamber in which it lives. But it's strength in numbers that produces a reef. New polyps can bud off the old, securing their own skeletons in the interstices and atop older polyps. Some species beget offspring that smother their parents and use those skeletons as foundations on which to cement their own. Over thousands of generations, millions of polyps work together to create an intricate limestone reef.

Life Zones

Reefs are divided into life zones defined by depth, water temperature, and light. Distinct corals inhabit each zone. They come in a profusion of forms: massive brain corals; gracefully curled wire corals; elkhorn coral, resembling an elk's antlers, which can span 10 feet (3 m); and pillar coral, which sends its cylindrical columns shooting sunward as high as 15 feet (4.5 m).

Each reef is a subaqueous metropolis that is also home to a multitude of other creatures: sea urchins, moray eels, lobsters, octopuses, anemones, tube sponges, conchs, and, of course, fish large and small. Huge groupers and cubera snappers hang suspended as if by invisible strings. Stingrays, manta rays, and hawksbill and loggerhead turtles cruise slowly by. Sharks lurk beneath ledges. Schools of permits and crevalle jacks stream past, glittering like foil. And an endless parade of brightly colored fish add to the beauty: blue tangs, queen angelfish, iridescent blue chromis, and black-and-white-striped sergeant majors, to name but a few.

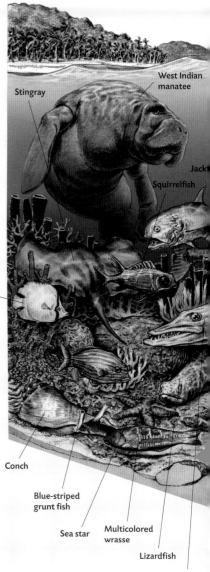

Laughing gull

West Indian manatee

Stingray

Jack

Squirrelfish

Spotfin butterfly fish

Conch

Blue-striped grunt fish

Sea star

Multicolored wrasse

Lizardfish

Great barracuda

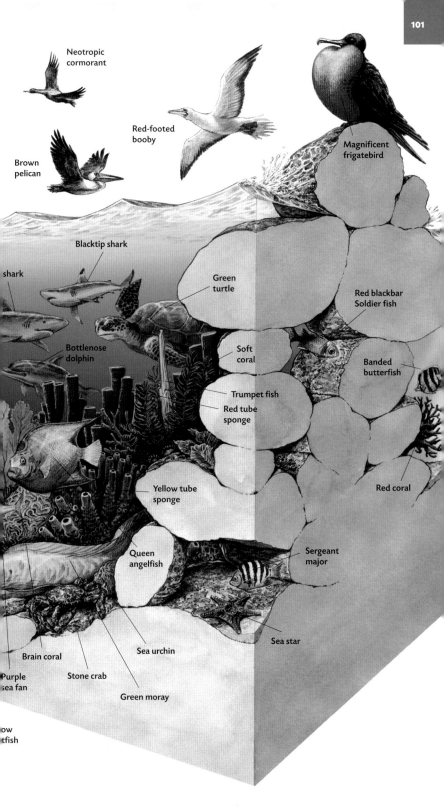

Neotropic cormorant

Red-footed booby

Brown pelican

Magnificent frigatebird

Blacktip shark

shark

Green turtle

Red blackbar Soldier fish

Bottlenose dolphin

Soft coral

Banded butterfish

Trumpet fish

Red tube sponge

Yellow tube sponge

Red coral

Queen angelfish

Sergeant major

Sea star

Brain coral

Sea urchin

Purple sea fan

Stone crab

Green moray

ow tfish

Parque Nacional Cotubanamá

Occupying a peninsula dangling off Hispaniola's eastern tip, this dry-forest region known for its fabulous birding was once a center of Taíno culture. Day travelers now zip out to Isla Saona to wade and swim in the waist-deep water that laps crystalline beaches.

The boat ride to Isla Saona is half the fun of visiting the isle.

Parque Nacional Cotubanamá

🏞 91 E1

✉ National Park office beside marina in Bayahibe

☎ 809/467-4083

💲 $

The park (formerly Parque Nacional del Este)—named to the UNESCO World Heritage List in 2001—covers 162 square miles (420 sq km), of which one-third is oceanic. Rhinoceros iguanas and hutias and solenodons (small, endangered mammals) scurry around in the leaf litter of tropical humid and seasonally dry deciduous forest. The 112 bird species include 11 endemics, not least the Hispaniolan parrot and Hispaniolan lizard-cuckoo. Red-footed boobies and frigatebirds inhabit the mangroves around **Bahía de Calderas,** a bioluminescent lagoon. Manatees are often seen close to shore. And four species of turtles lay their eggs in sands along

the western shore, where rich blue waters beckon with coral reefs. The limestone landscape is pocked with caves holding pre-Columbian pictographs. You can hire guides ($$) at the park office in Bayahibe. Two trails grant access. No overnights allowed; bring water and insect repellent.

The Asociación de Guías de Padre Nuestro *(tel 866/588-6856)* offers tours. Scubafun *(Calle Principal 28, Bayahibe, tel 809/833-0003, scubafun.info)* provides dive trips.

Western Sites

The main entrance to the national park is at **Guaraguao,** 3 miles (5 km) south of Bayahibe by dirt road. From here, a one-hour trail

At the Cueva de Berna, let a guide show you the Taíno petroglyphs carved near the cave entrance.

—ALICE SAMSON
National Geographic field researcher

leads to **Cueva del Puente,** with curtainlike stalagmites and stalactites. A ranger must guide you into **Cueva de José María,** deeper in the park. Its 1,200 splendidly preserved Taíno pictographs feature a Spanish galleon.

South of Guaraguao, the coastal track leads to **Playa Tortuga,** where a trail connects to a ranger station at La Palmilla via **Cueva de Panchito:** The low, slippery entrance is guarded by a Taíno figure, arms upraised.

Eastern Sites

The park can also be entered at the ranger station 1.5 miles (2.4 km) west of **Boca de Yuma,** a river-mouth fishing village atop wave-beaten cliffs at the park's extreme northeast. Close to the entrance is **Cueva de Berna,** with pictographs. Bring a flashlight. For a fee (*$*), rangers will guide you to **Manantial del Guano,** a cave with an underground lake and Taíno ceremonial stone circle. A clifftop trail with sheer drop-offs leads 7 miles (11 km) to a blowhole—**Manantial de Tulio.**

Listen to *bachata* music and eat grilled fish at seafood restaurants with magnificent views in Boca de Yuma. **Playa Blanca,** 1 mile (1.6 km) west of Boca, can be reached on foot or by boat (*$$$*)—and a boat is necessary to reach **Playa Borinquen,** a fishermen's beach beyond the Río Yuma.

Isla Saona

This picture-perfect isle is a 45-square-mile (116 sq km) escape for day trippers from the resorts. Many tours stop off at **Piscina Natural,** a lovely lagoon enclosed by a sandbar.

Boats pull in at **Mano Juan,** a palm-thatched village on the

Manatees

Resembling a gray tuskless walrus, the manatee is a herbivorous aquatic mammal that inhabits warm, shallow coastal lagoons and estuaries in North and South America. These gentle creatures grow to 10 feet (3 m) long, weigh up to 1,200 pounds (544 kg), and can live to be 60 years old. Females reach maturity at five years old and give birth every two to five years. Although protected, the population is threatened by pollution, habitat loss, and accidents with boats.

south coast. Blaring music in the vicinity detracts from the enjoyment, as do the vendors plying cold drinks and hair braids. To escape the crowds, follow a dusty trail west past **Laguna de los Flamencos** (with flamingos) to the fishing hamlet of **Punta Gorda** (*9 miles/14.5 km*). A second trail leads east 8 miles (13 km) to **Cueva Cotubanamá.** ∎

Punta Cana & Around

Shaded by stately palms, Punta Cana and its neighbors beckon with a seemingly endless strip of sugar-fine sands dissolving into reef-protected waters in peacock hues. Served by Aeropuerto Internacional de Punta Cana and the center of the deluxe hotel boom sweeping the country, this shore receives the lion's share of visitors to the Dominican Republic.

Flamingos take a stand at Manatí Park.

Punta Cana
◭ 91 F2

Bávaro
◭ 91 F2
Visitor Information
✉ Oficina de
Turismo Bávaro,
Plaza El Tronco
☎ 809/552-0142

The white beaches and turquoise waters here make up a tropical playground of unsurpassed beauty, with coconut palms towering over sands that stretch virtually unbroken for 40 miles (64 km).

La Costa del Coco (the Coconut Coast) is crooked at 90 degrees around **Cabo Engaño**, the nation's easternmost point. High winds whip up whitecaps that tempt surfers, though ferocious tides preclude swimming at the point. Pinned by a lighthouse, the headland separates the two main beach resort centers, with newly emerging resort regions sprinkled along the shore farther north. The Bulevar Turística del Este highway (currently under construction) will eventually link the main resorts.

Punta Cana

South of Cabo Engaño, lovely and sedate **Playa Punta Cana** birthed the region's tourism boom in the 1970s with the creation of today's **Puntacana Resort & Club** (see p. 212). The resort encompasses the 1,500-acre (502 ha) **Indian Eyes Reserve** *(locals & hotel guests only)*, a tropical forest reserve dotted with 11 freshwater lagoons fed by an underground river. A 45-acre (15 ha) section—the **Punta Cana Ecological Park** (tel 809/ 959-9221)— offers a sanctuary for local flora and fauna, including the endangered rhinoceros iguana. You can stroll through a botanical garden and traditional Dominican farm; kids will enjoy the petting zoo. Guided tours and horseback riding *($$$)* are available, and the resort hosts the Oscar de la Renta Tennis Center, opened in 2015.

Tourist development is rampant in the area, notably visible in the construction of the **Cap Cana** megaresort. This 15-year-project will add three signature golf courses, the Caribbean's largest marina—Marina Cap Cana—and superdeluxe hotels and villas separated from the jade-colored sea by shimmering **Playa Juanillo**.

Bávaro

Poorly regulated development marks the haphazard district of

Bávaro, north of Cabo Engaño, and its ungainly service center known as El Cortecito. Making amends are **Playa El Cortecito** and, immediately south, **Playa Bávaro**—together a seemingly endless stretch of whiter-than-white sand lined with hotels. Freestyle Catamaranas (tel 829-894-4636, freestylecatamarans .com) will whisk you to the reefs for snorkeling. Helicopters, ultra-lights, and Dominican Balloons (tel 809/977-8877, dominican balloons.com) trips by hot-air balloon add to the beach buzz. **Manatí Park** keeps the family entertained with wildlife exhibits, from crocodiles and flamingos to dolphin and sea-lion shows—and even an equestrian display. The new-in-2016 indoor sports facility at Hard Rock Hotel & Casino (tel 809/687-0000, hardrockhotelpuntacana.com) helps keep visitors happy on rainy days.

South of El Cortecito, reached by a separate access road, **Cabeza del Toro** is backed by a sleepy village where fishermen still haul in their boats, and by **Refugio de Vida Silvestre Lagunas Bávaro y El Caletón**—a mangrove and swamp forest reserve.

There's plenty to do inland, from horseback riding and ATV tours to Bávaro Runners (tel 829/599-0621, bavarorunners.com) jeep safaris, zip line adventures, and tours of the region.

Punta Macao

Playa El Cortecito merges north with **Playa Arena Gorda**, unspooling like a ribbon of silver lamé to Punta Macao, a rocky headland thrashed by surf. Golden **Playa Macao**, 7.5 miles (12 km) north of Bávaro, draws noisy groups of ATV riders and has a cove suitable for sheltered swimming beneath the dramatic bluffs. ■

Manatí Park
⚠ 91 F2
✉ Carretera Manatí, Bávaro
☎ 809/221-9444
$ $$$
manatipark.com

Punta Macao
⚠ 91 E3

Higüey
⚠ 91 E2
Visitor Information
✉ Oficina de Turismo Jarabacoa, Ave. Santana 51
☎ 809/554-2672

Higüey

This provincial capital (map p. 91 E2), founded in 1503 by the conquistador Juan de Esquivel (1480–1519), is the gateway to Punta Cana. The grimy city has little to recommend it other than the spectacular, avant-garde **Basílica de Nuestra Señora de la Altagracia** (Calle Agustín Guerrero 66, tel 809/554-4541), the largest church in the country. The modernist concrete cathedral was designed in 1950 by the French architects André Dunoyer de Segonzac and Pierre Dupré and is dominated by a 246-foot-tall (75 m) arch representing hands clasped in prayer. The stunning interior has inverted-V columns and a beautiful stained-glass wall framing the altar, with murals by José Vela Zanetti to each side. No shorts or bare shoulders are allowed.

The basilica hosts the **Festividades en Honor a la Virgen de la Altagracia** each January 21, when pilgrims honor the patron saint of all Dominicans, kept in effigy within a glass case.

The more intimate **Iglesia San Dionisio** (Calle Agustín Guerrero & Calle Pedro Livio), five blocks east, dates from 1567. It has a frescoed dome above the altar.

Overflowing with color, the **Mercado de Higüey** (Higüey Market; Ave. La Libertad bet. Calle Guerrero del Rosario & Calle Las Carreras) offers a sampling of local life.

Drive: Punta Cana to Sabana de la Mar

Facing northeast toward the open Atlantic, the Costa Esmeralda north of Punta Cana boasts gorgeous beaches. Carretera 104 parallels the palm-fringed shore inland. Although relatively lightly trafficked, in places the road has vehicle-devouring potholes. Side roads connect to lonesome beaches linked by a sandy track that runs virtually unbroken for some 20 miles (32 km). A four-wheel-drive vehicle is required for this shoreline drive.

Tortuga Bay Hotel, one of the many resorts lining the beaches at Punta Cana

Begin at **Bávaro** ❶ and head north along the new Uvero Alto-Miches highway (Carretera 105). Arriving at the Texaco gas station, turn right and follow the dirt road 1 mile (1.5 km) north to **Playa Macao** ❷. Turn left and follow the shorefront 400 yards to the Macao Surf Camp, and head inland to rejoin the highway.

Turn right and follow the highway to the next major intersection, signed for Playa Uvero Alto. The road snakes north past Dreams Punta Cana, Breathless Punta Cana, and Sirenis Punta Cana resorts. Beyond the Excellence Punta Cana resort, you can turn right at Rancho Caribeño restaurant to relax on the beach before continuing inland from Rancho Caribeño.

The route cuts through sugarcane fields and rice paddies. Ascending a rocky hill to **Boca de**

NOT TO BE MISSED:

Cabo Engaño • Playa Macao • Playa Lava Cama • Playa del Muerto

Maimón, enjoy the lovely vista over the countryside. The road then connects with the main Uvero Alto-Miches highway (now Carretera 104) in the community of **Las Lagunas de Nisibón.** Two miles (3 km) north of town, turn right onto a dirt road that leads through cattle pasture to **Playa Lava Cama** ❸, a magnificent expanse of white sand. Here, **Rancho Mar Taíno** (tel 809/554-2072) has a restaurant, horseback tours, a small zoo, and cabins.

Strewn with palm leaves and coconuts, the sandy track parallels the coast north to **Playa del Muerto ❹**, so named for the Dominicans who died trying to raft from it to Puerto Rico**.** After about 6 miles (10 km), at **Playa Nisibón,** turn left to access Carretera 104. You'll pass through a series of pretty hamlets as the road undulates through emerald meadows via the communities of Sabana de Nisibón and Las Lisas. Beyond Las Lisas, **Laguna Limón ❺** (see p. 108) comes into view. A stop here for birding may add hours to your journey; it's accessed from the hamlet of Los Güineos de Miches, about 1 mile (1.6 km) beyond Las Lisas.

Passing the dirt road that leads to scimitar-shaped **Playa Esmeralda,** the road descends to **Miches,** an undistinguished town set in a bay good for bonefishing. On the west side of town, climb the hill to **Hotel La Loma ❻** (see pp. 211–212) for spectacular views.

West of Miches, the potholed road passes through an impoverished region, relieved by a lovely view across palm-studded meadows to **Bahía de la Jina.** You'll arrive at a T-junction (Carretera 103) at the entrance to the town of **Sabana de la Mar,** gateway for boat tours to Parque Nacional Los Haitises (see p. 109) and ferries for Samaná. The Miches–Sabana la Mar highway was in construction in 2016.

EXPERIENCE:
Voluntourism

Nothing is as soul satisfying as knowing that you have contributed to ecological and cultural welfare at a grass-roots level. Here are some of the organizations that make that possible:
Go Overseas *(415/796-6456, gooverseas.com/volunteer-abroad)* lists almost 20 different volunteer programs in the Dominican Republic, from education and health to horsemanship.
International Student Volunteers *(714/779-7392, isvonline.com)* seeks volunteers to spend two weeks teaching and building rural projects.
Punta Cana Foundation *(809/959-9221, puntacana.org)* gets guests of Puntacana Resort & Club involved in maintenance of the Punta Cana Farm and ecological reserve.

Ⓜ See also area map pp. 90–91
► Bávaro
🕓 6 hours
↔ 95 miles (153 km)
► Sabana de la Mar

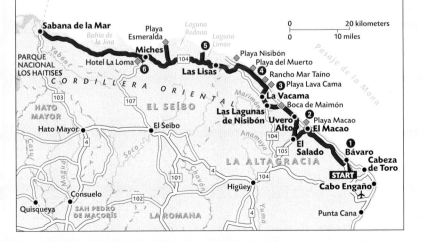

La Costa del Coco

Wild beaches along the coast north of Punta Cana are as yet mostly untapped for their tourist potential. They're backed by a watery world of swampy bayous filled by rivers washing down from the Cordillera Oriental, feeding mangroves and marshland that in turn support profuse birdlife. The new Uvero Alto-Miches highway has eased access to the region.

La Costa del Coco
◩ 91 E3 & F3

Uvero Alto

North of Punta Macao, the sands ease north toward remote **Boca de Maimón,** a wild, tangerine-colored beach backed by a labyrinth of lagoons and mangrove marshes. The region, known as Uvero Alto, is newly emerging and still reached via a maze of mostly dirt roads.

North of Uvero Alto, a rugged dirt road skirts the shore, parallel to the unbroken beach where marine turtles plod ashore in the spring-summer nesting season. The Coconut Coast is so called for the vast coconut plantations that extend for miles, merging into the Costa Esmeralda.

Reserva Científica Lagunas Redonda y Limón

Two shallow freshwater lakes are the foci of the Round & Lemon Lagoons Scientific Reserve *(Carretera 104, Los Icacos & Las Lisas),* extending out to sea. The wetlands form a refuge for waterfowl such as herons, egrets, and spoonbills. Manatees are often to be seen moving amid the mangroves.

Laguna Limón seeps into the sea at the south end of **Playa Limón,** a lovely miles-long sliver of golden sand. You can follow the sandy beach track south as far as **Boca de Limón,** the river mouth where visitors can rent boats *($$$)* for exploring the park. A ranger station and trail *($)* are accessed from Carretera 104, on the south side of the hamlet of Los Güineos de Miches.

Laguna Redonda can be reached by four-wheel drive from the community of Los Icacos, located some 6 miles (10 km) east of Miches. There are no facilities available, but you can rent boats in Miches.

Montaña Redondo rises from the plain inland between the lagoons. A trail leads to its summit for a bird's-eye view. ∎

Mogotes

The product of uplift and erosion over millennia, mogotes owe their genesis to a limestone seabed formed during the Jurassic period, beginning some 200 million years ago. Gradually the great plateau was thrust from the sea. Over ensuing eons, rainfall eroded the limestone mass to form classic karst scenery. Many mogotes are freestanding and conical in shape, like upended bullets, soaring an average of 100 feet (30 m) into the air.

Parque Nacional Los Haitises

Beguilingly scenic and biologically diverse, this wild and isolated 316-square-mile (826 sq km) park protects the nation's largest mangrove system. Its cinematic backdrop is formed by *mogotes*—dramatically eroded hillocks and sheer-faced cliffs that form a labyrinth of razor-sharp scarps and crags.

Named a national park in 1976, Parque Nacional Los Haitises encompasses the southwest quarter of Bahía de Samaná (Samaná Bay), some 15 miles (24 km) of rugged shoreline, and a vast swath of even more rugged inland terrain. Wildlife is visible in abundance here. Great blue herons, northern jacanas, and double-crested cormorants pick for food among the dense mangrove forests, also a habitat for manatees.

Rocky islets stud the waters offshore, including **Isla de los Pájaros** (Bird Island), a nesting haven for roseate terns, pelicans, and many other species of seabirds. The 112 bird species that have been recorded here also include the endangered endemic Ridgway's hawk, found solely in the park's tangled subtropical humid forest. The mogotes are riddled with caves—most notably **Cueva de la Linea**—containing Taíno pictographs. Swallows swarm around **Cueva de las Golondrinas.**

The park can be accessed by half-day boat trips (*bring hat & sunscreen, $*) from Samaná, Sabana's *muelle,* and Embarcadero Caño Hondo ranger station and pier (*7 miles/12 km W of Sabana).* Nearby, the ecohotel Paraíso Caño Hondo (*tel 809/259-8549, paraisocanohondo.com*) offers boat trips, horseback rides, and guided hikes (*$*) in the park. Caribbean Dream (*tel 809/552-6862, puntacanatours.com*) leads excursions from Punta Cana.

Carved out over centuries by an underground river, **Cueva Fun-Fun,** on the park's southeast side, features three miles (5 km) of chambers filled with incredible dripstone formations and pre-Columbian pictographs and petroglyphs. Tours of the cave begin at Rancho Capote in Yerba Buena (*14 miles/ 23 km W of Hato Mayor).* A horseback ride leads you to the cave, which visitors must rappel down to explore, the start of a memorable adventure that includes wading along an underground river. ■

Parque Nacional Los Haitises

 90 B3 & B4

Visitor Information

✉ National Park office, Ave. Los Héroes 54, Sabana de la Mar; park mainly accessed by boat from Sánchez, Santa Bárbara de Samaná, or Sabana de la Mar

☎ 809/556-7333 or 809/720-6035

Cueva Fun-Fun

✉ Rancho Capote, Calle Sánchez 5, Hato Mayor

☎ 809/481-7773

🕐 Reservations recommended

$ $$$$$ (tour)

cuevafunfun.net

Mogotes lend the landscape a dramatic quality.

More Places to Visit in the Southeast

Casa de Ponce de León

This fortified, two-story stone house built in 1505 served as the plantation home of the Spanish conquistador Ponce de León and his wife and three daughters. León accompanied Columbus on his second voyage in 1494 and later served as provincial governor. His home, standing in a tended garden, is now a museum containing his suit of armor and other period items. Signs are in Spanish only. The place is kept locked; a custodian opens it for visitors and gives Spanish-language tours for a tip.
🅜 91 E2 ✉ Calle Los Jobitos, San Rafael del Yuma, 14 miles (23 km) SE of Higüey ☎ 809/551-0118 🕒 Closed Mon. 💲 $

Cueva de las Maravillas

This fascinating anthropological reserve centers on a complex of vast caves and grottoes with magnificent dripstone formations and underground pools. The cave system also protects galleries with 472 Taíno pictographs and 19 petroglyphs depicting humans and animals. Recently reopened after being rehabilitated, the cave features 820 feet (250 m) of well-maintained paths with motion-sensor lighting; the rest of the galleries are off-limits to visitors. One-hour guided tours. Wheelchair accessible by elevator.
🅜 91 C2 ✉ Carretera 3, Ramón Santana, Boca de Soco ☎ 809/390-8180 🕒 Closed Mon. 💲 $$

Monte Plata & Around

Set amid ranchland interspersed with pineapple plantations, Monte Plata is a provincial cattle town famous for its patron saint festival, a tamer version of its colonial-era fiesta, when livestock were set loose in the streets like a mini-Pamplona. The nearby town of **Bayaguana** *(9 miles/14.5 km E of Monte Plata)* also hosts one of the country's foremost patron saint festivals from December 28 to January 1, with *topes* (horseback parades), brass bands, and a running of the bulls. **Rancho Comatillo** *(5 miles/8 km NE of Bayaguana, tel 809/547-9004, comatillo.com.do)* has horseback rides and camping.
🅜 90 A3

EXPERIENCE: Where to See Baseball in the D.R.

In a nation where one in four people lives below the poverty line, sugar-mill workers and field hands see baseball as a ticket to a better life. Dominican boys grow up swinging a bat. What they lack in equipment, they make up in talent and fierce determination. Scouts from the American leagues are ever present, on the lookout for Red Sox or Yankee wannabes.

Twenty-five major league teams maintain programs in the Dominican Republic. For further information, see *dr1.com/forums/dominican baseball*, or contact the Dominican League *(tel 809/563-5085, lidom.com).*

The following are the republic's major baseball venues:

Estadio Quisqueya *(Calle Tiradentes & Ave. San Cristóbal, Santo Domingo, tel 809/540-5772, estadioquisqueya.com.do)* is the nation's foremost stadium.

The Toros del Este play at **Estadio Francisco Micheli** *(Ave. Padre Abreu, La Romana, tel 809/556-6188, lostoros deleste.com).*

Estadio Tetelo Vargas *(Ave. Circunvalación & Carretera Mella, San Pedro de Macorís, tel 809/246-4077, estrellas orientales.com.do)* hosts the Estrellas Orientales.

A wild, palm-fringed peninsula boasting stupendous beaches, cascading waterfalls, and whales

La Península de Samaná

The manicured beach of the Gran Bahía Principe de Samaná resort

La Península de Samaná

An oblong peninsula reaching 30 miles (48 km) into the Atlantic Ocean, this slender sliver is large in appeal, featuring some of the country's most beautiful sands. The best beaches face northeast and receive cooling trade winds head on. The stars of Samaná, however, are the humpback whales that arrive every winter.

Even schoolchildren get about on the popular *motoconchos*.

These regular visitors to the Bahía de Samaná travel in from their summer feeding grounds in northern waters. Then, the bay-shore highway is thronged with sightseers as whales frolic so close to shore you could literally swim out to touch them.

There's plenty to do when the whales depart. Divers get raptures of the deep about the shallow bay that Columbus named the Gulf of Arrows—a graveyard for treasure-laden Spanish galleons. In fact, Samaná offers some of the best diving along the Atlantic coast, with 23 named dive sites and no shortage of dive shops. The reef-lined north shore, framed by high cliffs, plunges into an extraordinary underwater world of pinnacles and drop-offs teeming with colorful fish.

Inland, the narrow coastal plains ease up to low-lying marmoreal mountains. There's a heart-catching loveliness to the Cordillera Samaná,

LA PENÍNSULA DE SAMANÁ

Area of map detail

Cayos
las Ballenas

Playa Punta Po
Playa Bonita
La
Terre

Bahía Escocesa
Playa Cosón

NORTH
COAST
p. 125

Cayo Jackson

La
Majagua

Los Puentes
CORDILLERA SAMANÁ

Sánchez
Las Gar

EL CIBAO
p. 143

PARQUE
NACIONAL
MANGLARES
DEL BAJO YUNA

A   B

swathed in lush tropical forest. The prevailing winds lavish the mountains with rain, and streams cascade down through the spine where horseback treks lead to the Salto del Limón waterfall. Lush with thick foliage, most of the rugged region is accessible only to strong hikers or visitors on horseback.

It's the beaches, however, that garner the most accolades. Cayo Levantado, floating in the bay east of the orderly town of Santa Bárbara de Samaná, has some of the most spectacular sands. The seaside town of Las Galeras, at the peninsula's eastern extreme, retains a fishing-village atmosphere. On the north coast, laid-back Las Terrenas is a node for resident Europeans promoting kiteboarding, intimate guesthouses, and a lively nightlife, although upscale all-inclusive hotels are sprouting like mushrooms on a damp log.

In pre-Columbian times, the peninsula was a base for the Maguá tribe of Taíno Indians. Many of the residents wear a Taíno heritage on their faces, while others are descendants of African Americans who settled here in the 1820s. The latter are known for their Afro-Caribbean cuisine as well as dances such as the *chivo florete* and the *olí-olí*. Some elders even

cling to *inglés del muelle*—a form of Spanglish.

Booming tourism is adding a modern face to this wild spit of land. The government has invested heavily in Samaná in recent years. El Catey International Airport opened in 2006 west of Sánchez, boosting the region's fortunes, as did a new highway between Santo Domingo to Samaná. Meanwhile, cruise ships have begun to unload passengers at a custom-built port at Samaná, which boasts a new marina and convention center; and a ferry intermittently connects the town to Sabana de la Mar. ■

NOT TO BE MISSED:

Santa Bárbara de Samaná

This busy and orderly little port town (known locally simply as Samaná) is set in a beautiful natural harbor—the Golfo de las Flechas—backed by lush, green mountains. The old fishing village has blossomed in recent years due to a tourist boom, but remains placid, except in the winter when tourists flock for the humpback whale spectacle.

Santa Bárbara de Samaná

🗺 113 D2

Visitor Information

✉ Oficina de la Secretaría de Turismo, Calle Santa Barbara 4

☎ 809/240-6363

Golfo de las Flechas (Gulf of Arrows) was so named by Christopher Columbus for the fierce reception given him by the Taíno when he anchored here on January 12, 1493. Founded in 1756 by Gov. Francisco Rubio Peñaranda (1700–1773), the town was initially settled by immigrants from the Canary Islands, joined in 1824 by two shiploads of freed American slaves. Most historic structures

Samaná's La Churcha was brought piece by piece from England in the 19th century.

were destroyed by a fire in 1946. In the 1970s, President Joaquín Balaguer initiated a development plan that replaced many of the remaining historic homes with buildings in grim concrete style. Today, city fathers are funding a thoughtful remake, including the new waterfront **Pueblito Caribeño** commercial plaza in Caribbean vernacular style.

La Churcha *(Calle Desereaux & Calle Rubio Peñarada)*, a prim Nonconformist church prefabricated in England in 1823, is one of the few buildings to escape the 1970s modernization. Originally ministering to the freed American slaves, it today serves as the Dominican Evangelical Church. The slaves' descendants, concentrated in the **Barrio Wilmore** district, still speak an old form of English and have retained many of their traditions, expressed in harvest festivals every Friday, August through October. **Tour Samana With Terry** *(tel 809/538-3179, toursamanawithterry.com, $$$$$)* offers community tours.

The bustling four-lane waterfront **Malecón** *(Ave. de la Marina)* is abuzz at night when candlelit restaurants and cafés—many run by French émigrés—lend a Gallic feel. Yachts bob at anchor at the marina from where Transporte Maritimo *(tel 809/538-2556)*

INSIDER TIP:

While in Samaná for the whales, ask a local guide to take you to the Salto del Limón [see p. 124].

—MAGALY TORIBIO
Vice minister, Dominican Republic Ministry of Tourism

passenger ferries depart for Sabana de la Mar when conditions permit. The town is also a base for deep-sea fishing and for boat trips ($$$$$) to Parque Nacional Los Haitises (see p. 109).

In the bay, the **Bridge to Nowhere** links the mainland to the island of **Cayo Vigía** *(off-limits to visitors except guests at Gran Bahía Principe Cayacoa hotel; see p. 214).* The **Museo de las Ballenas** *(tel 809/538-2042, closed Sat.–Sun., $),* located at the western end of the Malecón, has exhibits on whales.

Cayo Levantado

This jewel of an isle rises from the bay 4 miles (7 km) offshore of Samaná. Famous as the setting for early Bacardi Rum ads, Cayo Levantado is fringed by a white sand beach lapped by warm, jade-colored waters. Stone paths lead from the dock to **Playa Pública,** which on weekends is crowded with day visitors. It has gift shacks and a bar-restaurant. The Gran Bahía Principe Cayo Levantado hotel (see p. 213) occupies most of the island. Ferries ($) depart the Malecón and private boats can be rented at the town of Carenero *(5 miles/8 km E of Samaná).*

Whale Sanctuary

The eastern third of the 25-mile-long (40 km) by 13-mile-wide (20 km) bay is protected as the Santuario de las Ballenas Jorobadas en la Bahía de Samaná, part of the Sanctuary for the Marine Mammals of the Dominican Republic (see p. 142). More than 1,500 humpbacks visit the bay in mating and calving season, January through March. As many as 300 may be present at any given time. Aggressive males compete for females in the rough, deep cobalt outer bay.

EXPERIENCE:
Enjoy Sportfishing

You don't have to worry about the big one that got away in Dominican waters. Blue marlin, tuna, and wahoo all jostle to bite on your hook. The Atlantic and Caribbean waters that surround Hispaniola are considered one of the world's premier sportfishing venues.

It's especially easy to get hooked on angling in the Mona Passage, east of the Samaná Peninsula, where the action is year-round. Escape Tours (tel 849/206-9361, escapetoursamana.com) **will take you sportfishing aboard the 48-foot (14.6 m) Getaway from Samaná's new Puerto Bahía Marina.**

Females give birth in the calm inner bay, where newborn calves frolic alongside their mothers. Peak month is February, when the whales often come within 300 feet (91 m) or so of shore. Strict viewing regulations are in effect when humpback whales are present. ■

Cayo Levantado
⚠ 113 D1

Santuario de las Ballenas Jorobadas en la Bahía de Samaná
⚠ 113 D1

Las Galeras & La Bahía del Rincón

A beach lover's dream at the eastern end of the peninsula, this area is renowned for its whiter-than-white sands washed by waters of heartbreaking clarity. Many of its beaches are reached by unmarked roads that wind through tunnels of shrub.

A fisherman plies the tranquil waters of the Bahía del Rincón.

One of the least disturbed coastal areas in the republic, the Bahía del Rincón is held within tall headlands. On its southeast shore, the fishing village turned resort of Las Galeras nestles up to a gently curving bay backed by tousle-topped palms. A tourism boom is changing this once sleepy region, although the village still clings to its laid-back charm.

Accessible on foot from town, virginal **Playa Playita** lets you wade in off the beach to swim nose to nose with yellow-tailed snappers, rainbow-hued parrot fish, and even an occasional turtle. Hidden east of town at the tip of Cabo Samaná are **Playa Madama** and **Playa Frontón.** A beach trail begins at the Casa Marina Bay all-inclusive resort on Playa Las Galeras, but it's about 5 miles (8 km) to Frontón. Rudy's Rancho (*tel 829/305-3368, rudysrancho .com*) offers horseback excursions to Playa Frontón.

Bike Las Galeras (*tel 829/930-0443, labellaventura.net*) offers biking excursions.

Playa del Rincón

A spectacular beach at the western head of the bay, Playa del Rincón requires a four-wheel-drive vehicle for access. The hilly road from the community of **Manuel**

What to Know About Riptides

Ferocious ocean currents called riptides are a potential hazard while swimming at many beaches in the Dominican Republic. Riptides are associated with beaches subject to heavy surf action. They form when the volume of incoming water is so great that it prevents the water's retreat. Any weak point in the waves is sufficient to form a fast-moving channel for egress, drawing excess water from up and down the beach. Swimmers and waders caught in the current will be dragged out to sea.

The natural instinct is to strike for shore. Riptides are so powerful that even the strongest swimmer can quickly tire and drown. Since the riptide channel is usually relatively narrow, the key is to swim parallel to shore, perpendicular to the current.

Riptides aren't static. They migrate along the beach, and can form and dissipate quickly. Their presence is often betrayed by a still, glassy surface in the midst of waves.

INSIDER TIP:

Try a piece of roasted *casabe* (flatbread made from cassava root) and taste history. Columbus liked it so much he took it as tribute from the Taíno.

—BRIAN RUDERT
Retired Foreign Service officer

Chiquito *(5 miles/8 km S of Las Galeras)* offers stupendous views. Alternately, boats *($$$$)* can be chartered in Las Galeras. Rimmed by the cliffs of **Cabo Cabrón,** the 3-mile-long (5 km) beach unspools like silver thread. At its western end, locals swim in the cool waters of the **Río Frío,** where thatched shacks sell freshly grilled seafood.

The dirt road to Playa del Rincón passes the **Iguanario Los Tocones** *(Los Tocones, km 6, tel 809/771-7661)*, where rhinoceros iguanas are bred for release to the wild. Nearby trails lead to **Laguna Salada,** a freshwater lake (despite its name—Salt Lake) with turtles, frogs, and waterfowl. At night, bulldog bats scoop up fish on the wing. And **Laguna del Diablo** *(2 miles/3 km S of Rincón)* is set like a jewel within a rare tract of virgin forest, drawing waterfowl and 12 endemic bird species. Samana Xtreme Buggy *(tel 829/542-3005, samanafun.com)* offers excursions by four-wheel drive from Samaná.

Dive Heaven

Scuba divers in Las Galeras are blessed with several good choices. **Cabo Cabrón,** a short boat ride from Las Galeras, features plunging cliffs with tropical fish, moray eels, and lobsters. An underwater pinnacle called **The Tower** is laden with sponges. **Piedra Bonita** offers the thrill of dives in clear waters patrolled by reef sharks, turtles, and barracudas. And a well-preserved container ship lies in a shallow grave close offshore. See Travelwise (p. 228) for scuba diving outfitters. ∎

Las Galeras & La Bahía del Rincón

🗺 113 E2 & E3

Visitor Information

✉ Tauro Tours

☎ 849/658-8997

taurotours-excursion samana.com

Drive: Samaná to Sánchez via Las Terrenas

The loop through the Cordillera Samaná takes in some delightful scenery, heightened by a break to visit the Salto del Limón waterfall. Spectacular beaches await at Las Terrenas and farther west, while the mountain road that connects Las Terrenas to Sánchez culminates with take-your-breath-away views. Reports of this latter section being suitable for four-wheel-drive vehicles only can be discounted, as it is now paved.

Fishing still provides a livelihood for inhabitants of Santa Bárbara de Samaná.

Begin in **Santa Bárbara de Samaná,** where the junction for El Limón is signed 0.75 mile (1 km) west of town. The paved road snakes uphill, delivering the first beautiful view over the bay after 3 miles (5 km), with the *mogotes* of Parque Nacional Los Haitises (see p. 109) floating on the hazy horizon. The ridgeline offers grandstand perspectives of the coast.

Dropping down toward the community of El Limón, beware of huge potholes in the road. If you wish to visit the nearby magnificent waterfall, **Salto del Limón ❶** (see p. 124), arrange your trip in advance through Santi Rancho *(tel 829/342-9976, cascadalimonsamana.com),* found in the heart of the village. Continuing onward, turn right at the T-junction beside Santi

NOT TO BE MISSED:

Salto del Limón • Playa las Ballenas • Playa Bonita

Rancho and follow the road 1.5 miles (2.4 km), then turn left and take the dirt road to **Playa Morón** *(4WD required),* where fishing boats festoon orange sands.

Return to El Limón and travel another 5 miles (8 km) to emerge by the shore at windswept **Playa Punta Popy ❷**. Stop to watch the kiteboarders. The Carretera Portillo follows the palm-fringed shore, passing Aerodrome Portillo.

INSIDER TIP:

Las Terrenas not only has some of the best beaches in the Dominican Republic, it is also a culinary mecca.

—RAUL TOUZON
National Geographic
Traveler *magazine photographer*

In the center of the town of **Las Terrenas** (see pp. 120–121), turn right onto Avenida Alberto Caamaño, which runs along exquisite **Playa las Ballenas ❸**. After spending some time snorkeling, backtrack into town, following the one-way system along Calle Principal. Turn right onto Calle Fabio Abreu, which merges into Carretera 133. After 200 yards, turn right on Calle Mariano Vanderhorst to reach **Playa Bonita ❹** *(signed route)*. You might wish to linger here, enjoying a chilled Presidente beer and grilled seafood with your feet in the water.

Return to Carretera 133 and follow it east for half a mile (0.8 km); turn right onto Ave. Juan Pablo Duarte (Carretera Las Terrenas–Sánchez). The road switchbacks uphill past

Vivero Las Colinas ❺, a plant nursery that clings to the mountainside. Four miles (7 km) after leaving town, you reach a ridge atop the Cordillera Samaná, with a superb coastal vista.

Cresting the mountains at the village of **Los Puentes** at about 1,475 feet (450 m), the road drops in sweeping curves through a series of farmed vales. You are now in the midst of mogotes—a dramatic landscape that suddenly opens to views of the **Bahía de Samaná** far below. If you pull over for photos, beware of the traffic. The largest coconut plantation on the island spreads out below.

The road switchbacks sharply, with stupendous views over the palm-clad foothills and bay as you coil down the steep grade. Some 11 miles (18 km) south of Las Terrenas, you emerge onto Carretera 5 on the east side of the town of **Sánchez.**

🅰	See area map pp. 112–113
▶	Samaná
🕐	3 hours
↔	31 miles (50 km)
▶	Sánchez

Las Terrenas & Around

Midway along the north shore of the peninsula, this easygoing beach town has blossomed in the past few decades from a ramshackle fishing village into one of the country's foremost resorts. Smack in the center of the boutique-hotel trend now sweeping Samaná, it beckons with a still mellow mood and superlative sands, despite "downtown" congestion and unregulated growth that continues apace.

Colorful paintings brighten the street scene in Las Terrenas.

La Terrenas
🗺 112 B3

Visitor Information
✉ Oficina de
Turismo,
Calle Libertad
(opposite the
Policia Nacional)
☎ 809/240-6141

**Playa Bonita &
Playa Cosón**
🗺 112 B2

The settlement of Las Terrenas was founded in 1946 after President Rafael Trujillo ordered that impoverished citizens from Santo Domingo be resettled there as fishermen and farmers. The village expanded in the 1980s, when Europeans—predominantly French, German, and Swiss—arrived to settle into a life of ease. With its relaxed daytime ambience and a laid-back nightlife, it's still quite popular with independent travelers who prefer zesty bars and low-key hotels. Gourmet restaurants and Haitian art galleries add notes of color.

The town's beachfront street—Avenida Alberto Caamaño—is lined with thatched restaurants clustered in **Pueblo de los Pescadores** (Fishermen's Village). Here, you can settle with your feet on the sand, listen to a Dominican string band, and relax with a chilled Presidente. Calle Principal hosts an open-air weekend street fair.

Beach activity revolves around **Playa las Terrenas**, a palm-shaded, coral-colored beach unfurling to each side of town. To the east, at **Playa Punta Popy**, kiteboarders skim reef-protected peacock blue waters. Playa Las Terrenas curls west to **Playa las Ballenas** and filters into the mangroves of **Laguna Marico,** a swampy habitat for purple gallinules and roseate spoonbills. Sandpipers scurry across the sands while stilt-legged herons and egrets patrol the swamps.

Offshore of Playa Las Ballenas and accessible by boat *(SS),* the three whaleback-shaped **Cayos las Ballenas** rise from multihued waters, enthralling divers with an underwater cave. The emerald coral flats, good for snorkeling, are a veritable hive of activity, with a rainbow host of tropical fish adding to the chromatic displays. Brown boobies and white-tailed tropicbirds nest here. Samana Diving *(Calle Francisco Caamaño Deño, tel 809/786-1043, samana diving.com)* arranges dives.

French-run Bahía Tours *(Ave. Duarte 237, tel 809/979-1564, bahia-tours.com)* offers excursions. KiteWorld *(tel 809/769-4978, kite worldlasterrenas.com),* at Hotel Beach Club Palapa, has windsurfing and stand-up paddlesurfing. Adventure Helicopter Samaná *(tel 829/645-7278, adventurehelicopter samana.com)* offers sightseeing flights from Playa Cosón. And French-run Flora Tours *(Calle Principal Duarte 278, tel 809/240-5482, flora-tours.net)* boasts a wide range of excursions, from ATVs and horseback-riding to kayaking.

Playa Bonita & Playa Cosón

South of Laguna Marico, well-named Playa Bonita—Pretty Beach—curls around the shores of **Bahía Escocesa** like a scallop shell. Charming boutique hotels nestle up to the palms behind the powdery sands, which stretch for miles. You can hike a narrow, marshy coast trail linking Las Terrenas to Playa Bonita via the rocky point of **Punta Caño del Jobo.**

EXPERIENCE:
Fly Like a Bird

Got a board? Bring it! Trade winds whip the republic's north-facing shores, providing thrills for the kiteboard and windsurf set. Conditions at Cabarete and Las Terrenas—the two main centers—are perfect for beginners and experts alike. More than two dozen schools can teach you how to hang ten or take to the air. Whether you want to try your hand at kiteboarding, surfing, or windsurfing, the following can show you the ropes:

Cabarete Windsports Club *(Hotel Villa Taina, Calle Principal, Cabarete, tel 809/571-0784, cabaretewindsports club.com)*

Laurel Eastman *(Calle Principal, Cabarete, tel 809/571-0564, laureleastman .com)* sets the standard at Cabarete for kiteboarding.

Pura Vida *(Calle Libertad 2, Las Terrenas, tel 809/915-7750, puravidaplanet.com)* offers kiteboarding and surfing instruction.

Playa Bonita merges west into Playa Cosón. Less crowded (except on the sands in front of the Viva Wyndham Hotel), this filament of snow-white talcum seems to stretch to infinity. Offshore a coral reef is patrolled by red soldier fish, blue-striped grunts, and trumpet fish that stand on their noses. ■

Whales Ahoy!

Valued for their precious oils and meat, Atlantic humpback whales have been devastated by commercial hunting. The species gained protection in 1962, but is currently listed as endangered. Fewer than 12,000 of these benign creatures are estimated to exist in the western North Atlantic, out of 30,000 humpbacks worldwide, although the population appears to be increasing.

Like all whales, the humpback is a warm-blooded, air-breathing mammal. These leviathans can weigh up to 50 tons (45 metric tons) and reach up to 50 feet (15 m) long. Cobalt gray above, they have speckled white underbellies, slender white flippers, and long jaws with knoblike bumps atop the snout. Though not actually humped, they appear so when preparing to dive.

The animals of the Atlantic population spend spring, summer, and autumn feeding in the cold waters of the northern Atlantic, where three main groups exist: one in the Gulf of Maine and Nova Scotia; one off Newfoundland and Labrador; and one around Greenland and Iceland. Here, in relatively shallow waters above the continental shelves, they feed on krill and schooling fish such as anchovies, mackerel, and sardines. Humpbacks lack teeth. Instead, they filter their food through bristlelike baleen plates. These intelligent creatures have evolved an ingenious means of harvesting food. After diving deep, they spiral upward while releasing a stream of air that forms "bubble nets" to trap their prey near the ocean surface. With a final burst of speed, the whales explode upward, jaws agape, to capture a great gulp of food.

As winter days shorten, the whales slip south on long migrations to warm, shallow Caribbean waters where they mate or give birth to young conceived the previous year. The most important of the calving and nursing areas is the Sanctuary for the Marine Mammals of the Dominican Republic, created in 1986. The different Atlantic populations intermingle in the breeding grounds from mid-January to mid-March, but later return to their respective northern feeding areas.

Both genders reach maturity at nine years. The males are true Pavarottis of the deep. During mating season, they assume head-down angled postures, hanging motionless, flippers outstretched, while performing elaborate and haunting arias to attract females.

Dramatic surface displays, such as breaching (giant leaps clear of the water), serve to warn off competitors eager for a piece of the action. Their boisterous tussles might involve six or more 30-ton (27 metric tons) bulls. Though aggressive toward each other during mating season, the males are solicitous to females, whom they caress with bubbles blown from below. Following a 12-month gestation, the mothers give birth to 15-foot (4.5 m) calves, which they nurse for the first year.

EXPERIENCE:
Whale-watching

For eyeball-to-eyeball encounters with whales, take to the waters on whale-watching excursions from Samaná. Options range from rubber dinghies to sportfishing vessels and flat-hulled craft with viewing platforms and covered decks. Whale Samaná (Calle Mella & Ave. La Marina, tel 809/538-2494, whalesamana.com, $$$$) **has twice-daily trips, mid-January to mid-March. Multiday trips also operate to the Silver Bank** (see p. 142). **With luck, the captain will lower a hydrophone into the water so you can hear the elaborate songs of male humpbacks.**

Humpbacks are easily identified by their long white pectoral fins and elongated jaws.

More Places to Visit on La Península de Samaná

Garganta del Diablo

The gaping Throat of the Devil blowhole, also known as **Boca del Diablo** (Mouth of the Devil), spouts a hissing blast of spray under extreme pressure. It's accessed from Carretera 5 by a greenery-shrouded, pot-holed road *(turnoff 5 miles/8 km E of Punta Balandra)*. You can set out for the blowhole along the **Sendero Ecoturístic Playa Frontón,** a shoreline trail that leads 3 miles (5 km) to Playa Frontón (see p. 116) via the **Cueva del Agua.** This cliff-face cavern burrows down to a brackish lake at sea level within the protected natural area, **Monumento Natural Cabo Samaná.**

🅰 113 E2 ✉ 12 miles (19.3 km) E of Samaná via Carretera 5

Salto del Limón

Crashing down through the palm-studded mountains, the Lemon Waterfall tumbles

---

Mamajuana

The infamous Dominican mamajuana cocktail enjoys mythical status as a fabled aphrodisiac, as well as a general cure-all for everything from *gripe* (the common cold) to menstrual pains. Mamajuana is drunk as a shot or even as a postprandial liquor. It tastes like sherry or port wine and is sold in bottles at *botánicas* and by the shot in working-class bars. The drink's individual ingredients depend on the maker but usually involve various sticks, leaves, and roots steeped in rum, with the addition of wine, honey, fruit juice, and a range of other natural elements. Popular ingredients include the bark of *anamú, caro,* and *marabeli;* a creeping vine called *bohuco; canelilla* (from cinnamon); plus twigs of several kinds of herbs.

---

130 feet (52 m) into a pool at its base. The muddy 1.2-mile (2 km) trail from the village of El Limón fords a river and rises steeply, ascending almost 1,000 feet (305 m). The trail is purgatory after rains and it is best to take a guided horseback excursion *(1 hour each way)* rather than hike. The final stage requires a steep descent on foot. Roadside *boscones* (touts) attempt to hustle arriving visitors onto one of their tours; book directly with established operators. Santi Rancho *(tel 809/343-0716),* in El Limón, is recommended. Tour operators in Samaná and Las Terranas offer half-day trips.

🅰 113 C2 ✉ 0.75 mile (1.2 km) SE of El Limón, midway between Las Terrenas & Samaná 💲 $

Samaná Zipline

Imagine the thrill of whizzing down between rainforest treetops within sight of white beaches and the azure Atlantic. The Samaná Zipline, at Tree House Village, in the hills above Playa El Valle, features 12 cables and offers a thrilling start—the first run is more than 1,000 feet (304 m). Local tour operators offer excursions.

dominicantreehousevillage.com ✉ 2 miles (3 km) S of Playa El Valle ☎ 805/850-3848 or 829/542-3005 💲 $$$$

Taíno Park

If you're interested in Hispaniola's indigenous culture, this recently opened theme park provides intriguing exhibits. Most are alfresco life-size recreations of the society as it lived at the time of the Spanish arrival, including scenarios showing their conversion to Christianity. Exhibits also include pottery, plus wood and stone motifs. MP3 audio narratives are available in various languages.

tainopark.com 🅰 113 C2 ✉ Los Róbalos, 6 miles (10 km) W of Samaná on the road to Sánchez ☎ 829/693-4267 💲 $

A wind-caressed shoreline, mountains where precious amber is found, and beaches with world-class windsurfing and kiteboarding

North Coast

Templo de las Américas, near Luperón, built to commemorate Columbus's arrival in Hispaniola

North Coast

Fringed by a lovely shoreline, the Amber Coast is framed to the south by the Cordillera Septentrional, separating the coastal plain from El Cibao and the Valle del Yaque. The palm-swathed mountains slope north to magnificent beaches and impossibly clear sapphire seas. Winds whip up the excitement for surfers, windsurfers, and kiteboarders, while treasures await below the waves.

Beneath gathering storm clouds, a fisherman casts his line in the waters of Playa Grande, east of Río San Juan.

Named for the valuable fossil resin found in the mountains inland, the Amber Coast was the republic's original center of tourism. Upstaged of late by La Costa del Coco, the north coast remains first choice for active vacationers. Development—not all of it pretty—is encroaching on the remaining patches of virgin coast, and the innocence most areas once knew is gone. All-inclusive resorts coalesce around Puerto Plata, but elsewhere small boutique and budget hotels cater to an independent-minded clientele.

Cabarete—the undisputed kiteboarding and windsurfing capital of the Caribbean—draws wind-seeking pilgrims from around the world. With thatched gourmet restaurants and lively bars spilling out along the beach, Cabarete is also party hearty, with a no-holds-barred, alcohol-focused nightlife spilling onto the sands. Sosúa, which has the unique distinction of having been founded by German Jews, is the scuba-diving capital of the north coast, while diving off the cape around Río San Juan is equally sublime. Sosúa has also long been known in the Caribbean for its rather seamy nightlife (although the scene is not half what it once was).

The all-inclusive resorts cluster around Puerto Plata, a 16th-century port city steeped in the past. This invitingly historic city boasts fine Victorian architecture and the Caribbean's only cable-car ride—up mist-shrouded Pico Isabel de Torres. Tour operators offer excursions into the mountains, from bike trips to waterfall canyoning and cascading. The rippling fairways of Playa Dorado and Playa Grande serve golfers. And Puerto Plata's family-friendly Ocean World Adventure Park lets kids swim with dolphins, while a new cruise port at Amber Cove that opened in 2015 has given the local economy a further boost.

West of Puerto Plata, the scant remains of La Isabela—site of the first Spanish settlement in the Americas—recall Columbus's maiden landing on December 4, 1492. Beyond, long strips of deserted sands accessed by rugged dirt roads fringe a countryside whose pastoral scenes carry you back in time. The jewel in the crown is magnificent Playa Punta Rucia, launch site for speedboat trips to Cayo Paraíso, a tiny sun-bleached cay ringed by coral reef.

The ocean waters north and east of Río San Juan are protected within the Sanctuary for the Marine Mammals of the Dominican Republic—a breeding and calving ground drawing the largest congregations of humpback whales anywhere on the planet.

Carretera 5 runs along the shore almost the entire way, although west of Luperón the going gets tough and Playa Rucia is accessed off of the autopista, DR 1. ■

NOT TO BE MISSED:

Chilling by night on Playa Cabarete **130**

Kiteboarding at Cabarete **130–131**

Day trip into the Cordillera Septentrional **133**

Checking out prehistoric amber at the Amber Museum **135**

Cable-car ride up Pico Isabel de Torres **137**

A walk in Puerto Plata **138–139**

Columbus's settlement at Parque Nacional Histórico y Arqueológico de Villa de La Isabela **141**

Around Río San Juan

A relatively recent tourism region that offers a tranquil escape from the thronged beaches farther west, the area around Río San Juan—a somnolent town that still has a working fishing harbor—boasts some stupendous beaches. Some of the country's best diving draws visitors to the translucent waters off the northeastern nape of the country.

Coconut trees provide shade on the hot sands of Playa Preciosa in Parque Nacional Cabo Francés Viejo.

Surrounded by cattle pastures, the town of Río San Juan, in a sheltered bay at the extreme northeast of the island, enfolds **Laguna Gri-Gri,** a small fresh-water lake lined with tangled mangroves. Calle Duarte, the unremarkable main street, leads to the lagoon, where boats wait to take you on trips through the mangroves. The jade lagoon is fed by subterranean waters stained by tannins from the mangrove forest, where croco-diles lurk in the channels. Early morning is best for fabulous birding. White egrets roost in the treetops, while swallows nest in the thousands in **Cueva de las Golondrinas** (Swallows' Cave). A sandy trail leads from the lagoon's north shore to **Playa Caletón;** the shallow waters are good for snorkeling.

Wind-whipped **Playa Grande,** 9 miles (14.5 km) east of Río San Juan, tantalizes with its mile (1.6 km) of soft, golden sands melding east to wave-pounded **Playa Preciosa.** Beach chairs and boogie boards can be rented at Playa Grande. Swimming is not advised due to ferocious riptides, but the rough sea is nirvana for surfers. Overhanging Playa Grande, the rippling fairways of the clifftop **Playa Grande Golf Course** (playagrande.com) are

INSIDER TIP:

One of the culinary highlights of the D.R. is a plate of *tostones* (fried plantain slices), a squeeze of lime, and an icy bottle of Presidente.

—ALICE SAMSON
National Geographic field researcher

among the Caribbean's best. The cliffs are at their most dramatic at Cabo Francés Viejo, a cape topped by subtropical forest within **Parque Nacional Cabo Francés Viejo,** where trails are simple goat tracks. In its lee, to the south, a staircase leads down to **Playa Bretón,** enclosed by white cliffs.

Offshore, divers are spoiled for choice. The waters teem with life. There are shallow wrecks to explore and possible encounters with humpback whales.

Emblazoned upon the limestone cliffs 4 miles (7 km) west of town is an image of the Virgen de Guadalupe; "holy" water from its base is sold to pilgrims.

Cabrera & Nearby

Caressed by Atlantic breezes at the very northeast tip of the isle, the clean and prosperous town of Cabrera is graced by colorful wooden houses. Cabrera is the gateway to **Playa Diamante** (6 miles/9 km S of Cabrera), a true gem of a beach. Tucked within a deep cove, this 200-yard-wide (183 m), snow white beach dissolves into neon blue waters.

You can wade out 100 yards (91 m) and still be thigh deep.

One mile (1.6 km) south, the **Santuario de la Virgen de la Piedra** draws pilgrims to the figure of Nuestra Señora de Lourdes carved into the stone face inside a chapel.

Cueva El Dudú (7 miles/ 12 km S of Cabrera) tempts divers to explore a freshwater jade blue *cenote* (sinkhole). Enfolded by rain forest, it resembles a set from Tarzan. The cool waters draw locals for dips from a rope swing. Buy your ticket for the cave at Restaurante Parador Dudú *($)*. A stone's throw away, the grotto of **Lago Azul** *($)* sparkles with aquamarine waters.

In the mountains west of town, Hotel/Restaurante La Catalina *(tel 809/589-7700 Cabrera or 313/279-3114 U.S., lacatalina.com)* offers horseback excursions for visitors. ∎

Río San Juan
▲ 127 D2
Visitor Information
✉ Oficina de la Secretaría de Turismo, Calles Muella & Capotilla
☎ 809/589-2831

Cabrera
▲ 127 E2

Sanky-pankys & Tigueres

The republic's tourist zones are crawling with sanky-pankys and tigueres. The former are male hustlers who pose as legitimate lovers and woo female tourists with *piropos* (compliments) and declarations of affection. Females who fall for a sanky-panky typically find themselves paying the man's costs and being solicited for money long after they've returned home. Marriage for the sake of a foreign visa is often the ultimate goal. Tigueres are hustlers who use artful guile to part tourists from their money. Some tigueres pose as police (often using stolen jackets): A favorite trick is to motion passing motorists—always tourists—to pull over before demanding a fine on the spot.

Cabarete

Cabarete, the Caribbean's hippest water-sports playground, was barely a speck on the map two decades ago. Today the tight little beach village has a red-hot rep and boasts plenty of low-key hotels and après-surf action, with ultracasual dining as well as a young, hip party scene.

Cabarete's always lively bars and restaurants spill onto the beach.

Cabarete

🗺 127 C3

Visitor Information

✉ Oficina de Turismo, Plaza Tricom, Calle Principal

☎ 809/571-0962

Cabarete is justly famous for its crescent-shaped beach and constant trade winds that blow inshore from the northeast. Its shallow bay is protected by a coral reef—ideal conditions for windsurfing and kiteboarding. Surfers also gravitate here for the best wave action in the country. The **Kiteboard World Cup championship** (worldkite tour.com) is occasionally held here in June, when the wind and waves are at their best.

Cabarete stretches along almost 3 miles (5 km) of shoreline. The beach—a setting for barefoot merengue by night—is lost to view from the road. Everything is laid out along the shore highway, lined by thatched bars, laid-back resorts, and surf shops. The drag is clamorous with traffic.

Crowded **Playa Cabarete** is the center for windsurfing action, with a score of outfitters along the beach. It merges westward, downwind, to **Playa Bozo**—a beach named for the beginner windsurfers who fail to tack and wash up here. The kiteboard action concentrates farther west, off **Kite Beach,** where kiteboarders perform acrobatics 30 feet (9 m) in the air. Beyond, the surfboard set heads to **Playa Encuentro,** a laid-back beach with reliably big waves. Take Off (Cabarete Center, tel

809/963-7873, *321takeoff.com*) is a well-respected surf school—one of many here.

Around Cabarete

After riding the wind, head to **Parque Nacional El Choco** *(Callejón de la Loma, 1.5 miles/ 2.4 km S of town).* Officially named Monumento Natural Lagunas Cabarete y Goleta, this park comprises 48 square miles (77 sq km) squeezed between the shore and the Cordillera Septentrional. Trails weave through marshes and forest to **Laguna Cabarete,** a good spot for birding. The lagoon is fed by freshwater springs that seep from three underground caverns whose formations form a canvas for pre-Columbian Taíno paintings. The main cave has a lagoon that's good for swimming. Active-adventure specialist Iguana Mama *(Calle Principal*

INSIDER TIP:

The D.R. is an adrenaline freak's dream, with the best windsurfing conditions east of Maui.

—TOM CLYNES
National Geographic contributing editor

74, *tel 809/571-0908, iguana mama.com*) offers trips to El Choco and into the Cordillera Septentrional (see p. 133).

Kayak River Adventures *(tel 829/305-6883, kayakriver adventures.com)* offers canyoning, plus kayaking and stand-up paddleboard trips on the Ríos Jamao and Yassica. And you can saddle up at **Wise Mountain** *(tel 829/769-5055, wisemountain.org),* a horse ranch in the mountains south of Gaspar Hernández. ■

EXPERIENCE: Learn the Moves

"Quien baila, nunca esta triste" ("Those who dance are never sad") is a popular Dominican saying. Life here moves to an infectious rhythm. The footloose Dominicans have a passion for music and dance—integral components of local culture. To watch elderly couples dancing cheek to cheek on a Sunday afternoon on the sands is to make you realize it's time to get into the rhythm.

These three dance schools teach you essential dance moves to make you feel *nunca triste* (never sad):

Alma Libre Dance School *(Millennium Resort, Cabarete, tel 849/272-2796)* Learn salsa, merengue, and *bachata* with dance professional Nina Ndjemba Elemba. Her

dance studio is in the Millennium Resort & Spa, a stone's throw from the beach and local discos, where by night you get to practice your moves.

Emily Watson School of Dance *(Sosúa Ocean Village, Sosúa, 809/777-1290, emilywatsonschoolofdance.com)* English-born Emily Watson and her Dominican partner Carlos Francisco teach various styles, from tap and ballet to salsa and even hip-hop.

Instituto Intercultural del Caribe *(tel 809/571-3185, edase.com/E_L08A _Dancing.htm)* This language school teaches bachata, merengue, and salsa for all levels of students. Programs are offered in Santo Domingo and Sosúa.

Sosúa

Known for its lively bar scene, Sosúa is popular with a laid-back breed of tourists and expats but gets crowded on weekends and holidays when Dominicans pour in to enjoy the golden sands lining a protected cove. Sosúa is great for mingling with locals and steeping in real island culture shared at beachfront restaurants and funky beach bars strung together with driftwood.

Sosúa's original synagogue is still active.

Sosúa

⚑ 127 C3

Visitor Information

✉ ASHORESOCA, Pedro Clisante 12

☎ 809/571-3440

Museo de la Comunidad Judía de Sosúa

✉ Calle Dr. Alejo Martínez & Calle Dr. Rosén

☎ 809/571-1386

🕐 Closed Sat.–Sun.

💲 $

Sosúa, between Cabarete and Puerto Plata, was a center for banana production in the late 19th century, when the United Fruit Company, a U.S. corporation, set up here. After the company abandoned the land in the 1920s, Sosúa reverted to a quiet coastal village before metamorphosing in the 1980s into a slightly decadent center for sex tourism. The scene has somewhat tempered since.

The twin sides of town differ greatly. **Los Charramícos,** in the west, is more authentically Dominican, with tightly packed streets

and humble houses. More jovial, touristy **El Batey,** to the east, was founded in the 1940s by Central European Jews given refuge here by Rafael Trujillo (see sidebar opposite) and is strongly European. Adjoining the wooden **synagogue** *(Calle Dr. Alejo Martínez & Calle Dr. Rosén),* still in use and bearing its Star of David motif, the tiny **Museo de la Comunidad Judía de Sosúa** tells the tale of Sosúa's Jewish community.

Between Los Charramícos and El Batey, lively cliffbound **Playa Sosúa**—a mile-long (1.6 km) strip of white sand—is lined with art galleries, bars, and simple restaurants along a tree-shaded path. And countless people offer banana-boat rides. To the east is **Playita Alicia,** a pretty half-moon strand backed by cliffs; the relatively deserted beach is accessed by boat or through the Casa Marina Reef Resort and lacks vendors.

This shore holds some of the country's finest offshore coral reefs, and scuba diving is well developed. More than a dozen dive sites include **Airport Wall,** which features swim-through caves with elkhorn coral. A resident moray peers out from the wreck of the *Zingara,* a cargo ship that was deliberately scuttled in 1993 to form an artificial reef. Merlin Dive Center *(Playa Sosúa, tel 809/545-0538, divecentermerlin.weebly.com)* and Northern Coast Aquasports *(Calle Pedro Clisante 8, tel 809/571-1028, northerncoastdiving.com)* offer dives.

Cordillera Septentrional

At the rural town of **Monte Llano** *(7 miles/12 km W of Sosúa),* badly eroded Carretera 25 climbs into the Cordillera Septentrional via Tubagua.

Nearby, **Tubagua Plantation Eco Village** *(tel 809/586-5761, tubagua.com),* an eco-resort integrated into the mountain community, offers an immersion into local lifestyles. And you can thrill to aerial rides between treetops at the **Yasika Zipline Adventure** *(tel 809/320-0000,*

yasikaadventures.com), with eight metal cables slung between ten treetop platforms.

South of Tubagua, the road snakes uphill into the mountains proper, cresting at La Cumbre and the **Parque Ecológico Café La Cumbre** *(tel 809/533-1984),* a coffee finca with a small museum and trails through native forest. Amber workshops line the road, including **Ambar La Cumbre** *(tel 809/656-1499).* Turn east at the police station in La Cumbre for the tiny hamlet of

Jewish Refugees

In July 1938, President Rafael Trujillo attended a conference on refugees in France. Pursuing his agenda to "whiten" the Dominican Republic, he stated his willingness to accept up to 100,000 European Jews fleeing Nazi persecution. In 1939 the Dominican Republic Settlement Association was formed and suitable Europeans (priority went to able-bodied men) were settled on 26,000 acres (10,522 ha) that Trujillo purchased from the United Fruit Company. Some 600 Jewish settlers arrived; each received 80 acres (32 ha), cattle, and a mule. Their Productos Sosúa (now Mexican owned) remains one of the country's leading producers of meat and dairy products.

La Toca, where miners chip amber from narrow tunnels bored into the hills (see p. 134).

To the southeast of town is **Monkey Jungle,** a working farm named for the squirrel monkeys (native to Central America) that frolic in a botanic garden. It also has a shooting range and a 7-station zip line adventure. ■

Monkey Jungle

✉ Carretera El Chocó km 9

☎ 829/649-4555

💲 $$$

monkeyjungledr.com

Amber

Amber is a fossilized resin from the extinct prehistoric *Hymenaea protera* tree. The oozing sap hardened into a clear, rocklike polymer over millions of years. Although it is not a mineral, this translucent substance is considered a gemstone and is the Dominican Republic's national gem.

Amber typically ranges in age from 15 million to 40 million years old. Most comes from Estonia, Latvia, and Lithuania, where it was traded throughout ancient cultures, finding its way into Egyptian and Roman jewelry and figurines. The Taíno peoples also held amber in high esteem, using it for jewelry and burning it as incense to keep mosquitoes away. The Dominican Republic has some of the world's largest amber reserves, as well as the largest variety of colors, the largest concentration of insect fossils, and the highest quality, determined by level of transparency. Amber is graded by color, from rich golden yellow to claret, purple, and even black, with colors varying by source and also according to age. The youngest amber is usually the lightest. Rare "blue amber"—found principally in the Los Cacaos mine of the Cordillera Septentrional—is prized by collectors. Although not strictly blue, it gives off a bluish sheen when light hits it at just the right angles.

All amber has long been prized for making jewelry, but the most valuable amber pieces contain inclusions, such as insects or plants.

Amber Mines

Amber is usually found underground. There are three main amber mining sites in the Dominican Republic. About 95 percent comes from around La Toca (see p. 133), high in the Cordillera Septentrional, where it is tightly imbedded within sandstone mingled with marine deposits. Amber is also found in lesser quantities at Bayaguana and Sabena, in the southeast of the country. It is mined by mostly impoverished locals who earn a subsistence living chipping away at rocks in narrow tunnels. Entire villages, including children, make a living as miners.

Amber pieces are usually at most 2 inches (5 cm) wide, although occasionally bigger pieces are found. The largest piece discovered so far in the Dominican Republic weighed a whopping 18 pounds (8 kg). The most precious pieces contain creatures and flower petals—inclusions—that became trapped in the sticky tree resin, which eventually hardened to form a transparent tomb. Millions of years later, perfectly preserved inclusions range from ants and flies to small frogs. One amber piece displayed in the Puerto Plata Amber Museum (see opposite) contains a 17-inch-long (42 cm) lizard. Since 1987, no amber containing a fossil may be exported from the country without a license from the National Museum of Natural History.

The demand for amber has fostered a market for plastic counterfeits. When rubbed with cotton, real amber becomes statically charged. It also floats in saltwater and emits a pine scent when held over a flame, unlike most fakes.

Puerto Plata

The largest city along the north coast, Puerto Plata (Silver Port) has roots going back to 1502 and boasts a historic core—Zona Victoriana—with gingerbread buildings that are being renovated one by one. A harmonic blend of old and new, Puerto Plata is backed by the peak of Pico Isabel de Torres, with a cable car that whisks you up from the sultry coastal heat to a far cooler climate. The city now boasts a new cruise port that has revitalized local tourism.

Christopher Columbus arrived on January 11, 1493, giving the spot the name Silver Port, although Gov. Nicolás de Ovando actually founded the settlement in 1502. Protected by a fortress, Puerto Plata thrived as a smuggling center until 1605, when the Spanish crown expelled the populace and razed the town. It was resurrected in 1737 and in the following century entered a golden age of tobacco farming.

The town is laid out around **Parque Central,** a tree-shaded oasis that provides a setting for weekend concerts. Located at the park's heart is **La Glorieta,** a reconstruction of the original gingerbread bandstand made in Belgium in 1872. Dominating the plaza is the twin-steepled **Catedral San Felipe Apóstol** *(Calle José del Castillo & Calle Duarte),* a fine edifice that combines art deco with a traditional colonial structure.

The **Amber Museum,** a store housed in a 1919-era creole town house, displays an impressive collection of amber pieces, including an entrapped million-year-old lizard and a mosquito inclusion used in the movie *Jurassic Park.* For a rainy-day taster of Dominican rums,

An orderly array of colorful wooden houses fills Puerto Plata's core.

Puerto Plata

⬛ 127 B3

Visitor Information

✉ Oficina de
Turismo,
Calle José del
Carmen Ariza 45
☎ 809/586-3676
🕐 Closed Sat.–Sun.

Amber Museum

✉ Calle Duarte 61
☎ 809/586-2848
🕐 Closed Sun.
💲 $

ambermuseum.com

Casa Museo General Gregorio Luperón

✉ Calle 12 de Julio
54
☎ 809/261-8661
🕐 Closed Mon.
💲 $

head to the **Brugal rum bottling plant** *(Ave. Louis Gine-bra, tel 809/261-1888, closed Sat.–Sun.);* you'll witness the bottling process before being hustled into the gift store for a lackluster cocktail.

Fortaleza San Felipe *(closed Wed., $),* one of the oldest fortresses in the New World, stands guard over the harbor entrance at the west end of the Malecón *(Ave. Gregorio Luperón).* Completed in 1577 to deter marauding pirates, the bastion contains a small museum displaying weaponry. A statue of Gregorio Luperón—the Dominican general who led resistance to Spanish rule in the 1860s—stands outside. He is honored in the recently restored **Casa Museo General Gregorio Luperón,** with displays on local history.

The **Malecón** seafront boulevard comes alive for the merengue festival each October, when a jazz festival is also hosted. The boulevard parallels **Playa de Long Beach,** the

gorgeous in-town beach with an oceanfront bicycle trail.

Playas Cofresí, Costámbar, & Dorado

The community of **Costámbar** *(2 miles/3 km W of Puerto Plata)* has a relatively undeveloped beach popular with locals, who flock on weekends. Farther west, Playa Cofresí is set in a wave-swept horseshoe bay, its hillsides studded with villas. Dominating Cofresí, and not to be missed, is **Ocean World Adventure Park** (see sidebar below), where you can slip into warm waters to

---

EXPERIENCE: Fun With the Family

To keep the kids happy in the Dominican Republic, these three venues should do the trick:

Ocean World Adventure Park *(Puerto Plata, tel 809/291-1000, oceanworld.net)* has sea lion and dolphin shows, plus lagoons for snorkeling and swimming with rays, nurse sharks, and dolphins.

Museo Infantil Trampolín *(Calle Las Damas, Santo Domingo, tel 809/685-5551, trampolin.org.do)* is perfect for a rainy day.

This fascinating children's museum has superb interpretative exhibits spanning themes such as history, geography, sciences, and society.

Seaquarium *(Bávaro, Punta Cana, tel 809/688-9525, seaquariumpunta cana.com)* will fulfill your dreams of walking across the ocean floor like an undersea diver. You can don a state-of-the-art diver's helmet with an air tube attached to a floating tank, then walk the seabed.

A cable car travels over thick vegetation to the top of Pico Isabel de Torres, offering splendid views of the countryside.

swim with dolphins. This theme park also features an aviary and performing sea lions. Near Cofresí is **Amber Cove,** a cruise port with resort facilities that service Carnival Cruise Lines.

East of Puerto Plata, sinuous Playa Dorado is the setting for a sprawling megaresort complex with hotels arcing around the championship **Playa Dorado Golf Club** (tel 809/320-3472, playadoradagolf.com).

Pico Isabel de Torres

Puerto Plata is spread-eagled below a dramatic flat-topped formation, Pico Isabel de Torres (2,621 feet/799 m). An often overloaded teleférico (cable car) ferries visitors up the mountain, where a statue of Jesus Christ stands with arms outspread. After enjoying breathtaking views, you can stroll through a forested 334-acre (135 ha) reserve and botanic garden. Caribbean martins and Hispaniolan trogons trill in the treetops.

The cable car is often closed in bad weather, and the wait can be long in peak season. Freelance guides hustle visitors, but they are not required. Early morning is best, before the clouds form. The cable car closes at 5 p.m.

The hale and hearty can hike the mountain from Puerto Plata via a trail from **El Cupey,** a rustic community at the foot of the mountain. Iguana Mama (Calle Principal 74, Cabarete, tel 809/571-0908, iguanamama.com) offers guided hikes. ∎

Ocean World Adventure Park

✉ Cofresí, 3 miles (5 km) W of Puerto Plata

☎ 809/291-1000

💲 $$$$$

oceanworld.net

Teleférico Puerto Plata

✉ Calle Manolo Távarez Justo

☎ 809/970-0501

💲 $$

telefericopuerto plata.com

A Stroll Around Historic Puerto Plata

Replete with old creole houses laid out along a tight grid of streets, Puerto Plata makes for a delightful downtown walk. If you'd like some guidance, licensed tour guides in baby blue dress shirts lead tours for negotiable fees; ask at the tourism office. On weekdays, the crowded streets are abuzz with *motoconchos* and other traffic; stick to the sidewalks and use extreme care when crossing streets. Weekends are better for touring.

Restored and beautified, the tree-shaded Malecón wanders along Puerto Plata's oceanfront.

Begin your walk at the office of the **Secretaría del Estado de Turismo** (*Calle José del Carmen Ariza 45, tel 809/586-3676*), where you can pick up a map. Walk north half a block, passing on your right the **Casa Curial** (Bishop's House), a lovely structure with gingerbread trim. Immediately beyond, enter the symmetrical **Catedral San Felipe Apóstol ❶** (see p. 135), recently restored.

Exiting, turn right onto Calle Duarte. Follow Duarte east two blocks to the **Amber Museum ❷** (see p. 135) in the pink-and-white Villa Bentz. Enter to admire the fine jewelry,

NOT TO BE MISSED:

Catedral San Felipe Apóstol
• Amber Museum • Fortaleza
de San Felipe • Malecón

then retrace your steps to the cathedral. Turn right onto Calle Separación, noting the orange-clapboard **Casa de la Cultura** (*Calle Separación & Calle Duarte, closed Sat.–Sun.*), featuring an upstairs art gallery; it hosts music and dance workshops. Next door is the neoclassical, yellow-and-white **Ayuntamiento,** City Hall.

Cross into **Parque Central ❸** surrounded by Victorian gingerbread structures—those along Calle Beller, to the north, are most intriguing. After admiring the central gazebo (see p. 135), cross to the northwest corner, commanded by the gleaming white **Iglesia Cristiana el Buen Samaritano** (Calle José del Carmen Ariza 29) **❹**, a Pentecostal church housed in a magnificent Victorian mansion.

Turn left onto Calle Beller. One block brings you to the tiny **Museo de Arte Taíno** (Plaza Arawack, Calle Beller 25, tel 809/586-7601), a store exhibiting Taíno pottery and artifacts. Crossing Calle San Felipe, the **Canoa Gift Shop** (Calle Beller 18, tel 809/586-3965) **❺**, on your right, has a particularly fine collection of amber and larimar jewelry, plus exhibits. Return to San Felipe and turn left. Walk north five blocks, passing the **Galería de Ámbar** (Calle San Felipe & Calle José del Carmen Ariza,

tel 809/586-6467, $), displaying exhibits relating to coffee, tobacco, rum, and sugar.

Arriving at Avenida Gregorio Luperón, turn left and walk 400 yards (366 m) to **Fortaleza San Felipe** (see p. 136) **❻**, standing over grassy **Parque Luperón** at the west end of the Malecón. Guides are not required: It takes but a few minutes to explore the small museum, cannon, and dungeons where Juan Pablo Duarte was imprisoned. Across from the fort, to the south, note the restored **lighthouse,** erected in 1879. After admiring the bronze **statue of Gen. Gregorio Luperón ❼**, the 19th-century independence hero, exit Parque Luperón along the **Malecón,** lined with modernist buildings, beach bars, and hotels. Trees shade your path east as you stroll the pleasant beachfront promenade. En route, take a brief detour to **Casa Museo General Gregorio Luperón** (Calle 12 de Julio 54, tel 809/261-8661) **❽**, housed in a restored Victorian manse. Retrace your steps to the Malecón to end your walk at **Playa de Long Beach ❾**.

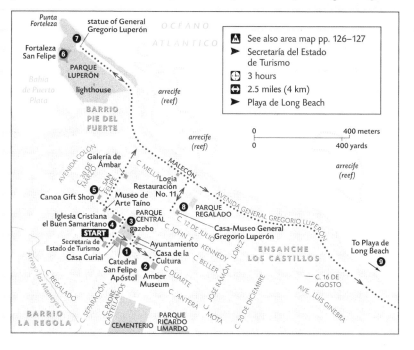

Luperón & Around

At the western reach of the Amber Coast, Luperón draws international yachters to its safe harbor. Nearby, the scant remains of the New World's oldest settlement are enshrined in a national park, while farther west manatees thrive in the lagoons of Estero Hondo within a stone's throw of one of the nation's most glorious beaches.

Early morning fog dissipates to reveal a cluster of motorboats at anchor off Punta Rucia.

Luperón
 126 A3
Visitor Information
✉ Oficina de Secretaría del Estado de Turismo, Calle Gen. Luperón 50
☎ 809/571-8002

Off the beaten track and somewhat somnolent, the small town of Luperón clings to a laid-back ambience. Long-touted plans for a deluxe resort have stalled. Guarding the east entrance to town is a life-size **statue of Gregorio Luperón,** the hero of independence from Spain. Luperón's main draw is as a hurricane hideaway: Its natural deepwater harbor is sheltered within a mangrove estuary made secure by surrounding hills. Catamaran tours of the mangroves are offered, as are sailing trips farther afield, from the slightly run-down **Marina Luperón Yacht Club** *(tel 829/771-2002),* 2 miles (3 km) west of Luperón.

Playa Grande is a sweeping swath of sands backed by the Luperón Beach Resort. Take care when wading and swimming, as the shallow and rocky waters host a veritable forest of spiny sea urchins. Scuba divers can explore the wreck of the *Manzanillo,* a 20th-century freighter lying in a watery grave 90 feet (27 m) down.

Parque Nacional Histórico y Arqueológico de Villa de La Isabela

This national park protects a promontory overlooking the placid bay that first welcomed Christopher Columbus in 1493. Here, the Great Discoverer established the first permanent settlement in the New World; the first Mass was held here on January 6, 1494. The settlement lasted five years until relocated to present-day Santo Domingo.

In 1952, Rafael Trujillo launched an archaeological project to excavate the site, which was named in honor of the Spanish queen. Alas, his instructions to "tidy up" were misunderstood: The overzealous crew bulldozed most of the site into the ocean. Only the barely discernible foundations remain, including the shell of Columbus's residence. A Taíno skeleton rests in an early cemetery; a tumbledown *bohío* represents a traditional Taíno dwelling; and a nearly decrepit **museum** displays cannonballs, Taíno artifacts, and exhibits on the Columbus landing, including a model of the *Santa María*.

The **Templo de las Américas,** half a mile (0.8 km) east, was built in 1990 in early colonial style to celebrate the 500th anniversary of Columbus's arrival. It contains lovely stained glass by Dominican artist José Rincón Mora (1938–).

Punta Rucia

With talcum white sands unspooling for miles, Playa Punta Rucia combines dramatic scenery with magnificent waters. Despite its relative obscurity, this enchanting beach combined with a rustic fishing village draws package excursions from far afield. It is separated by a headland from **Playa Enseñada,** lined with food shacks and luring Dominicans in hordes on weekends to play dominoes and jive to merengue. Irresistible and idyllic **Cayo Paraíso**—a perfectly circular coral island—studs the turquoise bay 6 miles (10 km) northwest of Punta Rucia. El Paraíso Tours *(tel 809/320-7606, Puerto Plata, paradiseisland.do),* at Punta Rucia,

Parque Nacional Histórico y Arqueológico de Villa de La Isabela

▲ 126 A3

✉ El Castillo, 9 miles (14.5 km) W of Luperón

💲 $

Punta Rucia

▲ 126 A3

Bumblebee Orchids

Visitors to the **Reserva Científica Villa Elisa,** near Punta Rucia, could be forgiven for doing a double take when they see its flowers. The dry forest reserve, 5 miles (8 km) north of Villa Elisa, was created to protect the Heneken's bee orchid *(Hispaniella henekenii),* or *orquídea cacatica,* a rare orchid endemic to the Dominican Republic. The tiny dark purple and yellow flower has evolved to mimic the form of a female bee, complete with false legs and wings. Male bees are fooled into attempting to mate and become smothered with pollen, which they take to the next plant. The orchid flowers from February to April.

offers excursions, including a stop at the cay on speedboat excursions to Parque Nacional Monte Cristi (see p. 159), farther west.

Punta Rucia is reached via a partially paved road from Villa Elisa, on Carretera 1, and in dry season only by four-wheel-drive vehicle from El Castillo via the village of La Isabela (this route requires a river fording). ■

More Places to Visit on the North Coast

Nagua

Nagua is an orderly coastal town and a tran-sit hub for *gua-guas* (buses) traveling between Samaná and the Amber Coast, as well as for Carretera 132, connecting Nagua to the Valle del Cibao and Santo Domingo. Hand-some beaches with surf washing up from a teal blue sea draw visitors; riptides, however, make swimming unsafe. At Boba, the old coast road (deteriorated to a sandy four-wheel-drive track) runs past wave-pounded **Playa Boba** and **Playa Laguna Grande.** Southwest of Nagua, the **Reserva Científica Loma Guaconejo** (*c/o Sociedad Ecológica del Cibao, tel 809/247-3833, soeci.org.do*) protects submontane rain forest on the easternmost slopes of the Cordillera Septentrional. **Centro Ecoturístico Cuesta Colorada,** at the gateway hamlet of Cuesta Colorada, has exhibits and an educational trail.
🅰 127 E1 ✉ 37 miles (60 km) S of Río San Juan via Carretera 5; Oficina de Turismo, Calle Coloso ☎ 809/584-3862

Refugio de Manatís Estero Hondo

This manatee refuge protects the mangrove forest and lagoon of Caño Estero Hondo. Sightings of manatees are virtually guaran-teed, depending on time of day, at this huge T-shaped lagoon. These endangered mam-mals move in and out of the estuary around dawn and dusk. Guides offer tours *(tip)* from the visitor center at **Playa Marisa,** where a boat is available.
🅰 126 A3 ✉ 2 miles (3 km) E of Playa Enseñada

Santuario de Mamíferos Marinos de la República Dominicana

The Sanctuary for the Marine Mammals of the Dominican Republic protects the largest mating and calving area in the world for Atlantic humpback whales. As many as 5,000 humpbacks gather in midwinter for rest, recreation, and romance. The sanctuary encompasses the shallow coastal waters off the Dominican shoreline between Cabo Francés Viejo and Bahía de Samaná plus the deeper ocean waters in between. Most important of these zones is the **Silver Bank,** a submerged limestone plateau located some 50 miles (80 km) due north of Nagua. Access is by permit only and visits are strictly regulated. Aquatic Adventures *(tel 954/382-0024 in U.S., aquaticadventures.com)* offers whale-watching trips out of Puerto Plata, January through April. Conscious Breath Adventures *(tel 305/753-1732 in U.S., consciousbreathadventures.com)* has weeklong trips from Cofresí.
🅰 127 E1 & E2 ✉ c/o Subsecretaría de Estado de Recursos Costeros y Marinos, Ave. John F. Kennedy, km 6.5, Autopista Duarte, Santo Domingo ☎ 809/732-3303

27 Charcos de Damajagua Natural Monument

An encounter with this series of waterfalls—protected since 2007 as the 27 Waterfalls of Damajagua Natural Monument—provides a thrilling adventure. Visitors can clamber to the top of the falls to enjoy whizzing down natural water slides and jumping into crystal-clear pools. From the entrance, the trail involves wading along a shallow riverbed (up to thigh-deep at certain times of year); appropriate footwear is recommended. The fee includes a guide, helmet, and life jacket and depends on the number of cascades visited (allow 4 hours for all 27 cascades). The natural monument, located 2 miles (3 km) south of the town of Imbert, has a restaurant. Iguana Mama *(Calle Principal 74, Cabarete, tel 809/571-0908, iguanamama.com)* offers trips.
🅰 126 B2 ✉ 16 miles (26 km) SE of Puerto Plata via Carretera 5 ☎ 849/276-4658
💲 $$–$$$$

A lush, fertile region laden with national parks and historically important agricultural towns

El Cibao

The popular figurines *muñecas sin rostros,* or faceless dolls, are made in El Higuerito.

El Cibao

Bounded by the Cordillera Septentrional and rugged Cordillera Central, the region known as the Cibao is comprised of the valley of the Río Camú and, westward, the valley of the Río Yaque del Norte. Lush and green in the east, arid and brown in the west, the Cibao is one of the republic's most fertile regions, and by far the wealthiest. It is full of historic cities, while a wealth of wildlife can be seen in parks from the mountains to the sea.

El Cibao is primarily associated with the broad valley of the Río Camú, extending east of Santiago de los Caballeros, the republic's second largest city. The eastern Cibao, the nation's most densely settled area, comprises a triangular plain christened La Vega Real (Royal Plain) by Christopher Columbus for its rich soils and ideal climate. During the 19th century, its wealthy middle class was the driving force in the quest for independence from Spain and Haiti. Later, the inhabitants supported democracy during the civil wars with the demagogic cattle barons of the southeast. As a result, the region's towns were ravaged during successive invasions.

Today, living history hangs by a thread. Most towns are heavily commercialized and choked with traffic. Santiago de los Caballeros alone among its cities boasts a fine collection of 19th-century structures, plus the nation's best museum and a fantastic monument bequeathed by Rafael Trujillo. Moca and La Vega feature intriguing latter-day churches, as does Santo Cerro, where colonial ruins dating back five centuries can be seen at La Vega Vieja.

The land around Santiago is quilted with bottle green fields where some of the world's finest tobacco is grown. Cuban émigrés settled in the Cibao in the late 19th century, seeding a tobacco industry. Cigar production centers around Villa González and Tamboril, where family-run factories welcome visitors for a lesson in Cigarmaking 101.

This region's population is distinct, with far more Spanish blood than is found in the rest of the country. Many natives of El Cibao consider themselves the country's social elite: They're proud of their European or Cuban heritage and their importance in national political life.

West of Santiago, the well-paved Autopista Duarte runs ruler straight, funneling through the fecund valley of the Río Yaque del Norte (the nation's largest river at 125 miles/ 201 km long), hemmed between the Cordillera Septentrional and Cordillera Central.

Relatively prosperous agricultural towns dot the highway's route.

In stark contrast, the far west is arid, culminating in the scorchingly hot delta of the Río Yaque del Norte. Goats munch on the cactus-studded flats while flamingos and ibises tiptoe around in hot pink. These floodplain wetlands are important staging and wintering sites for waterfowl and shorebirds, and manatees thrive in shallow freshwater lagoons. Parque Nacional Monte Cristi protects the habitat as well as the

NOT TO BE MISSED:

Marveling at handmade Carnaval masks   150–151

The collection of modern Dominican art at Centro León   151

A walk around historic Santiago de los Caballeros   152–153

Casa Museo Hermanas Mirabal   154

Taking in tobacco culture around Tamboril   157

Carnaval in Santiago de los Caballeros   160

Birding in Reserva Científica Loma Quita Espuela   160

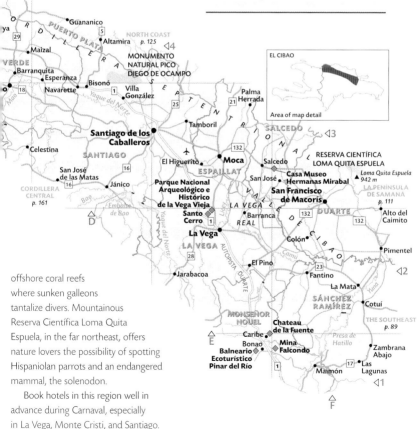

offshore coral reefs where sunken galleons tantalize divers. Mountainous Reserva Científica Loma Quita Espuela, in the far northeast, offers nature lovers the possibility of spotting Hispaniolan parrots and an endangered mammal, the solenodon.

Book hotels in this region well in advance during Carnaval, especially in La Vega, Monte Cristi, and Santiago.

Around Bonao

Flanked by the four-lane Autopista Duarte, Bonao has a long and storied history as a mining center. The town is shadowed by steep, forest-clad mountains that offer visitors splendid opportunities for hiking and adventuring to nearby beauty and swimming spots.

Bonao
△ 145 E1
Visitor Information
☎ 809/525-4454

Mina Falcondo
△ 145 E1
✉ Fundación Falcondo, Ave. Máximo Gómez 30
☎ 809/682-6041 ext. 2311
falcondo.do

Chateau de la Fuente
△ 145 E1
✉ Caribe, 3 miles (5 km) E of Bonao
☎ 809/575-4739 in Santiago
🕐 By appt. only
arturofuente.com

Dominating the small town's economy is the **Mina Falcondo,** 2 miles (3 km) east of Bonao, where locally extracted nickel ore is processed. Tours can be arranged with one week's notice through the **Fundación Falcondo,** which also promotes reforestation in the **Bosque Falconbridge Plan Sierra,** west of Bonao. The **Museo de Arte Cándido Bidó** (*Calle Padre Billini & Calle Los Santos, tel 809/525-7707, plazadela culturadebonao.com*), on the Plaza de la Cultura, displays the eponymous hometown artist's works as well as those of several other locals.

Chateau de la Fuente, at the village of Caribe, welcomes select visitors by advance notice to the showcase 200-acre (81 ha) plantation of the Tabacalera A. Fuente cigar company.

Maimón, located 11 miles (18 km) east of Bonao, enjoys a gorgeous setting in the midst of mountains near the head of **Presa de Hatillo,** a man-made lake good for fishing. Hire a local for boat tours to **Cueva de Sanabe,** which has pictographs. At **Balneario Ecoturístico Pinar del Río** (*Carretera Maimón km 3*), locals swim in river cascades.

West from Bonao, the snaking drive up the valley of the Río Yuna offers fine vistas, but casual hikers should beware: the area is prone to rains, fogs, and landslides. Some three miles (5 km) west of Bonao, the road passes **Balneario de la Confluencia del Ríos Yuna y Blanco,** an alluring riverside swimming spot. ■

Perico Ripiao

Perico ripiao (ripped parrot) is a form of merengue that evolved in the Cibao region in the 1850s. Known more respectfully as *merengue cibaeño* or *merengue típico* (traditional merengue), it is played with an accordion, tambora drum, and a metal scraper called a *güira*.

Until the 1930s, the music and its provocative dance form were considered salacious, and moralists tried to suppress it. When he seized power, dictator Rafael Leonidas Trujillo adopted the music, popularizing it as a national music beloved by all classes of Dominicans. It was later displaced by funk- and rock-influenced merengue as performed by Johnny Ventura and Wilfrido Vargas. It can still be heard, however, in working-class bars.

La Vega

Modern structures obscure this crowded and chaotic city's intriguing past, although its contemporary cathedral and a nearby pilgrimage site are well worth the visit. La Vega's February Carnaval celebration is considered the largest and most colorful in the republic.

Founded in 1494, La Concepción de la Vega was a base for the early gold-mining industry. It has since grown to become the country's third largest city, and a major agricultural center in the heart of El Cibao valley. The main draw is the postmodernist **Catedral de la Inmaculada Concepción de la Vega,** on the south side of **Parque Duarte** *(Calle Juan Bosch & Calle Padre Adolfo).* The cathedral's quasi-Gothic, neo-industrial style has inspired both praise and scorn.

The town's main park is surrounded by the beaux arts **Casa de la Cultura** *(Calle Independencia 32 & Calle Sánchez, closed Sat.– Sun.),* exhibiting Carnaval masks;

La Vega is known for its fierce demon masks, donned for Carnaval.

INSIDER TIP:

Visit a *colmado* (corner store), sit out in front, and share a one-liter bottle of Presidente with whoever is around.

—BRIAN RUDERT
Retired Foreign Service officer

and the neoclassical **Palacio de Justicia** *(Calle Sánchez & Calle Padre Adolfo);* and **Palacio Municipal** *(Calle Juan Bosch bet. Calle Independencia & Calle Padre Adolfo).*

Santo Cerro

Holy Hill, a few miles north of La Vega via Carretera Moca, offers a spectacular view over the city from the patio of **Iglesia Las Mercedes,** erected in 1886. Believers in Nuestra Señora de Las Mercedes say she worked a miracle here in 1495 to prevent Taínos burning a cross erected by Columbus himself. The church contains Santo Hoyo de la Cruz, a hole where Columbus's cross reputedly stood.

Parque Nacional Arqueológico e Histórico de la Vega Vieja, at the base of the hill, exhibits the original city's extensive remains. The fort's walls and watchtowers are still intact.

La Vega

🗺 145 E2

Visitor Information

✉ Oficina de Turismo, Calle Mella & Calle Durangé

☎ 809/242-3231 or 809/573-2811

Parque Nacional Arqueológico e Histórico de la Vega Vieja

🗺 145 E2

✉ Carretera Moca, 1 mi (1.6 km) NE of Santo Cerro

🕐 Closed Sun.

💲 $

Santiago de los Caballeros

The republic's second largest city, Santiago de los Caballeros (Santiago of the Gentlemen) holds on to its past glories as a tobacco boomtown and traditional center of agriculture. Its downtown streets are lined with charming yesteryear buildings, while the Centro León—combining a superb museum, art gallery, and tobacco factory—is not to be missed.

A mural in Fortaleza San Luís honors the women of the nation.

Santiago de los Caballeros

 145 E3

Visitor Information

✉ Gobernación, Parque Duarte & Calle del Sol

☎ 809/582-5885

🕐 Closed Sat.–Sun.

Founded in 1494 by Christopher Columbus (or possibly, as some historians claim, by his brother Bartholomew in 1495), Santiago was originally situated at the site of present-day Jacagua. The city was relocated to the eastern bank of the Río Yaque del Norte in 1562 following a devastating earthquake. It has since withstood the ravages of other temblors and several wars, including the civil war of 1912.

Today, the city of 650,000 is the leading entrepôt for produce from throughout El Cibao and is home to major tobacco

factories (most, however, are within Zonas Francas—free-trade zones—and are off-limits to visitors).

Santiago's vibrant nightlife reaches its zenith during Carnaval—famous for its fantastical devil masks *(caretas)*—when hotel rooms are sold out months in advance. Then, congested highways and a lack of directional signs on the roads produce a navigational nightmare extending into the suburbs.

Crowning a hill on the east side of town, the landmark **Monumento a los Héroes de la Restauración** *(Calle Daniel Espinal bet.*

Calle del Sol & Ave. Las Carreras) was commissioned by Trujillo as a tribute to himself. After his death, the neoclassical marble edifice was rededicated to heroes of the wars of independence. The monument is topped by a 230-foot (70 m) pillar spiraling up like a candy stick, with an allegorical figure of Victory balancing atop. The staircase to the top contains social-realistic murals by José Vela Zanetti. View it by night, when floodlit.

East of the monument is the modernist **Gran Teatro del Cibao** (Ave. Las Carreras 1, tel 809/583-1150), built in the 1980s as a reproduction of the Teatro Nacional in Santo Domingo. Life-size statues outside celebrate key literary figures of the early colonial epoch, including Calderón de

INSIDER TIP:

Find out why Dominicans eat plantains three times a day. For breakfast try *mangú*—mashed plantains with onions and olive oil.

—BRIAN RUDERT
Retired Foreign Service officer

la Barca (1600–1681), Lope de Vega (1562–1635), and Juana Inés de la Cruz (1648–1695). Architecture enthusiasts can also admire the modernist **Palacio Municipal** (Ave. Juan Pablo Duarte & Calle Ramón Mella), with a statue of Juan Duarte outside.

EXPERIENCE:
See You at the Car Wash

Sure, you can get your car hosed down and shined at a car wash. But in the Dominican Republic you can also get a beer. By night, a *cah wah* may serve as the local bar and dance club for impecunious locals. Many have DJs spinning the latest merengue and salsa tunes at volumes that make the beer bottles dance. Hostesses induce male patrons to order more drinks. In tourist venues, foreign patrons are likely to be hit upon by hustlers. Try the fun and hip **Engini Car Wash** (Calles Cáceres & Restauración, La Vega), with pool tables.

Centro Histórico

The colonial core, between Avenidas General López and Cuba, and Avenidas Las Carreras and Emiliano Tardiff, preserves scores of historically significant buildings, concentrated around **Parque Duarte.** Locals gather to gossip and flirt in this large tree-shaded plaza graced by Victorian lamp-posts. Horse-drawn carriages set out from here for sightseeing tours of the city. At its heart, the two-story, Victorian-era bandstand is a gingerbread dandy.

Rising to the south side, the late 19th-century **Catedral de Santiago Apóstol** combines Gothic and neoclassical elements with modern stained-glass windows by contemporary artist José Rincón Mora (1938–2016). Within, homeboy Ulises Heureaux—dictatorial president of the republic from 1882 to 1899—slumbers beneath a marble tomb. On the park's east side stands the two-story, pink-and-white neoclassical

Fortaleza San Luís

✉ Ave. Emiliano Tardiff & Calle San Luís

☎ 809/226-2029

Museo Folklórico Don Tomás Morel

✉ Ave. Restauración 174

☎ 809/582-6787

🕐 Open Sat. & Sun., by appt.

💲 Donation

Palacio Consistorial, the former town hall, dating from 1897. Next door, the **Centro de Recreo,** a private social club, is graced by an exotically Moorish facade. The handsome modernist **Gobernación,** municipal town hall, on the north side, features square marble pilasters. You can enter to admire the paintings by leading artists in the marble-floored lobby.

The crenellated **Fortaleza San Luís** is a French-styled remake, dating from 1805, atop the original castle. Within, the **Plaza de la Cultura** features a

---

Cigar Family Charitable Foundation

The Arturo Fuentes company is famous worldwide for its fine cigars. In the republic, it's also known for its charitable work. When the Santiago-based company established its Chateau de la Fuente tobacco farm in the Bonao region, it discovered that many local children weren't being schooled. It therefore set up a local school to provide free education, plus a health clinic, a sanitary system, and clean water for the village of Caribe, home of many of its workers.

The project is operated by the Cigar Family Charitable Foundation (*tel 813/248-2124, cf-cf.org*), funded by the J. Newman Cigar Co. and Tabacalera A. Fuentes y Cia.

---

four-square clock tower (erected in 1895) and a median lined with rusted cannon and busts of various national heroes. The fort's highlight is the **Museo Cultural,** displaying Taíno relics, eclectic works of art (from portraits of national heroes in battle

to Alberto Vargas's pinup females); and weaponry from colonial-era muskets, swords, and cannonballs to 20th-century machine guns. The modern sculpture collection is particularly impressive. English-speaking guides are available. Military hardware—vintage tanks, armored personnel carriers,

INSIDER TIP:

Local people create excellent reproductions of indigenous Indian pottery, which make great souvenirs.

—ALICE SAMSON
National Geographic field researcher

Howitzers, and the like—occupies the square's northeast corner.

Dusty and quirky **Museo Folklórico Don Tomás Morel,** founded in 1962 by poet, critic, and Carnaval promoter Tomás Morel, is chock-full of miscellany relating to Dominican folkloric life. The main draw is a fabulous collection of Carnaval masks, plus religious icons from Christianity and folkloric religions (including witchcraft), and battered musical instruments. A venerable *amapola* tree (the "tree of love") in the rear courtyard is a shrine to the theme of *amor.*

The leafy traffic circle at the junction of Avenidas General López and Hermanas Mirabal is anchored by the **Monumento Imbert**—a statue of Gen. José

Carnaval masks take center stage at the Museo Folklórico Don Tomás Morel.

María Imbert (1801–1847), a leader in the independence wars, on his charger.

Centro León

Housing perhaps the finest all-around museum in the country, the Centro León is a philanthropic venture of the Grupo León Jimenes tobacco company. The beautiful contemporary building showcases a stunning collection of modern Dominican art, presented in chronological order in a well-lit gallery on two levels. Works of note include Ramón Ovieda's "Lazaro Rising" (1970) and "Fish Sellers" (1967) by Elsa Nuñez. Below, the **Sala de Antropología** deals with ecology and biodiversity, plus Taíno culture, in thoughtfully presented dioramas and displays. Another section deals with local society from the colonial era to the modern day, with such themes as mulatto society, religious life, and the evolution of Dominican architectural styles. English-speaking guides (*$$*) are available.

Part of the same facility, the adjoining **Fábrica de Cigarros La Aurora** *(tel 809/734-2563, la aurora.com.do, closed Sat.–Sun.)* is a reproduction of the nation's oldest cigar factory, opened in 1903 when Grupo León Jimenes was founded. This showcase factory welcomes visitors in to view rollers pulling leaves into the company's trademark Preferidos, tapered at each end. A lector reads to the rollers as they work *(main factory next door closed to public)*. ∎

Centro León

- Ave. 27 de Febrero 146, Villa Progreso
- 809/582-2315
- Closed Mon.
- $

centroleon.org.do

A Stroll Through Santiago de los Caballeros

Delving into the heart of Santiago, this walk explores one of the nation's most complete colonial regions. The bustling street life is as intriguing as the structures in their various styles. An ongoing restoration is tidying up the region, which boasts plenty of delightful restaurants and bars.

Ficus trees grace Parque Duarte, a popular gathering place for locals and visitors alike.

Walking the main streets is safe by daylight. Nonetheless, parts of downtown Santiago pose risks for anyone venturing far from this route.

Begin at the Secretaría del Estado de Turismo office in the **Gobernación** on the north side of Parque Duarte. Cross to the west side of **Parque Duarte** ❶ and follow pedestrian-only Calle Benito Monción past the **Palacio Consistorial** (see pp. 149–150). Beyond, note the ornate Mudejar-style facade of the **Centro de Recreo** (see p. 150); if properly attired, you may be allowed in to admire the carved ceilings and ballroom.

Visit the **Catedral de Santiago Apóstol** ❷ (see p. 149), noting the carved mahogany doors. Exiting, turn left onto **Calle Duvergé**, lined with

NOT TO BE MISSED:

Catedral de Santiago Apóstol
• Fortaleza San Luís • Monumento
a los Héroes de la Restauración
• Museo Folklórico Don Tomás Morel

quaint buildings. Take Calle Duvergé one block and turn left on Calle España to the green-and-white **Mercado Modelo** ❸ *(main entrance Calle del Sol & Calle España)*. Explore the cavernous market, exiting on the south side onto Avenida Emiliano Tardiff. After 100 yards (91 m), cross the avenue to enter the **Fortaleza San Luís** ❹ (see p. 150), with its **Museo Cultural.**

Leaving the fort, cross to Calle San Luis, passing the neoclassical **Universidad Autónoma de Santo Domingo** *(Calle 16 de Agosto)*. Turn right onto **Calle del Sol**, the city's main commercial thoroughfare, where the best hotels and restaurants cluster. On the east side of **Parque de la Altagracia** ❺ ascend the steps to the **Iglesia de Nuestra Señora de la Altagracia** *(Calle del Sol & Calle Luperón)*. Continue four blocks, crossing Avenida Francia, and turn left on Calle Daniel Espinal. Turn left for the **Monumento a los Héroes de la Restauración** ❻ (see pp. 148–149).

Retrace your steps to Avenida Francia and head west along Calle Beller until it merges with Avenida Restauración. Continue west one block and turn left on Calle Benito Monción. Walk 50 yards (46 m) to visit **La 37 por las Tablas** *(Calle Benito Monción 37, tel 809/587-3033, closed Sun.)*, a small art gallery and, across the street, the **Casa del Arte** *(Calle Benito Monción, tel 809/471-7839, facebook.com/casa.de arte.9 closed Sun.)*. Returning to Avenida Restauración, turn left and walk 1.5 blocks to the corner of busy Avenida General López and the **Museo Folklórico Don Tomás Morel** ❼ (see p. 150) to marvel at the masks and knickknacks.

Turn south along Avenida General López to Calle del Sol. Turn left and walk past the **Fundación Educativa Acción Callejera** *(Calle del Sol 131, tel 809/581-0050, accioncallejera.org)*,

---

▲ See area map pp. 144–145
► Parque Duarte
🕐 4 hours
⬌ 1.5 miles (2.4 km)
► Parque Duarte

---

with its lovely mural; and the **Centro de la Cultura** *(Calle del Sol & Calle Benito Monción, tel 809/226-5222)*, hosting cultural activities. Finish at Parque Duarte, across the street.

Bachata

The distinctive and twangy guitar notes of bachata are a ubiquitous accompaniment to any journey around the country. This immensely popular musical genre evolved about five decades ago in the Dominican countryside and burst onto the nationwide scene only a decade ago. A Dominican equivalent of blues, it derives from traditional romantic bolero: *Bachateros* **(singers) croon about broken hearts and betrayal (bachata was originally called** *amargue,* **"bitterness"). The ever evolving genre has metamorphosed into a more fast-paced merengue style since José Manuel Calderón recorded the first bachata singles—"Borracho de Amor" and "Que Será de Mi"—in 1961.**

La Vega Real

Northeast of La Concepción de la Vega, the area that Columbus christened the Royal Plain occupies the heart of the Cibao region. Its prosperous (and traffic-choked) towns played important roles in the shaping of Dominican history.

San Francisco de Macorís
[M] 145 F3

Moca
[M] 145 E3

Casa Museo Hermanas Mirabal
[M] 145 F3
[✉] Conuco Salcedo, 2.5 miles (4 km) E of Salcedo
[☎] 809/587-8530
[$] $

The main city, **San Francisco de Macorís,** is surrounded by rice and cacao and blessed with intriguing buildings. Grassy **Parque Duarte** hosts the neoclassical **Ayuntamiento** *(Calle 27 de Febrero & Calle Restauración).* Triangular **Plaza de los Mártires** *(Ave. de los Mártires & Ave. 3ra)* holds a monument honoring locals martyred for independence. And twin-spired **Iglesia de Santa Rosa** *(Calle Colón bet. Calle Mella & Calle Restauración)* has fabulous stained-glass windows.

Faceless Dolls

El Higuerito *(5 miles/8 km W of Moca)* **is known for artisanal production of** *muñecas sin rostros,* **ceramic faceless dolls—the country's stylized mascot. The dolls portray Dominican** *campesinas cibaeñas* **(country women of El Cibao) dressed in straw hats or head scarves and carrying water vases or selling flowers. They're faceless, supposedly, so as not to favor any one racial group. The clay dolls are fired in traditional woodburning ovens, then painted in bright** *criollo* **colors. The cottage industry dates back to the mid-19th century.**

Well worth a visit in sprawling, hectic **Moca** is the **Iglesia de Corazón de Jesús** *(Calle Corazón de Jesús & Calle Morillo),* a multitiered confection with an impressive organ and marble altar.

Hermanas Mirabal Sites

The exquisite **Casa Museo Hermanas Mirabal,** a modernist 1954 home set in a garden near **Salcedo,** is a national shrine to the Mirabal sisters—María Teresa, Minerva, and Patria. The trio, who lived here, were beaten and strangled

INSIDER TIP:

Read Mario Vargas Llosa's novel *The Feast of the Goat* **for the experience of living in the last days of dictator Trujillo's regime.**

—BRIAN RUDERT
Retired Foreign Service officer

(along with Minerva's husband, Manolo Talveras) in 1960 for their leadership in the anti-Trujillo movement. The home is preserved as it was when they died. Guides lead tours.

Plazoleta Hermanas Mirabal, in the pretty village of **Ojo de Agua,** displays the twisted chassis of the sisters' car, which was thrown off a cliff after their murder. The sisters are also memorialized at **Jardín Memorial La Casa de Patria,** in San José de Conuco. Set in formal gardens, the home of Patria Mirabal was the site of the 1960 founding of the Revolutionary Movement June 14. ∎

Valle del Río Yaque del Norte

Autopista Duarte funnels traffic west from the city of Santiago through the valley of the Río Yaque del Norte, a lush Eden famous for producing half the republic's cigars. Westward, the highway is anchored by provincial and ranching towns that are way stations for travelers en route to Monte Cristi and the Haitian border.

The Río Yaque del Norte supplies a valley famous for its cigars.

The 25-mile-long (40 km) by 6-mile-wide (10 km) tobacco belt is centered on the town of **Villa González** *(8 miles/13 km NW of Santiago)*. **Proceadora de Tabaco Palmarejo** *(tel 809/754-9840)*, in nearby Jicomé, offers guided tours.

The best tobacco is grown along the foothills of the Cordillera Septentrional. **Monumento Natural Pico Diego de Ocampo** is a mountain reserve with trails and posts for birding.

Mao *(7 miles/12 km S of Autopista Duarte)* is a rice-growing and milling center with charming Victorian homes. Located in front of the military headquarters at the junction of Carreteras 18 and 29, the **Monumento al Machetero Heróica** celebrates fighters in the Dominican wars of independence.

At **Barranquita** *(4 miles/6 km N of Mao)*, the **Monumento a los Héroes de la Batalla La Barranquita** *(Parque de Recreo)* honors 18 citizens killed resisting the U.S. invasion in 1916.

Farther west, between Villa Elisa and Villa Sinda, tiny **Reserva Científica Villa Elisa** *(3 miles/ 5 km N of Villa Elisa)*, protects a forest festooned with endemic black orchids. ■

Valle del Río Yaque del Norte
145 D3

Monumento Natural Pico Diego de Ocampo
145 D4 & E4
✉ 5 mi (8 km) N of Villa González; Sociedad Ecológica del Cibao, Calle de la Restauración 116, Santiago

Cigarmaking 101

A fat cigar is a defining image of the Dominican Republic, as quintessential as rum and merengue. World-famous brands such as Arturo Fuentes, Davidoff, and La Flor Dominicana are acclaimed as the finest in the world, on a par with or even exceeding the cigars of Cuba.

Expert *torcedores* select the proper leaves as they hand-roll cigars at Fábrica de Cigarros La Aurora.

Although the island has been producing premium tobacco for more than a century, the quality and variety of cigars from the Dominican Republic have improved markedly in recent decades. Following the Cuban revolution in 1959, Cuba's communist government seized privately owned cigar factories, forcing their owners to flee. Many settled in the Dominican Republic, where they reestablished their brands using tobacco grown from their own Cuban seeds. Today, the country is the largest producer of cigars in the world. Production is centered on Santiago de los Caballeros, Tamboril

(see sidebar opposite), and Villa González.

The individual character of a cigar depends on the blend of the filler, binder, and wrapper leaf, or *liga*. Every cigar variety and brand has a recipe, and each factory has a tobacco master who ensures that the liga is appropriate to the specific cigar being rolled.

When dried and fermented leaves arrive in the tobacco factory, they are moistened to restore their elasticity, then flattened and stripped of their midribs. The rough leaves are sorted by size, classified according to color, texture, and quality (there are between 11 and 15 grades, and more than 75 colors in each category), then sent to the workshop to be rolled into cigars. First, the *torcedor*—the roller—rolls two or three *seco* (dry) leaves (for strength) in his or her palm. These are then wrapped in *ligero* (light) leaves (for aroma) and *volado* leaves (for even burning) to form the filler. The filler is enfolded by binder leaves, called *capotes*, and rolled until the familiar torpedo shape emerges. After being pressed in a tubular mold, this cylindrical "bunch" is

Freshly rolled cigars await pressing at the Fábrica La Caya, Santiago.

INSIDER TIP:

You can buy some of the best hand-rolled cigars in the world at their source in the factories around Santiago.

--LARRY PORGES
National Geographic Books author

wrapped in a pliable *corona* (crown) leaf, then rolled with the flat of a *chaveta,* a rounded, all-purpose knife that is the torcedor's only tool. Finally, a quarter-size piece of wrapper is folded and sealed at one end.

Dexterity is needed to ensure that the cigar is neither too tight nor too loose; otherwise, it won't draw. Torcedores usually follow in family tradition and, after an apprenticeship, graduate from petite Coronas to larger and specialist

sizes. An experienced roller can roll more than a hundred cigars a day.

A guillotine cuts the cigars to size. They are then fumigated, rechecked for quality, and sorted by color according to six categories ranging from greenish brown *(pariso verdoso)* to darkest brown *(oscuro)*. The cigars are stored in a cool room before being laid out in pine or cedar boxes—darkest on the left, lightest on the right—sealed with a label of guarantee. Each cigar wears a paper band imprinted with the brand's logo, and the boxes are adorned with richly emblazoned labels.

While export-brand cigars are hand rolled, many factories produce lesser quality, machine-rolled cigars for domestic markets.

EXPERIENCE: Tobacco Tours

Tamboril, 7 miles (12 km) east of Santiago, and Villa González, 8 miles (13 km) northwest of Santiago, are famous for producing the country's finest cigars. Several dozen small tobacco factories line the main streets. In Santiago, a guided tour at **Fábrica de Cigarros La Aurora** *(Ave. 27 de Febrero 146, tel 809/734-2563, laaurora .com.do)* puts you in reach of the *torcedores*.

The world's largest factory producing hand-rolled cigars, **Tabacalera de García** *(Ave. Libertad, tel 809/556-2127),* in La Romana, offers tours, as does the **Don Lucas Cigar Factory** *(Edif. Mundo Auténtico, Ave. Barceló, tel 809/466-1212, donlucascigars.com.do)* in Punta Cana.

Visitors receive an aromatic welcome at the **Museo Vivo del Tabaco** *(tel 809/320-4030)* outside Otra Banda, set amid rolling hills about 3 miles (5 km) northeast of Higüey, as prelude to a riveting tour of a cigar factory and museum.

San Fernando de Monte Cristi

Surrounded by arid wastelands and aromatic mangroves, the republic's most northwesterly city has strong affinities with Cuba and Máximo Gómez. Much of North America's table salt comes from here—garnered from seawater in the vast evaporative pans that stretch for miles north of town on the fringe of Parque Nacional Monte Cristi (see opposite).

San Fernando de Monte Cristi

⬛ 144 B4

Visitor Information

✉ Gobernación, Calle Mella 37

☎ 809/579-2254

venamontecristi.com

Casa Museo de Máximo Gómez

✉ Calle Mella 39

☎ 829/677-3648

Founded in 1501 but razed by Spanish authorities in 1606 to vanquish smuggling, the town was resettled in the 18th century by farmers from the Canary Islands. Although it suffered immeasurably during the 1860s War of Restoration, in time it became an important center for the export of precious woods, fruits, and tobacco. Monte Cristi's streets now vibrate with activity, notably during Carnaval in the last week of February, when the *civilis* (citizens) chase the *toros* (bulls) with bullwhips.

Paved **Parque Central** is pinned by the **Reloj de Monte Cristi,** a 19th-century Eiffel Tower–style clock tower imported from France; it still chimes every quarter hour. The most interesting site in town is the **Casa Museo de Máximo Gómez,** onetime home of the Dominican-born general (see sidebar). It was here, in 1895, that he and José Martí, leader of the Cuban independence movement, signed the Cuban declaration of independence—the Manifiesto de Monte Cristi—before setting out by boat to launch the war of independence. The small, gray building contains memorabilia recalling the duo's efforts.

The street of Calle San Fernando leads west out of Monte Cristi to **Playa Juan de Bolaños,** a narrow strip of gray sand where fishing boats draw up. An interpretive trail leads through the salt flats of **Salina Familiar Los García,** with a Centro de Interpretación.

Scimitar-shaped **Playa Buen Hombre,** 20 miles (35 km) northeast of Monte Cristi, offers tantalizing teal-colored waters whipped by winds. **Kite School Buen Hombre** *(Calle Principal 91, tel 829/923-8807, buen-hombre.com)* offers classes for beginners and downwinders for advanced kiters. ∎

Máximo Gómez

Máximo Gómez y Báez was born in Baní in the Dominican Republic in 1836. He joined the Spanish Army in 1856 and commanded Spanish calvary troops in Cuba. When the Ten Years War for Cuban independence broke out, the brilliant guerrilla strategist joined the cause and rose to be a general in the Rebel Army. When the war fizzled, he retired to his farm in the Dominican Republic. He returned to Cuba with José Martí on April 11, 1895, as generalissimo of the Cuban Mambisis. Following Cuba's independence in 1898, Gómez retired. He refused to be nominated as Cuba's president. He died in Havana in 1905 and is buried in Havana's Cementerio de Cristóbal Colón.

Parque Nacional Monte Cristi

This huge national park is one of the most varied in the nation, comprising coral reefs, beaches, desert badlands, lagoons, and mangrove-lined shores at the delta of the Río Yaque del Norte. Offshore, islands shudder with the caterwauling of seabirds, and galleons tempt divers with ancient treasure.

Covering some 212 square miles (550 sq km), two-thirds of it out to sea, the park protects 40 percent of the nation's mangrove forests—one of seven ecosystems in the reserve. More than 160 bird species are found here.

The access road ends at the park office, where a short trail leads to **Playa Detras del Morro,** with surf crashing ashore onto tangerine sands *(beware riptides).* The beach is clasped by unstable cliffs rising to 794-foot (242 m) **El Morro.** Pilgrims make the ascent each January 21 for the Día de la Virgen de la Altagracia (Day of the Virgin of Altagracia) via goat trails.

North of El Morro, creeks weave through mangroves sheltering manatees, while flamingos parade around **Laguna Quemado del Cojo** and **Laguna Saladilla.** The terrestrial zone south of Bahía de Monte Cristi covers a vast expanse of scrub, lagoon-pocked marsh, and mangroves accessible by unmarked trails off Carretera 45.

Isla Cabras, in the bay, is ringed with talcum white beaches. Sheltered off its eastern shore, the **Pipe Wreck** (named for the clay pipes that the 18th-century merchantman carried) lies 15 feet (4.5 m) down amid staghorn

Tall cliffs hem in lovely Playa Detras del Morro.

coral. Farther out, the **Cayos de los Siete Hermanos** (Seven Brothers Cays) form a coral necklace rising from the sea. The isles are nesting sites for American oystercatchers and boobies.

A barrier reef stretches east to Punta Rucia (see p. 141). Diving is world class. Park excursions are offered by Soraya y Santos Tours *(tel 809/961-6343, ssmontecristi tours.com),* and Club Naútico de Montecristi *(tel 809/579-2530).* ■

Parque Nacional Monte Cristi

🅰 144 A5 & B5

✉ National park office, Playa Juan de Bolaños

💲 $

More Places to Visit in El Cibao

Carnaval

The Dominican Republic's Carnaval evolved around Santiago de los Caballeros and La Vega as a celebration of the country's independence from Spain. Colorfully costumed *cojuelos*—evil spirits— are depicted with fantastical papier-mâché masks adorned with feathers and rhinestones, protruding horns, fangs, and bloodshot bulging eyes (many parts come from the slaughterhouse). The masks preserve an age-old tradition featuring a rivalry between two sides of town. Masks from Santiago's La Joya district feature multiple horns and a long curlew snout; those of Los Pepines represent *pepín*, an animal with an upturned snout like a duck's bill. The principal cast includes the *diablo cojuelo*, a devil prankster who walks with a limp; and *roba de gallina*, a transvestite who begs candies from shopkeepers to share with children. Revelers typically go around hitting people with balloons, but are otherwise entirely harmless.

Dajabón

This relatively prosperous border town surrounded by rice fields is an official crossing point into Haiti; all that separates the town from Haiti is the Río Dajabón. Time a visit for the Monday and Friday morning markets, when Haitians flock over the border to set up street stalls. **Los Indios de Chacuey** (*Carretera 18, 11 miles/18 km SE of Dajabón*)— billed as a Stonehenge in the tropics—was once an important Taíno ceremonial center. However, a community baseball field now partially obscures the ancient circle of rocks surrounding a stone slab carved with religious petroglyphs.
🅰 144 A3 ✉ 21 miles (34 km) S of Monte Cristi via Carretera 45

Monumento a los Héroes de la Restauración

This vast monument is set amid pines hard up against the Haitian border in the mountains south of Dajabón. On this site in August 1863, *independistas* Santiago Rodríguez, José Cabrera, and Benito Monción launched an armed revolt against Spanish occupation. Steps lead up from a paved plaza with Roman-style columns to a mezzanine with two huge concrete monuments: one a tall spired column engraved with the names of national heroes; the second a horizontal block featuring a bas-relief.
🅰 144 A3 ✉ 1 mile (1.6 km) N of Capotillo (10 miles/16 km SE of Dajabón)

Reserva Científica Loma Quita Espuela

This reserve protects virgin montane forest on the slopes of the Cordillera Septentrional. Hispaniolan parrots, cuas, and the *gallito prieto* are among 23 endemic bird species present; the endangered solenodon also exists here. The longest of the three trails, **Sendero de los Nubes** (1.75 miles/2.8 km), ascends into the cloud forest atop Loma Quita Espuela (3,091 feet/942 m). After a rigorous mountain hike, follow the **Sendero Balneario Rústico La Roca** to a *balneario* (swimming hole) for a cooling dip. **Sendero del Bosque del Cacao** leads through cacao forest at the edge of the reserve. Call ahead for a guide (*$$*). The ranger station and entrance is 1 mile (1.6 km) up a rugged dirt road from the hamlet of Alto La Cueva. The reserve includes a restaurant.
flqe.org.do 🅰 145 F3 ✉ Alto La Cueva, 7 miles (12 km) NE of San Francisco de Macorís ☎ 809/588-4156 💲 $

A major mountain range abounding in dramatic landscapes, from fertile vales to the mist-shrouded heights atop Pico Duarte

Cordillera Central

Wildflowers in Valle Nuevo

Cordillera Central

Running northwest to southeast, the country's mountainous backbone tapers down toward the edge of the capital city. Beginning barely 50 miles (80 km) from the lowland heat of Santo Domingo, the cool uplands of the country's interior rise to the highest point in the entire Caribbean. Though they lack snow-clad peaks, these grand mountains are promoted locally as the Dominican Alps, and they provide backcountry adventures.

Rugged in the extreme, the vast Cordillera Central is a world of plunging gorges and razorback ridges that extend west into Haiti as the Chaîne de Vallières. Three peaks surpass 10,000 feet (3,048 m). Towering over the cordillera is Pico Duarte (10,417 feet/3,175 m), its massive blue-green hulk looming overhead, drawing hikers and birders to its rarified heights. The nation's most challenging trek is a three-day hike to the summit, where frost sparkles at dawn and the entire island is laid out at your feet.

The air is crisp, even chilly, atop these towering mountains, where in winter temperatures can fall below freezing. On sunny days, the dark green forests are framed against intensely blue sky. By noon they're often fogbound. Drenching rains soak the cordillera, with the northeastern slopes receiving the brunt. This mountain chain forms the headwaters of the island's main rivers. Tumbling from forests redolent with the fresh scent of pines, sparkling waters as effervescent as champagne offer white-water thrills, plus cooling dips at the base of waterfalls crashing through shady ravines. Ecotourism and adventure are the main draws to the mountains, which form a perfect complement to a beach vacation.

A remote habitat of runaway slaves during past centuries and, more recently, of poor peasants who practiced slash-and-burn agriculture, the mountains have suffered from deforestation over two centuries. In 1956, the Dominican government created two national parks to protect the remaining forests. Parque Nacional José Armando Bermúdez (north) and Parque Nacional José del Carmen Ramírez (south) safeguard the largest remaining areas of virgin forest on the isle. To the southeast, recently created Parque Nacional Valle Nuevo

completes the trio: Access via four-wheel-drive is an Indiana Jones–style adventure that delivers the bonus of the most spectacular scenery in the entire country.

Of the handful of towns in the mountains, two stand out for visitors. The cool hillside retreat of Jarabacoa, at 1,732 feet (528 m), is a vibrant agricultural town that also thrives on tourism. A base for white-water rafting, Jarabacoa is the main gateway for climbs up Pico Duarte from the trailhead at La Ciénaga. Tranquil Constanza, set in a Shangri-la valley in the heart of the mountains at 3,940 feet

(1,200 m), is a place of heart-stopping beauty, resembling a piece of Switzerland dropped into the tropics. Strawberries and arable crops thrive in the gentle climate of mid-elevation slopes.

Autopista Duarte, the main highway between Santo Domingo and Santiago, provides easy access to both Jarabacoa and Constanza. Each is just a two-hour drive from the capital. Beyond these two towns, the default mode of transport for countryfolk is a donkey; visitors to the area will need a sturdy four-wheel-drive vehicle to negotiate the rugged mountain roads. ■

NOT TO BE MISSED:

A hike to Salto de Jimenoa Alto **165**

White-water rafting on the Río Yaque del Norte **166–167**

Trekking to the summit of Pico Duarte **170–171**

The drive to Constanza **172–173**

A four-wheel-drive trip through Parque Nacional Valle Nuevo **174**

Rare birds at Parque Nacional Montaña La Humeadora **176**

Rare plants at Reserva Científica Ébano Verde **176**

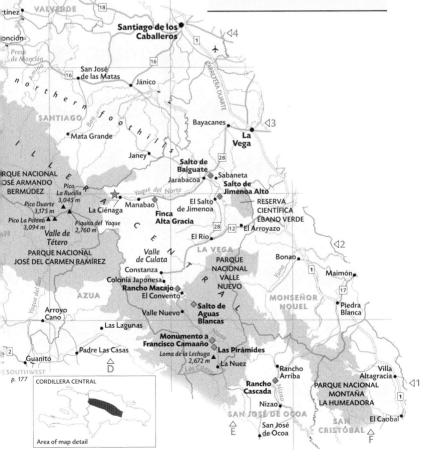

Around Jarabacoa

Considered a place of eternal spring, the farming town of Jarabacoa draws visitors from the capital seeking to escape the heat. Known as the adventure center of the Dominican Republic, Jarabacoa is a base for horseback rides, for birding and white-water trips, and for treks up Pico Duarte.

A swimmer takes the plunge at Salto de Jimenoa Alto.

Jarabacoa's town core rises over the Río Yaque del Norte, the country's major river. The central plaza, **Parque Mario Nelson Galán** (*Calle Mario Nelson Galán & Calle Colón*), is a haven of relative peace amid the beelike buzz of the town's scooters, the perfect place to stop and watch the world go by while enjoying a refreshing drink.

For travelers who like an adrenaline-spiced vacation, Jarabacoa's adventure center Rancho Baiguate (*tel 809/574-6890, ranchobaiguate.com*) offers a wide range of activities, including white-water rafting and a treetop canopy tour, plus hikes up Pico Duarte. Flying Tony (*tel 809/848-3479, flyindr.com*) offers paragliding. And golfers can get in the swing at the Jarabacoa Golf Club (*Quintas de Primavera, tel 809/854-2631, jarabacoagolf .com, $$$*).

Avenida La Confluence leads north 2 miles (3 km) to the **Balneario La Confluencia,** a natural swimming hole at the juncture of the Jimenoa and Yaque del Norte Rivers. West of town, the road passes the **Monasterio Santa María del Evangelio** (*tel 809/223-0591*), which has rooms for rent and where a trailhead has hikers puffing up **El Mogote.**

Jarabacoa bursts into colorful bloom each June for the Festival de Las Flores (Flower Festival), with parade floats and the crowning of a beauty queen.

The heights around Jarabacoa are corduroyed with coffee bushes. On the west side of town, the **Belarminio Ramírez Coffee Co.** coffee-processing mill welcomes visitors for guided tours. A café lets you savor its various Monte Albo coffees.

Waterfalls

The sheer beauty of forest-shrouded **Salto de Jimenoa** (*$*) draws gawkers to this waterfall above the hydroelectric station near Sabaneta, 3 miles (5 km) southeast of Jarabacoa. Frigid waters plummet 46 feet (14 m) into a pool within a rocky canyon. To reach it you'll need to thread your way across a series of swaying suspension bridges. Beyond the falls, the trail narrows, necessitating a dangerous climb over slippery rocks to reach the more spectacular **Salto de Jimenoa Alto,** tumbling 197 feet (60 m) and a setting in the movie *Jurassic Park;* an obligatory guide (*$$*) can be hired at the entry booth by the HEP station. Far better is to *descend* to the Alto cascade from the hamlet of **El Salto de Jimenoa** (*4 miles/7 km SE of Jarabacoa*), on the road to Constanza. The trail begins about 1,300 feet (400 m) west of **Don Felix Bar y Restaurante** (*Carretera Jarabacoa-Constanza km 7, tel 849/359-4442*), offering magnificent views over the forested

mountains toward Jarabacoa. Guided tours are offered through Turismo Rural (*tel 809/540-5304*).

Salto de Baiguate is signed off the Constanza road, 0.6 mile (1 km) east of the Shell gas station (*Calle del Carmen & Calle Deligne*) in town. From the trailhead, the narrow trail clings to the cliff face before descending via a staircase to a beach and natural pool, where the cascade suddenly crashes into view.

INSIDER TIP:

Among the ranches and arid pine forests of the Cordillera Central, you'll find that horses and mules are often the prevailing mode of transport.

—TOM CLYNES
National Geographic contributing editor

La Ciénaga

The end-of-the-road hamlet of La Ciénaga (*13 miles/21 km W of Jarabacoa*), at a crisp 4,500 feet (1,370 m), is the primary starting point for treks up Pico Duarte. The hamlet sits at the head of a deep vale. The snaking road from Jarabacoa is prone to landslides. En route, **Jarabacoa River Club** (*tel 809/574-2456, riverclubjarabacoa.com*) has river cascades and pools; you can also hike a short trail to visit the **Salto La Guázares** waterfall. ∎

Jarabacoa

▲ 163 E3

Visitor Information

✉ Oficina de la Secretaría del Estado de Turismo, Plaza Ramírez, Calle Mario Galán bet. Calle Duarte & Calle del Carmen

☎ 809/574-7287

🕐 Closed Sat.–Sun.

Belarminio Ramírez Coffee Co.

✉ Carretera Belarminio Ramírez

☎ 809/574-2618

🕐 Closed Sat.–Sun.

ramirezcoffee.com

La Ciénaga

▲ 163 D2

Rafting the Yaque del Norte

The Caribbean has barely been tapped for white-water rafting, an activity in which the Dominican Republic takes the lead. The Río Yaque del Norte is Hispaniola's Dom Pérignon of white water, a river that will have you laughing with sheer delight. The Cordillera Central's steep terrain and plentiful rain produces the perfect conditions for a thrill ride as you run the rapids.

The rapids of the Yaque del Norte can prove challenging at the height of the rainy season.

Below the mountains, the turbulent river settles down, flowing for mile after mile in solitude and peace. In the crisp mountain air and bright sunlight, the white water sparkles (although in places, the riverbanks are strewn with trash). You'll pass through several life zones as you cascade down the Caribbean's longest river. In general, the best times are fall and winter, at the end of the rainy season, when water levels are high. Whatever the time of year, you'll find a trip being offered. Most last two hours to half a day on the river.

Rivers are rated from Class I (flat water, considered a float trip) to Class V (high waves, suitable for experts only). Trips on the Río Yaque del Norte in the Jarabacoa area are Class II to Class IV, but a burst of rain can make a big difference, boosting the thrill quotient immeasurably. No prior experience is necessary for Class III, although beginners are usually accepted for the more rigorous Class IV trips even when the river rockets from the Dominican Alps at full throttle. You'll hang on tight for the 12-foot (3.7 m) vertical drop called Mike Tyson. And finesse is required to weave safely through The Cemetery—a long cascade named for the rocks poking up like tombstones amid the churning waters. The Río Yaque del Norte also offers easy stretches that allow quiet contemplation of nature.

The compact D.R. allows you to pack in a continent's worth of outdoor adventure— canyoning, rafting, climbing— in just a few days.

—TOM CLYNES
*National Geographic
contributing editor*

Most adventure companies offer paddle trips where you and your raftmates do the work of powering through a slalom course while your guide controls things from the rear. The sturdy, inflatable rafts can accommodate up to eight people. Life vests and helmets are mandatory, but the tour operator will supply all equipment (plus expert guidance).

All you need to wear is a swimsuit, a T-shirt, and river sandals or sneakers that you don't mind getting wet. Expect to get drenched—that's half the fun! Remember

Placid stretches allow rafters plenty of time to contemplate the valley's scenic beauty.

to take plenty of sunscreen—you'll be out in the sun all day—as well as a set of dry clothes and shoes to change into at float's end.

EXPERIENCE: Learn Rafting Basics

Raft trips on the Río Yaque del Norte are working trips. You get to participate fully in powering and steering, and everyone aboard gets to work equally.

Straddling the buoyancy tubes either cowboy style or sidesaddle, you'll revel in the adventure and the camaraderie of the shared experience. Your river guide sits at the rear. He or she will guide you after first demonstrating how to develop strong forward, backward, and "draw" (sideways) strokes. Since rapids require fast, decisive action, the key is for every- one to be working in unison, with the same goal. Communication is paramount. Commands are kept simple: "Forward!" "Backpaddle!" "Draw right!" "Draw left!" etc. Your skipper should have you practice all the strokes and

commands before reaching any rapids.

A good captain can read the water far ahead and get passengers to position the raft for the safest routes through the rapids. Even the best plans can go wrong, however. If you're thrown out of a raft, don't panic. Float with your feet out in front of you to ward off rocks. Breathe during the wave troughs; hold your breath in the crests. If you're ahead of the raft, swim away from it—you don't want to be caught between the raft and a rock! When the water calms, try to swim to the raft or (if it has flipped) to the riverbank.

Several outfitters take rafts down the Yaque del Norte (see p. 230), includ- ing **Iguana Mama** (Cabarete, iguanamama .com) and **Rancho Baiguate** (Jarabacoa, ranchobaiguate.com).

Parques Nacionales José Armando Bermúdez & José del Carmen Ramírez

The José Armando Bermúdez and José del Carmen Ramírez National Parks were created in 1956 to forestall deforestation and preserve the montane watersheds of 12 major rivers. The Caribbean's tallest peaks are enshrined within these contiguous parks, which span 7,500 feet (2,286 m) of elevation, offering alpine vistas and challenging hikes to the summits.

Crossing the Río Yaque del Norte near La Ciénaga is one way to start your journey up Pico Duarte.

Parque Nacional José Armando Bermúdez
 163 C3
✉ Park ranger office in La Ciénaga
☎ 809/974-6195 or 809/472-4204 ext. 223 (Sabaneta)

Covering 591 square miles (1,530 sq km), these twin parks are accessed via a few small towns. They claim the three highest mountains in the Antilles—Pico Duarte (10,417 feet/3,175 m), Pico La Pelona (10,151 feet/3,094 m), and Pico La Rucilla (10,003 feet/3,049 m). All three peaks can be conquered by climbing steep, muddy mule tracks.

Predominating at the parks' lower elevations are broadleaf subtropical humid forests of *palo amargo* (wild olive) and West

Indian cedar and walnut. Here, the thick undergrowth is rich with epiphytes and orchids. This ecosystem gives way above 4,000 feet (1,219 m) to the feathery-leafed *palo de cotorra,* or parrot tree, and the *palo de cruz* pine. Above that, mists swirl through cloud forests dripping with mosses. Creolean pines predominate above the cloud forest. Higher still, marshy alpine meadows are emblazoned with wildflowers.

Wild pigs *(puercos cimarrones)* forage the forests, and the parks are habitat to some 50 species of birds, among them the rufous-throated solitaire, Greater Antillean elaenia, and Hispaniolan parrot.

Pico Duarte

Climbing Pico Duarte (named for 19th-century founding father Juan Pablo Duarte) is a source of national pride to Dominicans. More than 3,000 hikers trek to the summit every year.

Most hikers enter the park at La Ciénaga (see p. 165). You must register at the ranger station, the Centro de Visitantes del Valle de Lilís, on the north side of the village. The station has crude dorm accommodations (*$$, up to 4 people*). A guide (*$$ per day*), or *arriero*, is obligatory for all hikes within the park, and a mule (*$$ per day*) to carry gear is highly recommended. You will need to also provide food and water (and toilet paper, plus carryout bags or camp trowels) for yourself and your guide. Sleeping bags, tents, and ponchos can be rented in the village. The 14-mile (23 km) trail (see pp. 170–171) has seven simple cabins. Camping is free.

You can also hike to the summit from the south side of the park, where an arduous 17-mile (27 km) trail begins at **Los Ingenitos**, on the north side of Embalse de Sabaneta (*N of San Juan de la Maguana*). An alternative 12-mile (19 km) route begins at **Las Lagunas**, northeast of Padre Las Casas, and leads via the **Valle de Tétero**—accessible, too, from **Constanza**. And a rigorous 8-mile (13 km) trail begins at **Arroyo Cano** (*N of Guanito, on Carretera 2*). On the north side of the mountain, a 28-mile (45 km) trail begins at **Mata Grande** (see p. 175). Regardless of trail, allow three days.

There are ranger stations at La Ciénaga, Sabaneta, Mata Grande, and Las Lagunas. Guides can be hired from the Brigada Cimarrón Sebastián Lemba (*tel 829/568-3544*) in La Ciénaga. ∎

Parque Nacional José del Carmen Ramírez

163 C2 & D2

400 yards (366 m) S of Presa Sabaneta, Carretera San Juan Sabaneta

809/557-3996 (Sabaneta)

EXPERIENCE: Lace Up Your Boots

Pico Duarte looms over the center of the republic as if beckoning visitors to rise to its challenge. But there are other, and easier, environments to explore as well.

Parque Nacional Cotubanamá (see pp. 102–103), close to the main beach resorts, is perfectly positioned for a day excursion from Bayahibe or Punta Cana. A network of trails allows visitors to easily discover *cenotes* (sinkholes) and Taíno caves. Ten distinct habitats are home to more than 110 species of birds.

Reserva Científica Loma Quita Espuela (see p. 160) has short, easy trails into cloud forest of the Cordillera Septentrional. The local cooperative supplies guides, and meals are served at a kitchen at the ranger station.

27 Charcos de Damajagua (see p. 142) guarantees a hike with a difference. After wading across and up the waist-deep Río Damajagua, you hike upstream from waterfall to waterfall.

Iguana Mama (*Cabarete, tel 809/571-0908, iguanamama.com*) is a reputable tour company with hiking trips, including hikes to 27 Charcos de Damajagua and multiday hikes up Pico Duarte.

A Walk in the Clouds

Pico Duarte lures intrepid hikers seeking the satisfaction of hiking to its peak, the Caribbean's highest. This nontechnical ascent, leaving from La Ciénaga, demands no more of you than stamina, determination, good hiking shoes, and overnight camping gear sufficient for nights that can fall below freezing atop cloud-hung heights.

The hike is best done December through March, the dryer months when the trails are least muddy. Give yourself at least two days; slower hikers might even take four days. (See p. 169 for details about planning your trip.)

The Trek

Begin at dawn, as the first day's trek takes six to twelve hours depending on the weather and your physical fitness. From **La Ciénaga,** the 14-mile (23 km) trail to the summit follows the **Río Los Tablones ❶,** hemmed in by broadleaf forest. The first few miles are relatively flat within the valley bottom. Gradually the trail becomes steeper, passing through carpets of ferns and stands of *palo de cotorra* (parrot tree) as you ascend past the Los Tablones ranger station to **La Cotorra ❷** (The Parrot), an area named for the birds often seen barreling past in jet-fighter formation. Savor the view down the mountain before continuing to **La Laguna ❸** rest area, where you can fill up on water (which you should boil or treat with chlorine tablets) and listen to the flutelike song of the mountain whistler, the trillings of the rufous-throated solitaire, and the whistling of the wind in the pines. Mists swirl overhead as you enter the dense cloud forest at 6,000 feet (1,829 m).

From La Laguna, a steep climb will have you puffing up to **La Cruce ❹,** where a side trail leads into the **Valle de Tétero ❺,** a scenic valley where Taíno petroglyphs can be seen. Beyond La Cruce, the Aquita Fría path ascends 3 miles (5 km) along a pine-clad ridge to **Aquita Fría ❻.** Water trickling from a large bog in this area of marshy alpine grasslands

The morning and twilight skies are the hikers' reward for climbing Pico Duarte.

NOT TO BE MISSED:

La Cotorra • Valle de Tétero • Aquita Fría • Vallecito de Lilís • Pico Duarte summit becomes the Río Yaque del Norte and Río Yaque del Sur. Skirting the summit of **Pico La Rucilla** (9,990 feet/3,045 m), the trail then descends. After 9 miles (14.5 km) you reach **La Compartición ➐**, where you should stay overnight *(warning—rats frequent cabin at night in search of food)*. The hut in this location has a small kitchen with a cast-iron stove, plus two solar-powered pay telephones.

INSIDER TIP:

The Constanza valley and the country's highest mountain, Pico Duarte, offer amazing landscapes for photographers.

—RAUL TOUZON
National Geographic
Traveler *photographer*

After a chilly night at the cabin, be back on the trail at dawn to beat the fogs that usually shroud the peak by mid-morning. It's an exhausting, undulating three-hour ascent to the summit via the **Vallecito de Lilís ➑**, a small valley with lily-strewn meadows. Beyond, you pass a surreal landscape littered with massive boulders. Arriving at the rocky **summit ➒**

Resting point: The hut at La Compartición

while, with luck, the sun still shines, you can enjoy the views in every direction. A photograph of you standing beside the bronze bust of Juan Pablo Duarte and a wind-whipped national flag will prove you were here.

Clouds will appear soon; head back to La Compartición for the second night before descending to La Ciénaga on day three.

🅰 See area map pp. 162–163
► La Ciénaga
⏱ 2–4 days
⬌ 29 miles (46 km) round-trip
► La Ciénaga

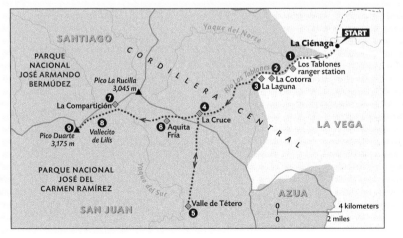

Constanza & Around

Set in a broad, fertile valley, this peaceful town enjoys a stupendous setting within a huge bowl created by a meteor strike eons ago. Constanza's alpine vistas keep visitors enthralled, streams sparkle in the fresh air, and you'll be glad for blankets at 4,000 feet (1,219 m) in this high-mountain valley.

A shopper visits a Constanza convenience store.

Constanza
🗺 163 D2
Visitor Information
✉ Calle Antonio María Garcia 43
☎ 809/539-2900
🕐 Closed Sat.–Sun.

Isolated throughout the colonial era, Constanza was connected by a basic road to the outside world only at the turn of the 20th century. In the 1950s, President Rafael Trujillo invited Japanese farmers to settle and boost the region's fortunes by starting the local vegetable and fruit industry. Dark, fertile soils, a mild climate, and the farmers' hard work have combined to produce a paradise of lime-green meadows and fields of vegetables, strawberries, garlic, and flowers.

The agricultural bustle centers on a lively **farmers market** (*Calle Enriquillo bet. Calle Rufino Espino & Calle Gratereaux*). Other sites in town include triangular **Plazoleta de los Héroes**—at the east entrance to town—with busts of the leaders of La Trinitaria (see sidebar p. 29); **Fortaleza Patria** (*Calle Gaston Deligne & Calle Padre Billini*), a military headquarters; and the **Parque Central** (*Calle Salomé*

INSIDER TIP:

Even in the most remote corners of the country, people will invite visitors in for a *cafecito*, strained through nylon stockings and super strong.

—TOM CLYNES
National Geographic contributing editor

Ureña & Calle Miguel Abreu) with a delightful whitewashed, 20th-century church on its west side.

Ecoturismo Constanza *(tel 809/786-3681, ecoturismoconstanza .net)* organizes guided excursions into the **Reserva Científica Las Neblinas de Constanza,** which protects montane cloud forest at the east end of the valley. North of Constanza, the **Valle de Culata** features caves with Taíno paintings. West of town, wild horses charge through the savannas of the **Valle de Tétero.**

Japanese settlers (see sidebar) established **Colonia Japonesa,** 1.5 miles (2.4 km) south of Constanza. Many of their descendants still live here, removed to some extent from the larger community. Within walled compounds, traditional Japanese-style homes are surrounded by cherry and plum trees; most houses, however, are now occupied by impoverished Dominicans and are run-down, as is the village itself.

Constanza is reached by road from Jarabacoa, as well as from Bonao via Carretera 12, which offers easier and scenic access. The town is served by an airport.

South of Constanza

South of Colonia Japonesa, the road climbs over a ridge, revealing phenomenal views over the Río Grande Valley. Soon you are amid true alpine scenery. **Rancho Macajo** (see p. 230), about 6 miles (10 km) south of Constanza, has forest trails, horseback rides, and ATV rentals. The road soon deteriorates into a serious four-wheel-drive challenge as it ascends to

---

Japanese Dominicans

Constanza's low-profile Japanese community of about 900 individuals was started by Gen. Rafael Trujillo in 1955, when 1,300 Japanese settlers from Kyushu arrived, having been promised free land, among other things, by their own government. The Dominican government paid their passage. Other Japanese families settled in Jarabacoa, Azua, and Dajabón. Conditions were dire, however, and many families unsuccessfully sued Japan's government for making false promises. The first-generation Japones speak Spanish with a melodious Japanese accent and welcome visitors with the *cha-no-yo* tea ceremony.

Parque Nacional Valle Nuevo (see p. 174) via El Convento and **Salto de Aguas Blancas,** which plunges into an ice-cold pool. This 285-foot (87 m) three-stage cascade has a *balneario,* restaurant, and parking; your four-wheel drive will have to crawl in first gear up a daunting dirt track to reach the waterfall. ∎

Parque Nacional Valle Nuevo

Accessible by four-wheel-drive or other similarly rugged vehicle via a sky-high dirt road, this alpine wilderness rewards intrepid travelers with an off-the-beaten-track adventure that promises stupendous scenery, while birders will have a field day.

Parque Nacional Valle Nuevo

- 163 E2
- Valle Nuevo, 19 miles (31 km) S of Constanza; 36 miles (58 km) N of San José de Ocoa
- 809/974-6195 or 809/472-4204 ext. 223 (Santo Domingo)

One of the most beautiful high-altitude regions in the Caribbean, 351-square-mile (910 sq km) Valle Nuevo— officially called El Parque Nacional Juan B. Pérez Rancier— protects pristine pine forests with tree species found nowhere else and 64 bird species. Hiking the old logging roads, you might spy Hispaniolan trogons and, higher up, the Antillean siskin.

A single road runs through the park, connecting Constanza (see pp. 172–173) with San José de Ocoa. Vertiginous and denuded, it is a slow drive for four-wheel-drive vehicles only *(make sure you have a working spare tire).* The northern ranger station is at La Siberia, 12 miles (19 km) south of Constanza. The entrance is at Valle Nuevo, at about 7,250 feet (2,200 m) amid a rock-strewn plateau.

The tiny **Monumento a Francisco Camaaño** *(7 miles/ 12 km S of Valle Nuevo)* features a grave and flagpole rising from a meadow where hero Francisco Camaaño Deñó (1932–1973) was assassinated. Two miles (3 km) to the south, story has it that **Las Pirámides**—four concrete sections forming a pyramid—marks the central point of Hispaniola. Southward, the road crests beneath **Loma de la Lechuga** (8,766 feet/2,672 m) and begins a descent to **La Nuez,** a ridgetop hamlet with spectacular views. ■

Las Pirámides—a monument that time has forgotten

The Northern Foothills

Though badly deteriorated in places, Carretera 16 runs along the northern foothills of the cordillera, linking Santiago to Monción. Side roads that probe into the coffee-clad mountains lead to *presas* (reservoirs) good for fishing and hiking amid scenic settings.

San José de las Matas, an agricultural center, enjoys a lovely setting with views over a valley patterned like dark green corduroy in endless rows of coffee. Gaily colored horse-drawn *coches* operate from **Parque Manuel A. Tavarez,** the main square. A rough dirt road leads south 16 miles (25 km) from town to the village of **Mata Grande,** where guides and mules can be hired (*$$$ per day*) for the trek up Pico Duarte (see pp. 170–171). En route to Mata Grande, you can join locals for a dip in the cool river pools at **Balneario La Tomas del Río Antón Sape.**

Westward, relatively prosperous **Monción** straddles a ridge with beautiful vistas. The town is centered on a park with a pretty church and a bust of Juan Duarte. Southeast of town awaits the **Presa de Monción,** a vast

Cleared areas mark farms in the cordillera.

reservoir offering gorgeous views toward the Cordillera Central. Hidden in the hills above Monción, **Los Charcos de los Indios** waterfalls are best visited in wet season (June–Nov.), when the cascades are at their most impressive. Monción is known as the Capital of Cassava Bread and has dozens of bakeries. ■

San José de las Matas
🅰 163 D3

Monción
🅰 163 C4

Coffee

Coffee bushes, native to Ethiopia, were first planted in Hispaniola in 1735; the island has some of the oldest coffee farms to be found anywhere in the New World. The climate and rich soils are perfect for the plant, which grows best in well-drained soils at elevations of 2,500 to 3,500 feet (760–1,070 m), with temperatures between 59 and 82°F (15–28°C) and a distinct wet and dry season. The handpicked beans are shipped to *beneficios* (processing plants), where the fleshy outer layers are removed to expose the beans. The beans are then dried, their skins stripped, roasted, and sorted and . . . they're ready for your cup.

More Places to Visit in Cordillera Central

Parque Nacional Montaña La Humeadora

Swaddled in montane cloud forest on its upper slopes, this rugged park spans 162 square miles (420 sq km) at the extreme southeast of the cordillera. The park—officially called Parque Nacional Eugenio de Jesús Marcano—protects a key watershed. Hikers and birders are amply rewarded with the chance of rare bird sightings. It has no formal facilities, although trails access the park from El Caobal, to the southeast. A single rugged road traverses the park, linking Piedra Blanca (on the Autopista Duarte) with the towns of Rancho Arriba and, farther along, San José de Ocoa.
🔼 163 F1 ✉ 6 miles (10 km) NW of San Cristóbal

INSIDER TIP:

If you're hiking the hills and spot an animal resembling an overgrown shrew, keep calm: It's a solenodon, a rare and endangered mammal with a massive head and a Pinocchio nose. Keep your distance—this creature has a venomous bite.

—JUSTIN KAVANAGH
National Geographic Travel Books editor

Parque Nacional Nalga de Maco

Created in 1995, this park protects 108 square miles (280 sq km) of montane forests, including cloud forest, at the extreme west of the cordillera. The park tops out at 6,329 feet (1,929 m) with the twin-peaked **Loma Nalga de Maco** (Monkey Buttocks Hill). Guides and mules for the two-day hike can be hired in the community of Río Limpio, where the ranger station is found; advance permits are required from the park headquarters in Santo Domingo *(tel 809/472-4204 ext. 223)*. Trails ascend to the summit via **La Cueva de la Sidra,** a cave with Taíno pictographs.
🔼 162 B3 ✉ Río Limpio, 21 miles (34 km) SE of Dajabón via Carretera 45

Reserva Científica Ébano Verde

This 9-square-mile (23 sq km) scientific reserve that tops out at 5,135 feet (1,565 m) is named for the endangered native green ebony tree. A 4-mile-long (6 km) trail leads from the Fernando Domínguez Visitor Center into a forest containing more than 600 other species of plants, 2 endemic butterflies, and 90 bird species, including the vervain hummingbird—the second smallest bird in the world.
turismorural.do/es/portfolio/ebano-verde
🔼 163 E2 ✉ 4 miles (6 km) N of El Arroyazo (13 miles/21 km W of Autopista Duarte ☎ 809/565-1422 (Santo Domingo)

Cockfighting

Dominican men are fanatical about cockfighting, the national spectator sport introduced by the Spanish centuries ago. Bloody affairs, fights are held in *clubes gallísticos* or *galleras*—circular cockfighting pits—found in every community. Fights are normally held on Sunday afternoons, when frenzied crowds gather to wager large sums and indulge in the island's ultimate symbol of machismo. The combatants are matched by weight and size. Owners dote over their prized *gallos*, whose feathers are oiled and thighs shaved before combat. Roosters fight for up to 15 minutes (often to the death) with fake, razor-sharp spurs.

A region abounding in dramatic landscapes, from the lowest point in the Caribbean to desert coastal plains and misty cloud forests

The Southwest

An array of fishing boats along
Playa Quemaito

The Southwest

Spanning tremendous diversity, the rugged southwest ranges from montane pine and cloud forests to wetlands, beaches, and even cactus-studded plains. Three important national parks rank high on birders' lists. The green-swathed Cordillera Central bounds the region to the north, while two other mountain ranges divide it into distinct lowland and highland zones.

A conduit for the destructive Haitian invasions of the 19th century, the region suffered gravely and the towns are relatively devoid of historic interest. The coastal plains that extend west from Santo Domingo are farmed with vast swaths of sugarcane like an endless green sea. So, too, the flatlands around Barahona, a center for sugarcane cultivation thanks to irrigation fed by rivers pouring down from the mountains. Melons, mangos, even grapes are grown alongside bananas and rice in the broad, well-watered Valle de San Juan.

The climate becomes progressively drier westward. The Sierra de Neiba and the Sierra de Baoruco—the republic's second high-est mountain range—march over the Haitian border, forming a barrier to moisture-laden northeasterly winds. The desertlike landscapes of the Península de Barahona stand in contrast to the lush farmland of the Valle de San Juan. In summer the sun beats down hard as a nail and the Península de Barahona broils. Months can pass without rain.

Organ-pipe cacti, prickly pears, and jumping cholla cacti (the stems detach so easily they seem to jump onto you when brushed) stud the landscape of Parque Nacional Jaragua, the country's largest national park and boasting the region's best beaches. (Wildlife-rich Parque Nacional Jaragua is also a battleground in developers' efforts to establish new all-inclusive resorts.)

The Sierra de Neiba and Sierra de Baoruco also lend their names to national parks. Clad in cloud forest and, higher up, with pines, these mountains offer superb birding. Between the

ranges, Lago Enriquillo holds Isla Cabritos in the midst of a searingly hot basin that is the lowest geographical point in the Caribbean. This vast saltwater lake is a habitat for flamingos and hundreds of American crocodiles—plump olive-green saurians that sun themselves on the mudbanks, motionless as logs. Together, the three major parks make up Jaragua-Baoruco-Enriquillo Biosphere Reserve, the nation's only such UNESCO-designated site.

NOT TO BE MISSED:

Viewing ancient Taíno pictographs in Reserva Antropológica Cuevas del Pomier **181**

An excursion to Bahía de las Águilas **185**

The scenic drive from Barahona to Pedernales **186–187**

Birding in Parque Nacional Sierra de Baoruco **188**

Crocodile viewing at Lago Enriquillo **189**

Hiking or mountain biking in Parque Nacional Sierra de Neiba **193**

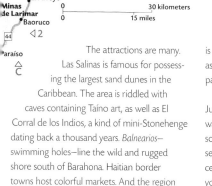

The attractions are many. Las Salinas is famous for possessing the largest sand dunes in the Caribbean. The area is riddled with caves containing Taíno art, as well as El Corral de los Indios, a kind of mini-Stonehenge dating back a thousand years. *Balnearios*—swimming holes—line the wild and rugged shore south of Barahona. Haitian border towns host colorful markets. And the region is known for its traditional music forms, such as *mangulina* and *carabiné,* performed during patron saint festivals.

Carretera 2 runs through the Valle de San Juan, while well-paved Carretera 44 makes its way along the coastal littoral, offering a terrific scenic drive south of Barahona, which is now served by an international airport. Major urban centers are relatively few, so it pays to keep your tank filled with gas. ■

San Cristóbal & Around

Seventeen miles (27 km) west of Santo Domingo, the Carretera Sánchez (Carretera 2) slices past sugarcane fields surrounding San Cristóbal, a town associated with dictator Rafael Trujillo. Nearby, the Caribbean's most important pre-Columbian cave art awaits at Reserva Antropológica Cuevas del Pomier.

La Iglesia Nuestra Señora de la Consolación, San Cristóbal

San Cristóbal

🗺 179 E3

Visitor Information

✉ Gobernación, Ave. Constitución 25

☎ 809/528-1844

🕐 Closed Sat.–Sun.

A traffic-choked industrial city straddling the Río Haina, San Cristóbal evolved from a simple stockade fortress built by Columbus on the riverbank. The nation's first constitution was signed here in 1844. Most famously, it's the former home-town of Trujillo, who named it the Meritorious City and turned it into a national shrine.

Parque Colón, the shady main plaza on Avenida Constitución, comes alive during the mid-June patron saint fiesta, when locals perform the traditional *carabiné* dance. The **Casa de la Cultura** *(Calle Mella),* on the south side of the plaza, hosts art exhibitions and literary and musical functions. The most interesting site in town is the mustard-colored **Iglesia Nuestra Señora de la Consolación** *(Ave. Constitución & Calle Padre Brown),* on the south side of **Parque Piedra Viva,** four blocks south of

Parque Colón. Its steeples topped by angels, the church is a domed confection built in 1946. Note the fine mural by Spanish artist José Vela Zanetti.

Beyond San Cristóbal

A curious legacy of the Trujillo era, the semicircular, hilltop **Castillo del Cerro** *(off Calle Luperón),* the Castle on the Hill, southwest of town, cost $3 million when built in 1947 as the dictator's private mansion. He apparently never spent a night in the four-story white elephant. Recently restored with the addition of jail cells, it now serves as a school for prison guards. It can be viewed from the outside only. **La Casa de Caoba** (House of Mahogany; *La Suiza, 2 miles/3 km NE of town*), is another abandoned Trujillo mansion. Built in 1938 of concrete faced with mahogany, it is in a sorry state. The guard offers informal Spanish-language tours for a tip. To get there, follow the signs for **Balneario La Toma** *(4 miles/ 7 km NE of San Cristóbal, $),* which draws locals to its natural swimming pools; to reach La Casa de Caoba, turn left through rusting wrought-iron gates beside the roadside water storage tanks.

Playa Najayo, 8 miles (13 km) south of town, as well as **Playa Palenque,** 4 miles (7 km) farther west, draw Santo Domingans to sun themselves and swim in the warm turquoise sea. Eastward, the sleepy coastal town of **Boca de Nigua** has several ruins, including the **Hermitage de San Gregorio,** a chapel built in 1785 for slaves and their owners.

Reserva Antropológica Cuevas del Pomier

The Caribbean's equivalent of France's Lascaux caves, the 54 caverns at Pomier have huge archaeological value. Currently being considered for UNESCO World Heritage status (only 11 are in

INSIDER TIP:

At La Casa de Caoba, feel the spirit of Minerva Mirabal, who rejected Trujillo's advances by slapping him on the dance floor.

—BRIAN RUDERT
Retired Foreign Service officer

the current reserve; the rest are in a huge marble quarry), the rocky galleries feature more than 6,000 Taíno pictographs and 500 petroglyphs dating back 2,000 years. Lizards crawl upon the walls alongside fish, mating birds, and spiritual symbols etched as if by the hand of Picasso.

The main caves have concrete paths and electric lighting, although they are often closed due to lack of electricity. The meager visitor center has no exhibits, and the entire site is virtually abandoned.

From San Cristóbal, take Avenida Constitución to La Toma, where the caves are signposted. After 1.5 miles (2.4 km), turn left at the T-junction to ascend the winding road to the caves. Tour companies in Santo Domingo offer excursions. ∎

Reserva Antropológica Cuevas del Pomier

🅰 179 E3

✉ Sector Villa Piedra, Los Cacaítos; 6 miles (10 km) N of San Cristóbal

☎ 809/472-4204 ext. 286 or 809/567-4300 (Santo Domingo)

💲 $

Taíno Cave Art

Panoramas of spiritual figures, powerful images of women in childbirth, ghostly six-fingered handprints of people who lived long ago—ancient Taíno artists daubed thousands of such images across the cave walls of Hispaniola. Scores of caves throughout the island contain drawings and carvings dating back 2,000 years.

Painted with various mixtures of charcoal, bat droppings, and animal fat, the crude images were daubed with shredded sticks. Other drawings were colored with white chalk or red clay or etched onto dripstones and limestone walls. Protected by the natural humidity and coolness of the caverns, they have lasted millennia.

Although the Taíno were a Stone Age people, they did not live in caves. These were considered sacred portals to the spiritual world. Most cave paintings represent spiritual beings, called *zemis:* Juracán, the powerful god who controlled storms; Yucahú, the god of cassava, represented with a three-pointed zemi; and the

Petroglyphs etched into porous rock at Las Caritas, near the north shore of Lago Enriquillo

rain god, Boiyanel, depicted with tears streaming from his eyes. A sun god also shines, as on the walls of Cueva de José María (see p. 103) in Parque Nacional Cotubanamá.

Some prosaic images represent food, but many are dedicated to fertility. Cueva Uno, at Pomier, for example, includes images of mating dogs. Lizards, frogs, and bats also appear, along with owls and other birds. Human heads are another common feature, often with two dots for eyes and a half circle for the mouth, staring out at visitors like smiley faces.

Most caves also depict the *cohoba* ceremony in which Taíno inhaled a hallucinogenic powder. Such ceremonies were intended as a means of communicating with spirits to ensure success in hunting, fertility, or cures. Pictographs in Cueva de Sanabe, near Presa de Hatillo (see p. 146), show humans trussed to poles. Six-foot-tall (2 m) images of powerful zemis and shamans suggest that these were caves used for healing.

Some caves, such as Las Maravillas (see p. 110) on the south coast, have vast panels of crowded drawings. The largest panels are within Reserva Antropológica Cuevas del Pomier (see p. 181), where 54 caves contain the largest collection of pre-Columbian rupestrian works in the Caribbean. Cueva de José María features among its 1,200 paintings a depiction of the sail of a Spanish galleon—a naive drawing presaging the extermination of an artful race.

Alas, some cave systems have been dynamited or bulldozed to make way for urban development. And images everywhere have been defaced with graffiti.

Fun Fun Cueva Tours *(tel 809/553-2656, cuevafunfun.net)*, in Punta Cana, offers Taíno-themed cave tours.

Baní to Azua

In the lee of the cordillera foothills, the coastal plain between Baní and Azua is smothered in sugarcane fields. During the *zafra* (harvest), they resound to a gallimaufry of tooting horns and the clanking carriages of diesel locomotives transporting the crop. Sands rise to fabulous heights atop the dunes of **Las Salinas.**

Fishermen put to sea near Baní.

Baní & Around

Baní is a thronged, unexciting, but prosperous town in the midst of sugarcane fields. At its heart, spacious **Parque Duarte** *(Calle Sánchez & Calle Mella)* offers repose beneath shade trees. Here, the **Iglesia de Nuestra Señora de Regla** hosts the patron saint festival each November 21. On the west side, the Ayuntamiento, or Town Hall, houses the meager **Museo Municipal** *(Calle Sánchez 1, tel 809/346-4300 ext 289, closed Sat.–Sun.)* on the first floor. One block north and two blocks east

of the plaza is **Casa de Máximo Gómez** *(Calle Máximo Gómez),* a small, landscaped park where a single post is all that remains of the birthplace of Máximo Gómez (1836–1905), the military figure who made Cuban independence his cause (see sidebar p. 158).

Playa Los Almendros, 3 miles (5 km) south of town, bustles on weekends when locals come to the sea to cool off. At Las Tablas, 9 miles (14.5 km) west of Baní, the hilltop **Santuario de San Martín de Porres** draws pilgrims; the rocky, cactus-strewn base is adorned with shrines.

Baní

 179 E3

Visitor Information

✉ Oficina de la Secretaría de Estado Turismo, Gobernación, Calle Sánchez

☎ 809/522-6018 or 809/346-4300

Azua

▲ 179 D3

Fruit farms line the route to **Las Salinas,** a fishing village famous for its massive wind-sculpted sand dunes, **Las Dunas de Baní.** Las Salinas Peninsula hooks around the Bahía de las Calderas, home of the Dominican Navy's main base, which you pass through to reach the dunes. On the bay's north shore, lovely **Playa Los Corbanitos** is set in a large cove hemmed in by mangroves; the green waters offer great snorkeling. Beyond lies **Playa Palmar de Ocoa,** at the head of the **Bahía de Ocoa,** a deepwater bay good for sportfishing; pleasant beaches line the eastern shore, where the nation's elite have vacation homes.

Azua

The commercialized town of Azua, straddling the highway 35 miles (57 km) west of Baní, holds few sites of interest, despite having been founded in 1504 by Diego Velázquez de Cuéllar (1465–1524), the conquistador who later conquered Cuba. Razed by earthquake and the Haitian army, the original city, now in ruins, can be seen at **Puerto Viejo de Azua,** in the shadows of an industrial complex 11 miles (18 km) southwest of Azua. A monument to independence marks pleasant **Parque Central** (*Calle Duarte & Calle Colón*). Two blocks west, on Calle Duarte, **Plaza 19 de Mayo** features a black marble monument and cannon memorializing the victory in 1844 over Haitian forces.

On weekends locals head to **Playa Monte Río** (*4 miles/6.4 km SE of Azua*) and the more pleasing white-sand **Playa Blanca,** which has hot springs. Dolphins frequent the reef-fringed bay.

Between Azua and Baní, the road climbs over **El Número,** a low mountain range whose sole pass framed by soaring cliffs was a latter-day Thermopylae in 1849, when Dominican forces defeated a Haitian army. Westward you drop to sweltering plains studded with cactus and impoverished settlements. Just east of El Número, Carretera 41 leads north to **San José de Ocoa,** a delightful hillside town surrounded by mountains. On weekends, locals flood **Rancho Francisco** (*tel 809/558-4099, facebook.com/RanchoFranciscoOcoa, $*), one of several *balnearios*—swimming complexes—with spring-fed pools south of the town. It hosts music concerts. ∎

EXPERIENCE:
Porres Pilgrimage

Time your visit to the **Santuario de San Martín de Porres** (*Las Tablas, 9 mi/14.5 km W of Baní*) for November 3rd, when Catholic believers make a pilgrimage to honor the Peruvian priest. Porres, a mixed Spanish and African friar in the Dominican order, lived an austere lifestyle and dedicated his life to the welfare of the poor. Many Catholics believe that he performed miracles, including levitation. If you're a believer, bring a candle to light in one of the shrines built into the rocky base. Note the **tomb of Juan Roberto Jaime,** a local priest responsible for construction of the sanctuary. The road to Las Tablas is best tackled in a four-wheel-drive vehicle.

Parque Nacional Jaragua

Occupying most of the Barahona Peninsula, the nation's largest park is a haven for many of the country's most critically endangered creatures. A thrilling ecotourism experience awaits visitors to the most southerly tip of the country.

Flamingos take flight over Laguna de Oviedo.

Flanked on two sides by the Caribbean and covered in sharp limestone, this 530.5-square-mile (1,374 sq km) park includes 349 square miles (905 sq km) of sea. Prickly pear cacti provide fruit for 3-foot-long (1 m) rhinoceros iguanas and endangered Ricord's iguanas.

The park was created to protect migratory flamingos in **Laguna de Oviedo,** a saltwater lake where more than 130 other bird species can be found. The **visitor center** at El Cajuil has a lookout tower. Compulsory guides lead two-hour tours *($$$)*, including tours to caves containing pre-Columbian drawings. The forest can be accessed by trail from a ranger station at **Fondo Paradí,** while tracks lead south from the hamlets of Manuel Golla and Oviedo to rustic fishing camps at

Trudillé and **Bucán Base.** On the west side of the park, **Bahía de las Águilas** beckons with a 5-mile-long (8 km) sliver of white sand. Boatmen *($$$)* will take you from **Rancho de la Cueva** (see p. 187).

Far offshore, scrub-covered **Isla Beata** and **Isla Alto Velo** and the **Los Frailes** and **Piedra Negra** cays are nesting sites for brown pelicans and boobies. Isla Beata is home to the world's smallest lizard—a minuscule gecko small enough to curl up on a dime.

Guides to the park are available through the Asociación de Guías de Naturaleza de Pedernales *(Calle Segunda, Barrio Alcoa, tel 809/771-9120)* or Grupo Jaragua *(Calle El Verge 33, Santo Domingo, tel 809/472-1036),* and La Perla del Mar Tours *(tel 809/545-0382, bahiadelasaguilas.net),* in Pedernales, offers tours. ∎

Parque Nacional Jaragua

🅜 178 B1
✉ El Cajuil, 46 miles (75 km) S of Barahona
☎ 809/501-1055 or 829/740-9072
💲 $

Drive: Barahona to Pedernales

Palm-fringed beaches pushed hard up against the sea by cliffs guarantee a spectacular drive along the rugged reef-fringed shore southwest of Barahona. The well-paved roller-coaster route is an official Vía Panorámica with good reason—it offers the most astounding coastal scenery in the republic. Carretera 44 runs south past fishing villages snug against sheer slopes before continuing to the border town of Pedernales.

The azure waters of the Caribbean draw swimmers to Playa Quemaito.

Begin your journey in **Barahona ❶**, the largest town in the region. Framed by sugarcane fields and mountains, the port town enjoys a lovely bay setting, although sights are few. Begin your drive at the Oficina de Turismo (*Carretera Batey Central*), where you can pick up a map.

The seafront Malecón boulevard becomes Carretera 44 south past **Punta Prieta ❷**, where a delightful tangerine-tinged beach is clasped by a cove adjoining the charming Playazul Hotel (see p. 221). The string of surf-washed beaches begins a few miles south with **Playa Quemaito,** at the hamlet of **Juan Esteban,** with fishing boats drawn up on the rough sands. Southward you'll pass through the hamlet of El Arroyo, where a sign points the way inland to Las Filipinas and the **Minas de**

NOT TO BE MISSED:

Punta Prieta • Playa Baoruco
• Balneario San Rafael • Enriquillo
• Bahía de las Águilas

Larimar (see p. 194); with a four-wheel-drive vehicle, you can climb the rugged 6-mile (10 km) mountain track to the oft cloud-shrouded mine site. Budget an additional 30 minutes each way.

The highway sidles south through **Baoruco,** a charming fishing village along a shingly beach shelving into unbelievably teal-blue waters. The rolling road then rises to a bend beyond which an awesome vista unfolds over **Playa Baoruco** 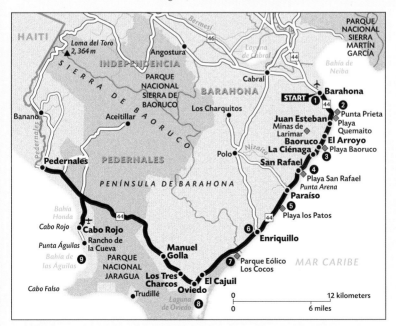. Farther south, the scene repeats above **Playa San Rafael** ❹, framed beyond by the foothills of the Sierra de Baoruco.

The road then dips down to **San Rafael,** where a waterfall cascades from the mountainside into an inviting *balneario* spilling into the sea. Two miles (3 km) south of San Rafael, the road steeples up to a *mirador* (vantage point) with fantastic views over the beach. Similar beaches await at the small coastal settlement of **Paraíso** and at **Playa los Patos** ❺, boasting a river-mouth balneario and palm-shaded sands.

Lined with pastel-painted clapboard houses, **Enriquillo** ❻, 34 miles (55 km) south of Barahona, is laid out atop a limestone plateau overlooking the azure Caribbean. Beyond, the scenery fades to scrub as the road cuts inland for Oviedo, passing **Parque Eólico los Cocos** wind farm ❼ and **Laguna de Oveido** ❽ (see p. 185) en route. Cattle munch penurious pastures in the slim shade of thorny acacias.

At Oviedo the road turns west, forming the northern boundary of **Parque Nacional Jaragua** (see p. 185). Sinuous as a snake, the rolling road provides spectacular views over the dry forests.

Seven miles (12 km) east of Pedernales, turn south for **Bahía de las Águilas** ❾ (see p. 185), accessed via the park entrance at **Rancho de la Cueva.** At this fishing village, cliff-face caves have been turned into barbecues—a great spot to enjoy a grilled lunch. Beyond, you can drive in a sedan to a clifftop mirador with spectacular views over the bay; you'll need a four-wheel-drive vehicle to tackle the rugged road that drops to the white beach. After sufficient time enjoying the sands and warm waters, retrace your route to Carretera 44 and continue west to **Pedernales** (see p. 194).

Ⓜ	See area map pp. 178–179
▶	Barahona
⊕	102 miles (165 km)
⏱	6 hours
▶	Pedernales

Parque Nacional Sierra de Baoruco

Lying between Lago Enriquillo and the coastal flatlands of the Península de Barahona, the rugged Sierra de Baoruco is considered the country's finest region for birding, with almost all the endemics present. The park protects some 310 square miles (800 sq km) of montane forests.

Forests filled with a bounty of birdlife carpet the Sierra de Baoruco.

Parque Nacional Sierra de Baoruco

🗺 178 B2

Visitor Information

✉ Calle 1ra 1, Puerto Escondido

☎ 809/515-0484

🕐 Closed Mon.

💲 $

Amigos de la Sierra de Bauruco

☎ 809/802-7273

Taíno leader Enriquillo's rebel forces hid in these wild, tangled mountains from 1519 to 1533 while they fought against the Spaniards. The region was named a national park in 1983. Former bauxite mines scar its southern slopes.

Antillean piculets, flat-billed vireos, and endemic bay-breasted cuckoos sing in the cactus-studded lowland dry forests. Above, broadleaf subtropical montane forest merges into pine forest with more than 160 orchid species. The pine forest is good for spotting endemic Hispaniolan crossbills and Antillean siskins, while La Selle thrushes flit about the park's cloud forest.

The park is being developed with trails. Access is off Carretera 44, to the south, via the paved **Vía Panorámica El Aceitillar.** En route, **La Charca** pond offers premium birding. The road climbs to the ranger station at El Aceitillar, where a 4.5-mile (7 km) trail leads to a visitor center and lookout at **Hoyo de Pelempito** (6,335 feet/ 1,931 m). From the north, a dirt road climbs from Duvergé to the Puerto Escondido ranger station; here, the **Sendero Sierra de Baoruco** trail *(4WD vehicles only)* connects to El Aceitillar. Permits from the Secretaría de Estado de Medio Ambiente, in Santo Domingo, are required to traverse this trail.

A mountain track parallels the Haitian border via **El Aguacate**—a remote post—and the isolated ranger station at **Loma del Toro** (7,756 feet/ 2,364 m) before dropping down to El Naranjo; it's a four-wheel-drive challenge.

El Aceitillar has camping, showers, and toilets. Tody Tours *(Calle José Gabriel Garcia 105, Santo Domingo, tel 809/686-0882, todytours.com)* offers ecological tours. ∎

Parque Nacional Lago Enriquillo e Isla Cabritos

Wildlife-rich Lago Enriquillo, an inland body of salt water covering an area equivalent to that of Manhattan, is the largest lake in the Caribbean and also its lowest point. The landlocked, hypersaline lake shimmers beneath the blistering Caribbean sun like a sort of dreamworld between hallucination and reality. Its waters support a host of wildlife, including crocodiles.

Cradled between the Sierra de Neiba to the north and the Sierra de Baoruco to the south, **Lago Enriquillo** is the remnant of a channel, linked to the bay of Port-au-Prince, that once divided Hispaniola into two islands. About one million years ago, the channel was sealed off by tectonic shifts and sediment dropped by the Río Yaque del Sur. Thereafter evaporation from the waters exceeded inflow and the surface of the 21-mile-long (34 km) lake is now about 150 feet (46 m) below sea level.

Though intensely saline, the lake supports prodigious amounts of wildlife, including a large population of American crocodiles. These carnivorous reptiles are most easily seen along the lake's north shore in cool marshy swamp fed by freshwater inlets.

Lake Enriquillo, with 62 bird species, is also a habitat for tens of thousands of sandpipers, herons, and terns. Its salty mirror reflects populations of roseate spoonbills and greater flamingos, the latter looking for all the world like feathered roses atop carnation stems.

Ship-shaped, 5-mile-long (8 km) **Isla Cabritos** (Goats Island) rises from the center of the lake. Rhinoceros iguanas crawl around among the ten species of cactus. The island, which has a visitor center, can be visited by registering at the ranger station at La Azufrada. Boats leave from the station on two-hour tours *($$–$$$$ depending on number of passengers)*. Take water and wear covered shoes to guard against scorpions. Ecotour Barahona *(Calle Enriquillo, Edif. 7, Paraíso, tel 809/243-1190, ecotourbarahona.com)* offers guided tours. ■

Crocodiles

American crocodiles grow up to 15 feet (4.5 m) long and weigh up to 2,000 pounds (907 kg). They prefer the fresh or brackish water of river estuaries, coastal lagoons, and mangrove swamps. The species is "vulnerable" throughout its North, Central, and South American range. Crocodiles spend much of the morning sunning on the mudbanks; once their bodies reach a certain temperature, they slither into the water to cool off.

Parque Nacional Lago Enriquillo e Isla Cabritos

 178 A3 & B3

✉ Ranger station at La Azufrada, 2 miles (3 km) E of La Descubierta

☎ 809/880-0871 or 809/472-4204 ext. 286 (Santo Domingo)

$ $

EXPERIENCE: Birding at Its Best

The Dominican Republic is the most popular destination in the Caribbean for serious birders. Wherever you are in the country, the birding is sure to astound. With so many distinct ecological zones, you're spoiled for choice. Still, some specific locales offer birding par excellence.

In 2009 the Dominican Republic formed a new national park–**Reserva Biologica Loma Charco Azul** *(on NW border of Sierra de Bahoruco National Park)*– to protect a vital last-refuge habitat for three endangered species (bay-breasted cuckoo, Hispaniolan cross-bill, and La Selle thrush) as well as five globally vulnerable species (chat tanager, golden swallow, Hispaniolan parakeet, Hispaniolan parrot, and white-winged warbler). Fat Birder *(fatbirder.com)* is an excellent resource.

Birding Tours

The following companies offer birding tours in the Dominican Republic:

Field Guides *(tel 512/263-7295, fieldguides.com)*

Focus on Nature *(tel 302/529-1876, focusonnature.com)*

Tody Tours *(tel 809/686-0882, todytours.com)*

Wings Birding Tours *(tel 520/320-9868, wingsbirds.com)*

Birding Hot Spots

Here are a few of the best places to tick off from the checklist of 306 species.

Lago Enriquillo

A supersaline lake (see p. 189) in a rain-forsaken valley 150 feet (46 m) below sea level is a venue for huge flocks of flamingos. Possible sightings of migrant warblers and waders also excite visiting birders.

Bay-breasted cuckoo

INSIDER TIP:

The drive from Lago Enriquillo to Pedernales gives you a chance to see almost all of the D.R.'s endemic birds.

—BRIAN RUDERT
Retired Foreign Service officer

Parque Nacional Los Haitises

The dramatic limestone formations of Los Haitises National Park (see p. 109) form a stupendous backdrop for birding. The park is renowned as the only refuge for the critically endangered Ridgway's hawk. Other must-see birds include the ashy-faced owl, ruddy quail-dove, and northern potoo.

Parque Nacional Sierra de Baoruco

The Sierra de Baoruco mountains (see p. 188), in the southwest, are considered the nation's premier birding site. Habitats range from dry deciduous forest to cloud forest. Enthusiasts flock to spot such species as the La Selle thrush, Antillean piculet, and Hispaniolan trogon.

Valle de Neiba

The Valle de Neiba is a low-lying region between the Sierra de Baoruco and Sierra de Neiba. Lago Enriquillo occupies much of the valley and is girded by a circular road, though the lake view is mostly obscured by scrub vegetation and the road runs well inland of the waters for most of the way.

Neiba, on Carretera 48 northeast of the lake, is the preeminent agricultural town and gateway. Neiba is surrounded by banana plantations and even grows grapes, sold roadside. The **Instituto Nacional de la Uva** *(Calle Proyecto & Calle Ángel Miro Santana, Neiba, fieldguides.com)* experimental station, north of town, works on perfecting sweet wines. South of Neiba, the receded lake bed—a world of salt pans and reed marshes—is thick with birds; stands of royal palms make for a perfect photo.

A pickup truck laden with goods heads for Haiti.

Carretera 48 west of Neiba is framed by a glade of flamboyants merging into the community of **Villa Jaragua,** full of colorful clapboard homes. A signposted roadside trail 200 yards (183 m) west of the town of Postrer Río leads to **Las Caritas;** it's a short uphill scramble to a cave overlooking Lago Enriquillo that is etched with Taíno petroglyphs, including *caritas* (tiny faces) with varied expressions.

Westward, **La Azufrada**—aka Cruce de Iguanas for the iguanas crawling around—is the entrance to Parque Nacional Lago Enriquillo e Isla Cabritos (see p. 189). La Azufrada is named for its sulfurous mineral waters; you can dip in the refreshing pools. A lakeside path ($) is good for spotting iguanas, while flamingos and crocodiles frequent the mouth of the Río Descubierta.

At the valley's western extreme is **Jimaní,** the principal border town with Haiti and setting for El Corte ("the cutting"), the genocidal massacre by machete of thousands of Haitians ordered by Trujillo in 1937. A dusty hilltop venue for an outdoor market, the town is notable for its color and bustle. Gaily painted Haitian buses called *tap-taps* honk their way through town. South of Jimaní, Carretera 46 runs through a series of small towns with Haiti's Massif de la Selle and the Sierra de Baoruco forming a backdrop. The hamlet of **Enriquillo** has a statue of the Taíno hero. ∎

Valle de Neiba

⧩ 178 B3 & C3

Visitor Information

✉ Gobernación, Calle 19 de Marzo 38, Jimaní

☎ 809/248-3330

Valle de San Juan

The region known simply as El Valle is a fertile oasis cut through by the Carretera Sánchez (Carretera 2). Hemmed between the Cordillera Central and the Sierra de Baoruco, the valley formed a natural conduit for invading Haitian armies, and many of the key battles with Dominican forces occurred here during the mid-1800s.

Children are drawn to the unique grounds of the cathedral of San Juan de la Maguana.

Valle de San Juan
🅰 178 B4 & C4
Visitor Information
✉ Ayuntamiento Municipal, Ave. Independencia #81, San Juan de la Maguana
☎ 809/557-2447

The main settlement is **San Juan de la Maguana,** founded in 1508 and the setting for several battles with Haitian forces; most of the original town was destroyed. The eastern entrance to this now prosperous city is spanned by an **Arco de Triunfo.** Adjoining are **Parque Duarte,** featuring a monument to Juan Pablo Duarte; the beautiful neoclassical, domed **Ayuntamiento** (City Hall); and the modernist **Palacio de Justicia.** In the heart of town, **Parque Central** *(Calle Independencia & Calle Duarte)* is surrounded by 19th-century buildings, notably the exquisite, pink-and-green **Catedral San Juan Bautista.** Rebuilt in 1958 in the shape of a Latin cross, it has baroque and rococo ornamentation. San Juan is famous for its patron saint festival, with two weeks of festivities culminating with a running of horses on **El Día de San Juan** each June 24; and for its **Festival de Espíritu Santo,** in early June, when the Catholic faithful make a pilgrimage from the small town of El Batey.

　El Corral de los Indios *(4 miles/7 km N of San Juan)* is the country's most complete ancient Taíno settlement. This 150-yard-wide (137 m) stone circle is centered on a slab etched with faces. Dating back more than one thousand years, it was used for ceremonial purposes and as a *batey,* or ball court. Nearby, a dirt road leads east from La Maguana via Maguana Arriba to **Templo Liborio,** a pilgrimage site for cultists of Olivorio Liborio, a faith healer murdered by U.S. troops in 1922.

Farther north, **Presa de Sabaneta**—a large artificial lake—is gateway to **Las Cuevas de Seboruco,** featuring pre-Taíno pictographs; it is also the trailhead for a challenging five-day hike to the summit of Pico Duarte (see pp. 170–171). Another trailhead begins at **Presa de Sebana Yegua** *(15 miles/25 km E of San Juan),* offering superb fishing. Ask at the military post to be escorted onto the dam for splendid views.

Westward, the potholed Carretera 2 connects San Juan to

Las Matas de Farfán, a sleepy market town that springs to life for the Saturday market. **Comendador del Rey,** a border town also known to locals as Elías Piña, boasts a colorful Haitian market every Monday and Friday. Farther north, **Bánica**—another border town—claims a charming redbrick church dating from 1514.

Parque Nacional Sierra de Neiba

Covering 158 square miles (407 sq km), this park protects the country's largest expanse of cloud forest. The broad Sierra de Neiba range separates Lago Enriquillo from the Valle de San Juan and rises to 7,477 feet (2,279 m) atop Monte Neiba. Dry forest at lower elevations rises to cloud forest and pines. The park is perfect for hiking, mountain biking, and birding. Its 83 bird species include 21 of the island's 22 endemics, including the Hispaniolan trogon. ■

Parque Nacional Sierra de Neiba

🗺 178 B4

Visitor Information

✉ Calle San Pedro 10, San Juan de la Maguana

☎ 809/567-4300 ext. 286 (Santo Domingo)

EXPERIENCE: How to Make *Bandera Dominicana*

The staple lunch dish of the republic, bandera dominicana (see p. 20) can be sampled around the country. A good place to try it out is **La Galería del Espía** *(Calle Independencia 7, San Juan de la Maguana, tel 809/557-5069).* Here's the recipe:

1. Marinate stewed goat meat or beef overnight, then chop into bite-size pieces. Sauté with garlic, onions, tomatoes and bell peppers, then add beef stock and seasoning. Simmer for two hours, adding tomato paste to thicken.

2. Stew red kidney beans in chicken stock. Add chopped sautéed celery and spices, plus a touch of tomato paste. Cook until the beans become creamy.

3. Cook white rice with water and a little oil in a skillet. Once the water is absorbed, remove the lid and let the rice continue to cook on low heat to create *concón* (burnt rice on the bottom of the pan).

Serve hot with concón to the side. Add a salad of lettuce topped with sliced tomato and avocado. Serve the four items "quartered" on the plate, symbolizing the Dominican flag. The beans and meat juice go atop the rice.

More Places to Visit in the Southwest

Minas de Larimar

The little-known semiprecious larimar gemstone (see sidebar below) has grown in popularity recently, spurring activity at larimar mines in the mountains southwest of Barahona. Impoverished miners burrow into tunnels dug into the natural hollow lava tubes with which the mineral is associated—strenuous and dangerous work. The turnoff from Carretera 44 is at the village of El Arroyo. You'll need a four-wheel-drive vehicle for the rugged dirt road to the mines.

◭ 178 C2 ✉ Las Filipinas, 9 miles (15 km) W of El Arroyo via dirt road

Larimar

Larimar is a beautiful blue rock found only in a small area around Barahona. Often mistaken for turquoise, this crystalline mineral is a pectolite: a secondary rock of volcanic origin, formed when lava pushing up through overlying rock absorbed various mineral compounds and was later superheated and crystallized. The mineral ranges in color from sky blue to deep blue, often interlaced with streaks of white, gray, even red. Larimar is priced according to color and purity.

Parque Nacional Sierra Martín García

Midway between Azua and Barahona, wrapped around the north shore of the Bahía de Neiba, this 103-square-mile (268 sq km) park encompasses lagoons, wetlands, beaches, and waters off Punta Martín García. Ecosystems include mangroves and subtropical dry forest. Eleven endemic bird species, 25 reptile species, plus 232 species of flora are represented. A pre-Columbian site and petrified lake with fossils are protected on the southeast side near the hamlet of Barreras, where you can reach the park via a dirt road.

◭ 178 C3 ✉ Loma El Curro, Barahona
☎ 809/567-4300

Pedernales

Pedernales is a remote border town where, on Mondays and Fridays, Haitians set up a market. With several modest hotels, Pedernales provides a base for exploring **Jaragua** (see p. 185) and **Sierra de Baoruco** (see p. 188) **National Parks**. The latter is accessed by a dirt road that crawls up to above 6,000 feet (1,829 m) before dropping down to the **Valle de Neiba** (see p. 191).

◭ 178 A2 ✉ 88 miles (142 km) SW of Barahona

Polo Magnético

In the forests of the Sierra de Baoruco south of Cabral, just past La Cueva, the "magnetic pole" is a point (marked by a roadside billboard) where the road appears to run downhill. Stop your car, however, release the brakes, and the car starts rolling backward up the hill. The phenomenon is an optical illusion, but locals swear that it is the result of magnetically charged ore or dark forces.

◭ 178 C2 ✉ 12 miles (19 km) S of Cabral on road that links Cabral and Polo

Reserva Científica Laguna de Cabral

The shallow Laguna de Cabral—the nation's largest freshwater lake—is famous for its endangered slider turtles, found only on Hispaniola. The lake (also known as Laguna del Rincón) and surrounding wetlands are protected as a scientific reserve. Guided boat trips (*$$$$*) can be arranged at the ranger station at the north end of Cabral, from where an interpretative trail extends toward the lake.

◭ 178 C3 ✉ Cabral

Travelwise

Motoring through Bahía de las
Águilas

TRAVELWISE

PLANNING YOUR TRIP

When to Go

The Dominican Republic has a warm and humid tropical climate year-round, but it varies by region. In general, November through April is dry season, when temperatures average a balmy 75 to 80° F (23–26° C). The hottest months are May through October, when temperatures in Santo Domingo average a humid 86 to 90° F (30–32° C). This is also the wet season, when almost daily afternoon showers occur. The end of the wet season is a good time to visit, when everything is lush. The country lies within the hurricane belt, and severe tropical storms are frequent in summer and fall, often causing flooding.

This close to the Equator, temperatures vary with elevation rather than with latitude. Regional variations are pronounced. The Cordillera Central and upper highlands enjoy year-round springlike climate. The southwest and parts of the Valle del Yaque receive little rainfall—much of this zone is cactus-studded semidesert. Elsewhere, be prepared for stifling humidity in the lowlands away from the coast. The Caribbean coast can be cooler in summer, when trade winds pick up. Most tourists visit in the dry season, when beach resorts can be sold out and rates for hotels and car rentals are high

Festivals occur year-round. Lenten week is the biggest holiday in the Dominican Republic, and much of the country shuts down; hotels in cities hosting festivals are usually fully booked.

What to Bring

The Dominican Republic has a tropical climate, so dress accordingly. Lightweight, loose-fitting cotton and synthetic clothes are best. Loose-fitting shorts and T-shirts prove comfortable and are acceptable everywhere, including Santo Domingo, although you'll want some more elegant wear for nighttime. A sweater and/or lightweight jacket are useful for the heavily air-conditioned restaurants and essential for visits to highland areas, where warm waterproof clothing is a must when hiking.

You'll want a comfortable pair of walking shoes for exploring the cities; sneakers work fine. Dress shoes are needed for upscale restaurants and most nightclubs. Hiking shoes will prove useful if you plan on exploring mountain trails or wilderness areas. Avoid bright colors (which can frighten away wildlife) if you plan on birding or taking nature hikes.

You'll need insect repellent, particularly for coastal areas and during wet season, even in cities.

Bring sunglasses, as the tropical light is intense, and wear a hat and sunscreen.

Medicines are widely available. However, you should bring a basic first-aid kit that includes aspirin, antidiarrheal medicine, antiseptic lotion, Band-aids, and prescription medications. Bring a spare pair of glasses or contact lenses rather than a prescription.

Insurance

Travel insurance is a wise investment. Companies that provide coverage for the Dominican Republic include:

Allianz, tel 866/884-3556, allianztravelinsurance.com

Assistcard, tel 866/477-6741, assistcard.com

TravelGuard International, tel 800/826-4919, travelguard.com

Entry Formalities

All foreign visitors need to present a passport, and most must also purchase a tourist card (US$10, good for 30 days), upon arrival. Citizens of Australia, Canada, the United Kingdom, and the United States, plus most Western European countries, are not required to obtain visas.

Tourist cards can be extended for an additional 90 days for US$4 (more for longer stays) by applying to the Department of Migration *(Ave. 30 de Mayo & Héroes de Luperón, Santo Domingo, tel 809/508-2555, migracion.gob.do).* The fee can also be paid at the airport upon departure. Officially, a return ticket is required of all visitors arriving by air. A US$20 tax is levied upon departure.

HOW TO GET TO THE DOMINICAN REPUBLIC

By Air

Most flights land at the chaotic **Las Américas International Airport,** tel 809/947-2225, 8 miles (13 km) east of Santo Domingo. Solicitors offering taxi, hotel, and other services await your arrival, and luggage theft is common. Most tourists heading to the beaches arrive either at **Punta Cana International Airport,** tel 809/959-2376, Puerto Plata's **Gregorio Luperón International Airport,** tel 809/291-0000, or the **Samaná International Airport,** tel 809/338-5888, at El Catey.

The following U.S. airlines all offer regular flights to the Dominican Republic:

American Airlines, tel 800/433-7300, aa.com
Delta Airlines, tel 800/221-1212, delta.com
JetBlue Airlines, tel 800/538-2583, jetblue.com
Spirit Airlines, tel 800/772-7117, spiritair.com
United Airlines, tel 800/864-8331, united.com.

By Sea
More than a dozen major cruise lines offer the Dominican Republic on their itineraries. Contact the **Cruise Lines International Association,** tel 855/444-2542, cruising.org.

Group Tours
Few travelers to the Dominican Republic choose a packaged tour. Most such tours cater to scuba divers, kiteboarders, and surfers. A few others focus on nature and cultural encounters. Contact **Dominican Republic Ministry of Tourism** (see pp. 201–202) for recommended tour companies.

GETTING AROUND
In Santo Domingo
By Bus
The city's relatively efficient public transport system is overseen by the Metropolitan Transit Service (OMSA). Large metropolitan buses cover the longer city routes; jam-packed minibuses connect city neighborhoods. Air-conditioned buses cost RD$15; buses without air-conditioning cost RD$10. Buses generally operate from 6 a.m. to 9:30 p.m.

By Car
Autopistas (highways) that lead into and out of Santo Domingo have tollbooths (RD$30). The autopistas and main roads into and out of the city are usually congested at rush hour and on

weekends and public holidays. Avenida John F. Kennedy and Avenida 27 de Febrero are often horrendously clogged during business hours.

By Metro
Santo Domingo has a state-of-the-art Metro. Two lines run north–south and east–west, linking the city center, with 29 stations. A standard RD$20 fare applies. Four additional lines are planned.

By Taxi
Taxis operate from Las Américas International Airport into Santo Domingo (about RD$1600). Licensed tourist taxis are yellow and have a Taxi Turístico logo. Agree on the fare with the driver before leaving.

In town, legal taxis display a brown certificate in the windshield. They are numerous, cheap, and safe as long as you stick to licensed taxis. Set rates apply according to distance.

Taxis do not have meters, so ask your hotel concierge for an appropriate fare before settling on a price with the driver. The minimum fare is RD$150. To hail a cab, call Tecni-Taxi *(tel 809/ 472-8895).* With radio taxis, you can set the fare with the radio dispatcher.

Most Dominicans travel in *carros públicos,* multipassenger taxis that often pack in as many people as can fit. Most públicos are not roadworthy and are usually driven recklessly.

Tours are available by horse-drawn carriage through Zona Colonial and along the Malecón. Negotiate a price before leaving.

Throughout the Dominican Republic
By Air
Air Century *(tel 809/846-4333,*

aircentury.com) provides small plane charters. Domestic flights arrive and depart from **Joaquín Balaguer International Airport** *(tel 809/826-4003),* in Santo Domingo, and connect with the regional airports listed above as well as:

Aeropuerto del Cibao, Santiago, tel 809/233-8000
Aeropuerto María Montéz, Barahona, tel 809/524-4144

By Boat
A regular passenger-only ferry operates between Santa Bárbara de Samaná and Sabana de la Mar. The ferries are often crowded. Water taxis ferry people between Boca Chica and Cayo Sabinal; Bayahibe and Isla Saona; and Santa Bárbara de Samaná and Cayo Levantado. Fishing boats can be rented for journeys to remote beaches and national parks.

By Bus
Three private companies compete and offer fast *(directo)* and slower *(regular)* service:
Caribe Tours *(tel 809/221-4422, caribetours.com.do)* has nationwide service.
Metro *(Calle Francisco Prats, 55 yards/50 m E of Ave. Winston Churchill, tel 809/227-0101, metroserviciosturisticos.com)* links Santo Domingo and the north coast.
Capital Coachline *(tel 809/ 530-8266, capitalcoachline.com)* connects the capital with Port-au-Prince, Haiti.

Long-distance service is typically by large, modern, air-conditioned buses with reclining seats. Minivans or pickup trucks (*gua-guas,* pronounced WAH-wahs) provide town-to-town service; they are usually overcrowded and unsafe.

Buses are crowded on weekends; reserve seats if possible, and guard against pickpockets and luggage theft. Fares are reasonable; the most expensive destination costs about RD$500 one way.

By Car

To rent a car you must be over 25 and hold a passport and a valid driver's license. You will also need a credit card and will have to leave a hefty deposit (at least RD$15,000/US$400). Check that the rental includes unlimited mileage. A loss damage waiver (enuncia a daños o perdida) and liability insurance are mandatory; some companies refuse to honor insurance issued abroad. Rental rates vary from RD$1,500 daily for small cars to RD$5,000 for four-wheel-drive vehicles (carro con doble). Rental cars cannot be taken into Haiti.

Rental insurance does not cover damage caused by falling coconuts. Do not park under coconut palms.

Most international rental car companies are represented in the D.R., including:

Avis, tel 809/535-7191 or 800/331-1084, avis.com

Budget, tel 809/549-0351 or 800/472-3325, budget.com

Dollar, tel 809/221-7368 ext. 40 or 800/800-5252, dollar.com

Hertz, tel 809/221-5333 or 800/654-3001, hertz.com

These agencies all have outlets at major airports.

Main roads throughout the country are in reasonably good condition. However, minor roads are in poor repair. A four-wheel-drive vehicle is recommended for remote areas, including the Cordillera Central and for access to most national parks. For off-road exploration, a rugged vehicle is essential.

The nation's drivers are capable of astounding recklessness—there is a high auto fatality rate, especially during Carnaval season. Some roads have speed bumps, and there are police/military checkpoints, especially close to the Haitian border.

A government campaign to end police corruption has had some success, and the incidence of police demanding bribes from tourists is much reduced. However, isolated cases still occur.

Gasoline is expensive. Many gas stations (bombas) close at 8 p.m., and they can be rare in remote parts of the country, where it is worth filling up at every opportunity. Many gas stations do not accept credit cards.

Talking on a cell phone while driving is illegal, and wearing a seatbelt is mandatory.

See pages 202–203 for what to do in case of a car accident.

By Taxi

There are plenty of taxis available in tourist resorts. Fares are negotiable and should always be agreed upon before setting off. Most locals use carros públicos, private cars that act as unmetered shared taxis picking up and dropping off along their routes. Though the cheapest option, they can get crammed and are unsafe. Look for a white seal on the front door. Avoid unlicensed taxis. Motoconchos, small motorcycles that carry passengers, are the default mode of transport for locals outside Santo Domingo. They are dangerous and should be avoided.

Group Tours

Once in the Dominican Republic, many visitors choose a packaged excursion. The country has several dozen reputable tour agencies, including:

Colonial Tours & Travel (tel 809/688-5285, colonialtours.com.do) has offices in Santo Domingo, Punta Cana, and Bayahibe.

Iguana Mama (tel 809/571-0908, iguanamama.com) specializes in ecological and adventure tours.

DomRep Tours (tel 809/686-0278) offers a wide range of specialist tours.

PRACTICAL ADVICE
Communications
Email & Internet

Most towns and villages have Internet cafés (usually charging between RD$30 and RD$60 per hour). Most have high-speed connections, but electricity outages are frequent. Most tourist hotels are wired for Internet use or have business centers. Some offer free service to guests; otherwise fees can be RD$150 per hour or higher. Upscale hotels usually have modems; some charge a fee. An increasing number of venues have Wi-Fi hot spots.

Post Offices

It costs RD$20 or more to mail a letter or postcard to North America, and RD$33 to Europe. Most towns have a post office, usually open weekdays from 8 a.m. to 5:30 p.m. Many gift stores and hotels sell prepaid letters and postcards. Allow at least 10 days for mail to the United States or Canada, and at least 14 days for mail to Europe. Never mail anything of value.

There is no home delivery in the Dominican Republic. Mail is delivered to postal boxes (apartados postales, abbreviated Apdo.), which can be rented through the **Instituto Postal Dominicano** (tel 809/534-5838, inposdom.gob.do) in Santo Domingo.

Service is unreliable and theft is common. Hence, most people use private mail and courier services. **DHL** (tel 809/534-7888, dhl.com.do) and **FedEx** (tel 809/565-3636, fedex.com/do) have offices throughout the Dominican Republic and offer express international and domestic service.

Telephones

Public pay phones accept prepaid phone cards, which can be bought at hotels, local stores, gas stations, and telecommunications centers nationwide. Sidewalk sellers also sell the cards to cars stopped at traffic junctions. Insert the card into the phone and the cost of your call is deducted. Local calls cost RD$1 per minute; national calls cost about RD$5 per minute.

Claro (tel 809/220-1111, claro .com.do) and **Tricom** (tel 809/476-6000, tricom.net) are among the major phone companies in the country that also operate walk-in phone centers, where it is possible to place international calls at a fraction of the cost of hotel-charged calls. Phone-center calls to North America typically cost RD$5 per minute. Some Internet cafés have cheaper rates. Hotels usually charge a high fee for calls from in-room phones; phone cards can be used from hotel phones.

For direct-dial international calls from the republic, dial 00, then the country code, the area code, and the number. For operator-assisted calls to countries outside the Dominican Republic, dial 0. For information, call 411. When placing a domestic call in the Dominican Republic, dial 1, then 809, or 829, or 849, and then the seven-digit phone number.

When calling from the United States, dial 1, plus one of the Dominican Republic's country codes, 809, 829, or 849, then the local number.

Visitors can activate their cell phones within the republic and then purchase prepaid phone cards or a phone plan. GSM (European) phones can be activated at Orange Dominicana outlets as well as at **Claro** stores (tel 809/220-1111, claro .com.do); CDMA (North American) phones can be activated at Verizon or Tricom stores.

Electricity

The Dominican Republic operates on 110-volt AC (60 cycles) nationwide, although a few more remote places use 220 volts. Most outlets use U.S. flat, two-pin (sometimes three-pin) plugs. Some of the remoter parts of the country are not on the electrical grid; here restaurants and hotels rely on generators or solar power. Blackouts are frequent; most major hotels, however, have their own generators. Power surges are common, and it is always a good idea to use a surge protector for laptops.

Etiquette & Local Customs

Dominican society is diverse. Life in Santo Domingo is cosmopolitan and relatively liberal, while smaller towns and rural villages are far more conservative. Society remains extremely class conscious. Dominicans respect professional titles and use them when addressing titleholders, such as engineers (e.g. Ingeniero Fuentes) and architects (Arquitecto Garcia).

Adults are addressed as Señor (Mr.), Señora (Mrs.), or Señorita (Miss). The terms Don (for men) and Doña (for women) are used for high-ranking or respected individuals and senior citizens.

Dominicans are courteous and gracious, except when driving. They pride themselves on their hospitable natures and are usually eager to help visitors. They normally use the formal usted form of "you," while the informal tu form is reserved for intimates. Women greet each other by kissing the air next to the cheek; there is usually no contact except between family members and close friends. Hugs are generally used only among close friends and family. Handshakes tend to be limp, and overly firm handshakes are often considered aggressive.

Life revolves around the family. Personal contacts are the key to success, particularly in business and politics.

The Dominican Republic is a macho society. Despite the advance of women in politics and business, gender roles are strictly defined. Younger women travelers may receive unwanted attention from Dominican men; usually this is limited to verbal compliments (piropos)—often salacious—and propositions.

Dominican society is unsympathetic toward gays and lesbians and open displays by homosexuals may result in harassment or worse.

Dominicans are extremely proud of their country and are sensitive to criticism by foreigners, particularly U.S. citizens, due to lingering animosities fueled by past U.S.–Dominican relations.

Outside the main tourist areas and business centers you may not be understood in English, so it is advisable to learn a few Spanish phrases. Most restaurants in cities have menus in English, although you may have to ask for them.

Holidays

In addition to Christmas, New Year's Day, and Easter, the Dominican Republic observes the following national holidays:

January 6—Epiphany
January 21—Our Lady of Altagracia
January 26—Juan Pablo Duarte's birthday (celebrated on the closest Monday)
February 27—Independence from Haitian occupation
March/April—Holy Friday
May 1—Labor Day (celebrated on the closest Monday)
May 26—Corpus Christi
August 16—Dominican Restoration Day (celebrated on the closest Monday)

September 24—Our Lady of Mercedes
November 6—Constitution Day.

The biggest holiday of the year is Carnaval—usually the four days leading up to Ash Wednesday. However, some towns hold festivals at other times of year (see regional chapters for details). You should avoid driving in areas where these festivals are being held, as the accident rate soars.

Most tourist sites and services stay open for these holidays, but banks and government offices will close.

Liquor Laws
The legal age for drinking alcoholic beverages is 18 in the Dominican Republic. Driving while under the influence of alcohol is illegal; a conviction of drunk driving will nullify any insurance coverage for rented cars. Liquor sales in tourist areas are allowed until 1 a.m. Sunday through Thursday and until 2 a.m. Friday, Saturday, and holidays.

Media
Newspapers & Magazines
The Dominican Republic has five major national newspapers, published in Spanish and available at newsstands around the country. The daily *Listín Diario* is the most conservative and complete and covers everything from politics to fashion; *Diario Libre, Hoy, El Caribe,* and *El Nacional* are also good.

Most such publications are sold at small streetside stands. Major U.S. magazines and dailies, such as *USA Today* and *Time,* are usually available at leading hotel gift stores.

There is no English-language newspaper. However, D.R. One *(dr1.com)* and Dominican Today *(dominicantoday.com)* publish news online in English.

Television & Radio
Television reaches everywhere in the country, which has almost 50 local TV stations. Most upscale hotels offer cable or satellite TV with U.S. and European programs. The Caribbean Travel Network (CTN) presents tourist information through Telecable Nacional.

The Dominican Republic has scores of radio stations. All but a few broadcast local news and Latin music. Reception is sporadic, with remote areas, such as the Cordillera Central, receiving only one or two stations. Cadena de Noticias (95.2 FM; *cdn.com.do*) broadcasts news in Spanish. The BBC World Service and Voice of America offer English-language news.

Money Matters
Currency
The Dominican currency is the *peso oro* (RD$), which is officially divided into 100 centavos. However, the tiny centavo coin has been withdrawn from circulation, leaving the 1-, 5-, 10-, and 25-peso coins in circulation. The U.S. dollar is widely accepted in main urban centers and is the preferred currency in tourist resorts. Euros and pounds sterling are not as readily accepted, but can be exchanged at banks.

The Banco de Reservas has foreign-exchange booths at major international airports. Some banks in larger towns also have foreign-exchange counters to serve travelers, but you shouldn't count on this. There are a few private exchange offices *(casas de cambio),* which offer similar rates to banks and are usually open longer hours.

Visitors may have trouble cashing traveler's checks anywhere but banks due to widespread fraud and holds imposed by banks. Many shops will refuse to accept them.

Avoid changing money on the street; such exchanges typically involve scams.

As of press time, the exchange rate was:

U.S. $1 = RD$46
€1 = RD$50

ATMs
Most banks have 24-hour automated teller machines (ATMs) for cash advances using credit cards or withdrawals from your account using a bank card. There is usually a small charge for using the ATM. Don't count on ATMs actually having cash; those at airports often run out. When heading to remote areas, be sure to have sufficient cash on hand.

Using ATMs during regular banking hours is advisable in case of problems (such as machines not returning cards). Avoid using ATMs in poor neighborhoods and in dark locations, where crime may be a problem.

Credit Cards
Credits cards *(tarjetas de crédito)* are widely accepted. Hotel and other major tourist entities accept most types of credit cards; other outlets usually accept only MasterCard and Visa. Banco de Reservas gives cash advances against MasterCard only.

Opening Times
Most stores are open Monday through Saturday, 9 a.m. to 6 p.m., but malls, supermarkets, and many souvenir stores have longer hours, and are also open on Sunday.

Banks are typically open Monday through Friday, 8 a.m. to 3 p.m., and Saturday 8 a.m. to 1 p.m. Businesses are typically open Monday through Friday 9 a.m. to noon, and 1:30 p.m. to 5 p.m.; travel agencies and tourist-related businesses also open on Saturday, 8 a.m. to noon, and do not close for lunch. Most government offices are open weekdays 7:30 a.m. to 4 p.m.

Places of Worship

Most communities have at least one Roman Catholic church and often a Protestant church. Local tourist information offices and leading hotels can usually supply a list of places of worship.

Restrooms

There are very few public restroom facilities *(baños)*. Most restaurants and bus stations have rest rooms, although standards of cleanliness vary.

Smoking

Many Dominicans smoke, and smoking in public places is neither frowned upon nor forbidden. Many upscale restaurants have nonsmoking sections, although rarely is this in a separate room. Elsewhere, "No Smoking" signs are regularly disobeyed. Surprisingly few Dominicans smoke cigars, despite the fame of the country's hand-rolled *puros*.

Time Differences

The Dominican Republic is on Atlantic Standard Time (AST), which is one hour ahead of U.S. Eastern Standard Time (EST), and four hours behind Greenwich Mean Time (GMT). The country does not observe Daylight Savings Time, so in those months its time is the same as EST.

Tipping

Tipping is not a fact of life in the Dominican Republic except in tourist areas, where many people in service jobs depend on tips to make ends meet. However, a tip is an acknowledgment of good service: If the service is not satisfactory, do not tip.

Restaurants add a 10 percent service charge onto bills, where an additional tip should be given for good service. Workers in many cafés and budget eateries do not expect to receive tips. Hotel porters should be given 15 pesos per bag (airport porters expect twice that), and room service staff RD$30 per day. Taxi drivers do not expect a tip.

In the countryside, park rangers, boat guides, and the like often provide services for which a tip is in order, and usually expected. Tour guides should be tipped for personalized services. A communally collected tip is often the norm on group tours (see sidebar p. 11).

Travelers With Disabilities

The Dominican Republic does not display great sensitivity to the needs of visitors with disabilities. No national law requires hotels to provide such facilities, and few buildings have wheelchair access or provide special rest room facilities. Buses are not adapted for wheelchairs, and few curbs are dropped at corners. Modern, upscale hotels and a few restaurants in major cities and tourist areas have wheelchair access, and a few hotels provide special suites.

The following agencies provide information on travel abroad for visitors with disabilities:

Asociación Dominicana de Rehabilitación, Calle Mary Pérez Viuda cnr. Leopoldo Navarro, Santo Domingo, tel 809/689-7151, adr.org.do

Fundación Dominicana de Ciegos, Ave. Expreso V Centenario *&* Calle Tunti Cáceres, Edificio 11, Santo Domingo, tel 809/538-4161

Gimp on the Go, gimponthego.com. Internet-based newsletter and forum for disabled travelers.

Society for Accessible Travel *&* Hospitality, 347 5th Ave., Ste. 605, New York, NY 10016, tel 212/447-7284, sath.org.

Visitor Information

The Dominican Republic's **Ministry of Tourism** maintains the following website: godominicanrepublic.com. The ministry is headquartered at Calle Cayetano Germosen cnr. Ave. Gregorio Luperón, Santo Domingo, tel 809/221-4660, and has the following offices abroad:

Canada: 2055 Peel Street #550, Montreal, Quebec H3A 1V4, tel 514/499-1918 or 800/563-1611

Germany: Hochstrasse 54, 60313 Frankfurt, tel 069/9139-7878

Spain: Serrano 114, 28006 Madrid, tel 091/417-7375

United Kingdom: 18–21 Hand Court, High Holbon, London WC1V6JF, tel 020/7242-7778

United States: 136 E. 57th St., Ste. 803, New York, NY 10022, tel 212/588-1012 or 888/374-6361.

The Ministry of Tourism also maintains regional information bureaus around the country:

Santo Domingo: Ave. Cayetano Germosén cnr. Ave. Gregorio Luperón, Santo Domingo, tel 809/221-4660

Boca Chica: Plaza Boca Chica, Calle San Rafael, tel 809/523-5106

Cabarete: Plaza Tricom, Calle Principal, tel 809/571-0972

Constanza: Calle Antonio María García #43, tel 809/539-2900

Higüey, Ave. Juan XXIII, Plaza El Naranjo, 809/554-2672

Jarabacoa: Plaza Ramírez, Calle Mario Galán bet. Calle Duarte *&* Calle del Carmen, tel 809/574-7287

La Romana: Ave. Libertad #7, Edif. Almodóvar, tel 809/550-6922

Las Terrenas: Calle Libertad (opposite police station), tel 809/240-6141

Monte Cristi: Gobernación, Calle Mella 37, tel 809/579-2254

Nagua: Gobernación, Calle Club Rotario, tel 809/584-3862

Puerto Plata: Calle José del Carmen Arizo 45, tel 809/586-3676

Punta Cana: Calle Friusa, Plaza El Tronco, Bávaro, tel 809/552-0142

Samaná: Ave. Santa Bárbara 4, tel 809/538-2332

San Cristóbal: Gobernación Ave. Constitución, tel 809/528-1844

Santiago de los Caballeros: Gobernación, Parque Duarte & Calle del Sol, tel 809/582-5885

Sosúa: Plaza Eric House, Calle Principal, tel 809/571-3433.

The ministry also publishes an excellent series of pocket-size guides (in Spanish only) on golf, protected areas, scenic drives and lakes, and individual regions. **Cuesta Litorería** (*Ave. 27 de Febrero 1 & Calle Abraham Lincoln, Santo Domingo, tel 809/473-4020*) and **Mapas Gaar** (*Calle Conde Peatonal cnr. Espaillat, Edif. Jaar, Santo Domingo, tel 809/688-8004*) are well stocked with maps, which can also be bought in main resorts.

The **Dirección Nacional de Parques** (DNP; *Ave. Cayetano Germosén cnr. Ave. Gregorio Luperón, Santo Domingo, tel 809/567-4300, medioambiente.gov.do*) publishes *Sistema de Áreas Protegidas de República Dominicana* (in Spanish only) and issues permits for visits to forest reserves (RD$100 per permit). It has a public information office at **Local 28** (*Plaza Naco, Ave. Tiradentes & Fantino Falco, Santo Domingo, tel 809/567-4300*).

Dominican Republic Vacation Planner is a tourist-oriented publication published annually in English. It can be ordered from the Ministry of Tourism offices; D.R.One (*dr1.com*) provides an online version.

Websites

Several excellent websites offer general information about the Dominican Republic. Among them are:

dominicanrepublic.com
dr1.com
hispaniola.com
popreport.com

EMERGENCIES
Crime & Police

The Dominican Republic is a poor country, and although violent crime against tourists is rare, caution should be exercised at all times, particularly in impoverished parts of Santo Domingo and other major cities. In towns and tourist areas there is a danger of pickpockets and snatch-and-grab theft. Be especially wary in crowded areas, such as buses and markets. Scams are common, especially in private street transactions; never take your eyes off any items you purchase. And keep your possessions in a locked suitcase in hotels, as theft by cleaning staff is common.

Never leave items unguarded on beaches. Avoid leaving luggage or valuables in cars; do not carry large quantities of cash or wear expensive-looking jewelry; avoid carrying your camera or purse loose on your shoulder; and keep passports and credit cards secure and out of sight. When using your credit card, try not to let it out of your sight, as credit card fraud in the Dominican Republic is pronounced. If anything is stolen, report it immediately to the police (expect a lengthy bureaucratic process) and/or your hotel; in the event of loss of your passport, contact your embassy immediately. And never hike alone or drive alone at night, if possible.

Tourism police—Politur, headquartered at Bloque D, Calle 30 de Marzo & Ave. México, Santo Domingo, tel 809/222-2026, politur.gob.do—patrol major tourist zones. Traffic police (*tránsitos*) patrol the highways, although they are very few in number.

Police corruption is on the wane; nonetheless, a few corrupt police still occasionally demand arbitrary bribes. Many tourists have reported receiving unjust treatment and arrest under false pretenses for refusing to pay a bribe. Few policemen outside Santo Domingo and tourist areas speak English.

Hustlers (*tígueres*) are a nuisance in tourist areas, although they usually accept a "No!." Some sell cocaine and other drugs; penalties for drug possession are harsh.

Embassies

U.S. Embassy, Ave. República de Colombia 57, Santo Domingo, tel 809/567-7775, santodomingo .usembassy.gov

Canadian Embassy, Ave. Winston Churchill 1099, Santo Domingo, tel 809/262-3100, canadainternational.gc.ca

British Embassy, Edificio Corominas Pepin, Ave. 27 de Febrero 233, Santo Domingo, tel 809/472-7111, gov.uk/government/world/organisations/british-embassy-santo-domingo

Emergency Telephone Numbers

Fire fighters (*bomberos*), police (*policía*), and public ambulance (*ambulancia*) can all be summoned by calling 911. In addition, **Movimed** (*tel 809/535-1080, movimed.com.do*) offers private ambulance service. The main Tourism Police station in Santo Domingo is at Bloque D, Calle 30 de Marzo & Ave. México, Santo Domingo, tel 809/222-2026.

What to Do in a Car Accident

In the event of an accident, do not move the vehicle or permit the other vehicle to be moved. Take down the license plate numbers and *cédulas* (legal identification) of any witnesses. Call the transit police and await their arrival; they will fill out a report that you will need for insurance purposes. If you suspect the other driver has been drinking, request that an *alcolemia* (breathalyzer test) be administered.

If someone is seriously injured or killed in the accident, contact your embassy immediately.

HEALTH

Most towns have private physicians and clinics. In Santo Domingo, many medical services are up to North American standards. The best private facility is the **Clínica Abreu** *(Ave. Independencia & Calle Burgos, tel 809/688-4411, clinicaabreu.com.do).* The **Hospital Padre Bellini** *(Ave. Sánchez bet. Calle Arzobispo Nouel & Calle Padre Bellini, tel 809/333-5656, hospitalpadrebillini.gob.do)* is among several public hospitals close to the tourist zone. **Clinic Assist** *(tel 809/541-3000, hospiten.com)* operates full-service clinics and ambulance service in Santo Domingo and Punta Cana.

Emergency care is free in hospitals. However, service and facilities are often rudimentary, and private medical service is preferable, albeit quite costly.

Government-run *centros de salud* (health centers) also serve virtually every town in the country and offer treatment for nominal fees. However, public health facilities are usually basic and visitors are advised to seek treatment at private facilities.

Take out full travel insurance, which should cover all medical costs, such as hospitalization, nursing services, and doctor fees. A medical evacuation clause is also important in case sufficient care is not available and you need to return home. Be sure to notify your carrier as soon as possible.

If you require medical help, consult your hotel. Most keep a list of doctors and medical centers, which can save time. Otherwise, consult the Yellow Pages of the telephone book. Keep any receipts or paperwork for insurance claims. Make a note of the generic name of any prescription medications you take before you leave home. They may be sold by a different trade name in the Dominican Republic. Most towns have well-stocked pharmacies, but check that the medicine is not a cheap, generic version and/or out of date.

The Dominican Republic's main health hazards—other than traffic accidents—relate to its tropical climate, where bacteria and germs breed profusely. Wash all cuts and scrapes with warm water and rubbing alcohol. Tap water should be avoided, including when brushing your teeth. Use bottled water. Always boil water when camping, and avoid ice unless it has been made from bottled water (most tourist resorts make ice from purified water). Take a pass, as well, on uncooked vegetables and seafood (except ceviche, which is normally safe), and fruits you don't peel yourself.

Be liberal with the application of sunscreen and drink plenty of water to guard against dehydration.

Biting insects abound, particularly in the humid lowlands. Malaria is present in lowland areas, and is a problem mainly on the Caribbean coast. Consult your doctor for a suitable malaria prophylaxis. Dengue fever is also spread by mosquitoes and occasional outbreaks are reported in the westerly lowland regions close to Haiti; there is no preventative medication, so it is wise to try to avoid being bitten. Use insect repellents liberally, and wear light-colored clothing with long sleeves and full-length pants, good for also guarding against chiggers *(coloradillas).* **Chitras** (tiny sand flies) are present on and near beaches and are most active around dawn and dusk.

The Dominican Republic has no venomous snakes. However, it does have scorpions and tarantulas. The tarantulas, found mostly in rural areas, rarely bite, but scorpions are more dangerous. Don't put your hand in crevices, and shake out shoes and clothing in the morning.

Stingrays abound in the shallows on both Atlantic and Caribbean shores. Shuffle your feet when wading to ward them off.

Riptides are a danger along much of the coast, particularly where high surf comes ashore (see sidebar p. 117).

And last but not least: Avoid sitting under coconut trees; falling coconuts can kill!

FURTHER READING

The Dominican Republic Reader: History, Culture, Politics (2014) by Erica Paul Rooda & Lauren H. Derby. Essential background on society.

The Feast of the Goat (2001) by Mario Vargas Llosa. Profound novel set in the months surrounding Trujillo's 1961 assassination.

How the Garcia Girls Lost Their Accents (1991) by Julia Álvarez. A deeply affecting novel profiling a Dominican family's struggles to adapt to a contemporary, U.S.-dominated world.

Reflections on the Spanish Isle: Glories of the Dominican Republic (2007) by Joseph L. Borkson. Coffee-table book about the island's history and architecture.

Trujillo: The Death of the Dictator (1998) by Bernard Diederich. The story of Trujillo's assassination and legacy.

Hotels & Restaurants

The Dominican Republic has more accommodations by far than any other Caribbean destination. Hotels are diverse and reasonably priced, although standards vary widely. The country offers excellent value for money, notably in all-inclusive resorts and especially in conjunction with air/land packages.

PRICES

HOTELS

An indication of the cost of a double room in the high season is given by **$** signs.

$$$$$	Over $200
$$$$	$100–$200
$$$	$50–$100
$$	$25–$50
$	Under $25

RESTAURANTS

An indication of the cost of a three-course meal without drinks is given by **$** signs.

$$$$$	Over $35
$$$$	$20–$35
$$$	$10–$20
$$	$5–$10
$	Under $5

HOTELS

There is a wide range of facilities available for visitors. Large areas of the country are remote and/or receive very few tourists, and accommodations are limited; more desirable rooms can fill quickly during busy months and especially during festivals such as Carnaval.

The Dominican Republic is blessed with some top-of-the-line hotels. These range from small, family-run hotels that combine intimacy and charm to high-rise international chain hotels, usually with business facilities. Several have casinos. Almost 95 percent of the country's hotels, however, are all-inclusive beach resorts, where the trend is toward deluxe boutique hotels. At all-inclusives, you normally get what you pay for. Less expensive resorts often serve monotonous buffets and lesser quality brands of beer and rum. More expensive resorts usually offer a choice of restaurants, including gourmet options, as well as luxurious accommodations. Some of the major chains are:

Barceló, tel 800/227-2356, barcelo.com
Iberostar, tel 888/923-2722, iberostar.com
Marriott Hotels & Resorts, tel 888/236-2427, marriott.com
Radisson, tel 800/967-9033, radisson.com
Sol Meliá, 888/956-3542, solmelia.com
Viva Wyndham, tel 877/999-3223, vivaresorts.com.

Reservations are essential for Christmas, New Year's, and Easter. The same holds for Carnaval in Santiago, La Vega, and Monte Cristi, when accommodations can be impossible to find. And hotels around Cabarete tend to fill up in midsummer when windsurfing and kiteboarding conditions are ideal.

Santo Domingo has some of the best accommodations in the country, ranging from inexpensive guesthouses to boutique hotels in restored colonial mansions to ritzy high-rises. The all-inclusive resort is king around Punta Cana, La Costa del Coco, and Playa Dorado near Puerto Plata. In the Cordillera Central, options are generally limited to simple country inns. However, certain areas of the country, such as the southwest, have relatively few hotels, and those often no better than mediocre. In these budget hotels sink plugs may be missing, showers are often cold, and mattresses are thin. Warm (tepid) water may be provided by an electric element above the shower. Insure windows and doors are secure.

The Dominican Republic has no true wilderness lodges, although several hotels in the mountains specialize in adventure activities. Some hotels around Cabarete and Sosúa serve surfers and kiteboarders and range from simple to ritzy. Camping is available in most national parks, but should be avoided on beaches.

You can also rent vacation and long-term properties—everything from beachfront bungalows to Spanish haciendas. Avoid *cabañas turísticas,* usually rented by the hour for sexual trysts.

Hotel rates generally are about 15 percent higher in high season (Nov.–April). In mid-range and budget hotels, ask to see several rooms, as the same price often applies to rooms of vastly different sizes and standards. Beachfront hotels are usually more expensive than those away from the beach, and oceanview rooms cost more than non-oceanview rooms.

Unless otherwise stated, all hotels listed here have dining rooms and private bathrooms and are open year-round.

A 16 percent sales tax and 10 percent service charge are added to all hotel bills.

RESTAURANTS

Eating out can be a great pleasure in Santo Domingo, which offers a wide variety of restaurants, including many world-class options. Some of the most cosmopolitan restaurants are associated with upscale hotels, especially those of La Costa del Coco and near Cabarete. Elsewhere, menus are typically restricted to traditional fare and seafood.

Seafood is the staple along the coasts, while chicken and goat (and to a lesser degree, pork) form the elements of traditional Dominican food. Opening hours vary widely; in Santo Domingo, restaurants typically open noon to 11 p.m. or midnight. Many restaurants close on Mondays. Make reservations for the more expensive restaurants, particularly on weekends. In Santo Domingo and major resorts, service is usually fast, but elsewhere it is often slow. It is considered rude to deliver the bill until the patron asks for it.

Local fare can be enjoyed for less than US$5. *Comedores,* local mom-and-pop restaurants, are found everywhere and offer simple (and usually delicious) dishes that include a cheap lunchtime *plata del día,* or daily dish—usually featuring rice and beans, *mangú* (see p. 20), and a meat. Streetside snack stands prepare cooked dishes on demand and are popular venues for simple empanadas and *chicharrones.*

A 16 percent tax is added to restaurant bills, and a 10 percent service charge is normal.

A selection of the best quality restaurants for each region is given below.

Credit Cards

Giving a card number is often the only way to reserve rooms in upscale hotels. Some hotels add a fee of up to 15 percent for credit-card payments. Most hotels and quality restaurants accept credit-card payments, but many budget properties do not.

Making Reservations

Please check details before booking restaurants or hotels. This applies particularly to the availability of facilities for disabled guests or nonsmoking rooms, acceptance of credit cards, and rates. Do not rely on the mail; fax or email your hotel reservation, and take your printed confirmation with you.

If a Dominican tour operator informs you that the hotel of your choice is full, check directly with the hotel; even the most reputable tour operators have been known to steer clients toward hotels that pay preferential commissions.

Organization

Hotels and restaurants have been grouped according to region, then listed alphabetically by price category. Hotel restaurants have been highlighted only if they are open to the public.

B=breakfast L=lunch D=dinner

Credit & Debit Cards

Abbreviations used are: AE (American Express), DC (Diners Club), MC (MasterCard), V (Visa)

■ SANTO DOMINGO

HOTELS

SOMETHING SPECIAL

🏨 **BILLINI HOTEL**

🍴 **$$$$**

PADRE BILLINI 256,

TEL 809/338-4040

billinihotel.com

A lovely boutique hotel that perfectly reflects colonial charm, this superb newcomer epitomizes how a tasteful avant-garde conversion can metamorphose a historic mansion into something sublime. Chicly furnished rooms enlivened by contemporary art boast modern perks, such as luxe toiletries, large-screen smart TVs, and Arne Jacobsen chairs. The elegant **Castil Restaurant,** surrounded by centuries-old columns, delivers gourmet fusion fare, and a rooftop terrace serves tapas.

🛈 24 🅒 🌊 🍴
🅒 All major cards

SOMETHING SPECIAL

🏨 **HOSTAL NICOLÁS DE**
🍴 **OVANDO**

$$$$$

CALLE LAS DAMAS

TEL 809/685-9955

accorhotels.com

A beautiful conversion of the early-16th-century governor's mansion, this class act combines historic ambience and contemporary style. The sumptuously appointed guest rooms come with complete amenities, plus 24-hour room service. Supported by weathered limestone columns, **La Résidence** restaurant, specializing in Mediterranean dishes, offers a romantic gourmet experience as a prelude to postprandial pleasures in the Cibao cigar lounge. The chef's fixed-price daily three-course menu is a relative bargain.

🛈 97 🅿 🅒 🅒
🅒 AE, MC, V

🏨 **RENAISSANCE**
JARAGUA HOTEL &
CASINO

$$$$$

AVE. GEORGE WASHINGTON 367

TEL 809/221-2222

renaissance-hotels.marriott
.com

A superb location on the Malecón within walking distance of the Zona Colonial, plus gracious appointments that include rooms with luxe linens, combine to make this one of the city's best large-scale hotels. Reopened in 2015 after a lengthy restoration, the all-new and

---

🅢 Nonsmoking 🅒 Air-conditioning 🌊 Indoor pool 🌊 Outdoor pool 🍴 Health club 🛈 Wi-Fi 🅒 Credit cards

ultra-contemporary hotel has a huge casino with a show-room, tennis courts, plentiful meeting space, and an inviting pool and sundeck.

🛏 300 🅿 🛗 🌐 🛗 🏊 🍽
💳 All major cards

SOMETHING SPECIAL

🏨 EMBASSY SUITES BY HILTON SANTO DOMINGO
$$$$

AVE. GEORGE WASHINGTON 500
TEL 809/685-0000
embassysuites3.hilton.com
This 21-story hotel overlooking the Malecón features five executive levels. The guest rooms are among the most stylish in Santo Domingo, with fresh contemporary furnishings and fabulous ocean views through walls of glass. The hotel has the largest casino in Santo Domingo and a full complement of amenities.

🛏 228 🅿 🛗 🌐 🛗 🏊 🍽
💳 All major cards

🏨 HOTEL FRANCES
🍽 $$$$

CALLE DE LAS MERCEDES
TEL 809/685-9331
accorhotels.com
This historic hotel is superbly situated in the heart of the Zona Colonial. A sister property to the more deluxe Hostal Nicolás de Ovando, it offers spacious guest rooms with a contemporary take on an Edwardian theme. Le Patio courtyard restaurant and gracious bar are pluses, and the hotel has Wi-Fi.

🛏 19 🅿 🛗 🌐 🛗 📶
💳 AE, MC, V

🏨 HOTEL OCCIDENTAL EL EMBAJADOR
$$$$

AVE. SARASOTA 65
TEL 809/221-2131
occidentalhotels.com

Set amid palm-shaded gardens on the west end of town, this modern hotel is best suited to business travelers and has all the required amenities. The 50-year-old property was recently updated in a classic Edwardian vogue, and while not as luxurious as competing hotels in this price range, is perfectly adequate.

🛏 286 🅿 🛗 🌐 🛗 🏊 🍽
💳 AE, MC, V

🏨 SHERATON SANTO DOMINGO
$$$$

AVE. GEORGE WASHINGTON 365
TEL 809/221-6666
sheratonsantodomingo.com
This classy deluxe high-rise hotel (formerly the Meliá Santo Domingo) on the shoreline drive draws patrons to its glittering casino. It has graciously appointed rooms and full amenities, including a sophisticated lobby bar and restaurant.

🛏 245 🅿 🛗 🌐 🛗 🏊 🍽
💳 All major cards

🏨 HODELPA CARIBE COLONIAL
$$$

ISABEL LA CATÓLICA 159
TEL 809/688-7799
hodelpa.com
This hotel has a handy, albeit noisy, location 55 yards (50 m) from Parque Colón. The lively cramped lobby in this faded art deco hotel is loaded with cosmetic touches. The small rooms are adequate and enhanced by draped beds, but will not suit claustrophobics; a suite is worth the splurge. It has a small restaurant and limited and awkward parking. Excellent service.

🛏 54 🅿 🌐 🛗 💳 AE, MC, V

🏨 HOTEL CONDE DE
🍽 PEÑALBA
$$$

CALLE EL CONDE & CALLE

ARZOBISPO MERIÑO
TEL 809/688-7121
condepenalba.com
Offering an unbeatable location on Parque Colón, this intimate three-story Mediterranean-style hotel is graced by wrought-iron balconies with bougainvillea. The recently refurbished rooms in four styles are stylish and comfortable; south-facing rooms have park views. The popular sidewalk restaurant is a great place for perusing the street life.

🛏 20 🅿 🌐 💳 AE, MC, V

🏨 HOTEL DOÑA ELVIRA
$$$

CALLE PADRE BILLINI 207
TEL 809/221-7415
dona-elvira.com
Renovated colonial home exuding historic charm with modestly furnished rooms, all with cable TV and Wi-Fi. Some have king beds. The patio garden in this intimate bed-and-breakfast, run by a bohemian Belgian-American couple,

includes a modern annex in traditional style.

🚹 12 ❄️ ❄️ 🏊 📶
❄️ All major cards

🏨 **BOUTIQUE HOTEL PALACIO**
$$
CALLE DUARTE 106
TEL 809/682-4730
hotel-palacio.com
Recently reincarnated as a hotel, the former home of 19th-century dictator-president Buenaventura Báez is a pleasing option. Spacious rooms around an atrium courtyard offer understated decor and contemporary bathrooms.

🚹 40 🏊 ❄️ MC, V

🏨 **HOTEL ATARAZANA**
$$
CALLE VICENTE CELESTINO DUARTE 19
TEL 809/688-3693
hotel-atarazana.com
This splendid Swiss-run budget option occupies a lovingly remodeled colonial structure graced by stylish decor. Blazing tropical colors add to the uplifting mood. Breakfast patio with kitchen for guests.

🚹 6 ❄️ ❄️ MC, V

🏨 **HOTEL DUQUE DE WELLINGTON**
$$
AVE. INDEPENDENCIA 304
TEL 809/682-4525
hotelduque.com
Secure, well-run, value-priced hotel in the relatively tranquil Gazcue district, within walking distance of Zona Colonial. Pleasant furnishings and modern bathrooms. It has a nice restaurant, travel agency, and pool set in a leafy courtyard.

🚹 29 🅿️ ❄️ ❄️ All major cards

🏨 **HOTEL PORTES 9**
$$
CALLE ARZOBISPO PORTES 7
TEL 849/943-2039
portes9.com
A tiny gem hidden in the southeast corner of the colonial city, this intimate family-run option is perfect for travelers who eschew large hotels. Guest rooms exude stylish sophistication, each on a theme. Designer toiletries, fine linens, and high-speed Wi-Fi are pluses.

🚹 4 ❄️ 📶 Free ❄️ MC, V

RESTAURANTS

SOMETHING SPECIAL

🍴 **VESUVIO DEL MALECÓN**
$$$$$
AVE. GEORGE WASHINGTON 521
TEL 809/221-1954
vesuvio.com.do
A longtime favorite of local cognoscenti, this Italian restaurant specializes in seafood and pasta. Classy ambience and top-notch service are hallmarks, as is the risotto with shrimp and squid, the lobster thermidor, and the to-die-for desserts. Choose outdoor patio dining with fairy lights twining the palms, or three separate air-conditioned indoor rooms.

🪑 350 ❄️ ❄️
❄️ All major cards

SOMETHING SPECIAL

🍴 **EL MESÓN DE LA CAVA**
$$$$
AVE. MIRADOR DEL SUR 1
PARQUE MIRADOR DEL SUR
TEL 809/533-2818
elmesondelacava.com
A magnificent romantic atmosphere is found at this predominantly surf-and-turf restaurant occupying a cave with dripstone formations and tables in various chambers and tunnels. International menu with favorites such as Black Angus steaks, stuffed chicken

roulade, and grilled lobster. While tourists go for the ambience, locals flock for some of the capital's most flavorful and rewarding dining. Start with the gazpacho, and leave room for the Crema Catalana dessert. Reservations are required. Take a sweater, because the cave is always cool.

🪑 120 🅿️ 🕐 Closed B
❄️ ❄️ All major cards

🍴 **MITRE RESTAURANTE & WINE BAR**
$$$$
AVE. ABRAHAM LINCOLN 1001
TEL 809/472-1787
mitre.com.do
Supersophisticated, this top-class lounge restaurant serves baby-back ribs, braised sea bass, *gambas tonatto*, and international fusion fare. A deck with table umbrellas takes the overflow. Valet parking available.

🪑 80 🅿️ 🕐 Closed B
❄️ ❄️ All major cards

🍴 **SAMURAI**
$$$$
CALLE SEMINARIO 57
TEL 809/565-1621
samurairestaurante.com
The city's finest Japanese restaurant satisfies sushi fans. The menu also includes tempura and hibachi entrées plus an excellent Sunday brunch popular with both locals and expatriates.

🪑 40 🕐 Closed B 🅿️
❄️ ❄️ ❄️ All major cards

SOMETHING SPECIAL

🍴 **EL CONUCO**
$$$
CALLE CASIMIRO DE MOYA 152, GAZCUE
TEL 809/686-0129
elconuco.com.do
One of the best city restaurants serving Dominican fare, this thatched restaurant is furnished in country fashion. The prix-fixe buffet is a bargain and

includes various steaks. *La bandera* (beef simmered with rice, kidney beans, and fried plantains) is a consistent winner. Waiters in costume. A folkloric troupe performs.

60 DC, MC, V

SOMETHING SPECIAL

MESÓN DE BARÍ
$$$

CALLE HOSTOS 302
TEL 809/687-4091
A lively, unpretentious bohemian bar with walls festooned with contemporary art, this atmospheric restaurant is always jam-packed with an eclectic crowd, from artists to the monied business elite. The traditional *criolla* cuisine features such dishes as chicken breast with onion, garlic, and peppers, and *cangrejo guisado* (fresh crab stewed in savory brown sauce). Stick to the house specials. Live jazz is often played.

60 Closed B All major cards

PAT'E PALO
$$$

CALLE LA ATARAZANA 25
TEL 809/687-8089
patepalo.com
Splendid outdoor ambience with views across the floodlit Plaza de España. Waiters in pirate costume. Try the Angus beef carpaccio starter and yucca gnocchi with sweet peppers in cumin sauce.

80 Closed B MC, V

SEGAFREDO ESPRESSO CAFÉ
$$

AVE. LOPES DE VEGA, EDIF. NOVO-CENTRO
TEL 809/683-1313
Newly relocated from Zona Colonial, this hip bar-café-restaurant retains its chic industrial styling but now

offers an exciting fusion menu of fresh seafood dishes, plus such staples as burgers, lasagna, and pizza. Clients rave about the hearty cocktails and specialty coffees. A DJ spins world-beat tunes, and live bands sometimes perform.

50 Closed B & Sun. MC, V

▇ THE SOUTHEAST

BÁVARO

🏨 GRAND PALLADIUM PALACE RESORT SPA & CASINO
$$$$$

PLAYA BÁVARO
TEL 809/221-0719 OR 888/237-1226
palladiumhotelgroup.com
A gracious, neocolonial-style all-inclusive resort set on the beach. Palatial rooms, suites, and villas have columned Jacuzzi tubs open to the guest rooms. Eleven restaurants; four swimming pools; a kids' club; tennis, basketball, and badminton courts; and casino.

364 P ⬆ 🔆 🔆 🏊 🔻 AE, MC, V

🏨 MELIÁ CARIBE TROPICAL
$$$$$

PLAYA BÁVARO
TEL 809/221-1290
melia.com
Supremely elegant all-inclusive all-suite resort. Gracious rooms blend contemporary and Edwardian styles. Facilities include 13 restaurants, a gorgeous swimming pool, two full-service spas, kids' club, and 14,000 square feet (1,300 sq m) of meeting space.

1,312 P ⬆ 🔆 🔆 🏊 🔻 All major cards

PRICES

HOTELS
An indication of the cost of a double room in the high season is given by $ signs.

$$$$$	Over $200
$$$$	$100–$200
$$$	$50–$100
$$	$25–$50
$	Under $25

RESTAURANTS
An indication of the cost of a three-course meal without drinks is given by $ signs.

$$$$$	Over $35
$$$$	$20–$35
$$$	$10–$20
$$	$5–$10
$	Under $5

🏨 THE GOLF SUITES
🍽 $$$$

AVE. REAL, BÁVARO
TEL 809/552-8888
thegolfsuites.com
Within the Cocotal Golf & Country Club (see p. 227), the hotel offers gracious one-, two-, and three-bedroom suites and apartments clad in coralstone and with private Jacuzzis, plus the superb *Ristorante Bacco* (see opposite; room delivery only), and a mini grocery for self-catering. Rush Personal Training Studio has Zumba classes, and the MakinGastronomy Studio offers cooking courses.

58 P ⬆ 🔆 🔆 🏊 🔻 AE, MC, V

🏨 IBEROSTAR BÁVARO
$$$$

PLAYA ARENA GORDA
TEL 809/221-6500
iberostar.com
A cavernous open-walled lobby sets the tone for this classy all-inclusive, low-rise

🏨 Hotel ⓘ No. of guest rooms 🍽 Restaurant ⬚ No. of Seats 🕐 Open/Closed Hours P Parking ⬆ Elevator

resort with elegant and spacious junior suites. An inviting walk-in pool plus complete amenities add to the appeal.

🛈 598 🅿 ⬆ 🌀 🌀 🏊 🏋
🆑 All major cards

🏨 NH REAL ARENA
$$$$

PLAYA ARENA GORDA

TEL 809/221-4646

nh-real-arena.hotels-punta-cana.net

Opened in 2008, this deluxe all-inclusive looked distinctly hip when it opened, but has been outclassed since. However, the tile-floored rooms feature lively tropical color schemes and are comfortable, if understated. It hosts cabarets and has a casino and a shopping plaza.

🛈 640 🅿 🌀 🌀 🌀 🏊
🏋 🆑 All major cards

🏨 OCEAN BLUE & SAND
$$$$

PLAYA ARENA GORDA

TEL 809/476-2326

oceanhotels.net

This elegant, family-focused all-inclusive resort adjoins the White Sands Golf Course. Decor, in white and Wedgewood blue, with cool coralstone floors underfoot, plays up Edwardian styling. A vast pool complex and a complete range of amenities are available. Activities offered range from archery and bowling to sailing and scuba diving. Exquisite suites.

🛈 708 🅿 ⬆ 🌀 🌀 🏊
🏋 🎧 Free 🆑 MC, V

🏨 BARCELÓ BÁVARO RESORT
$$$–$$$$

PLAYA EL CORTECITO

TEL 809/686-5797 OR

800/277-2356

barcelo.com

Megaresort spread along 3 miles (5 km) of beachfront,

with 2,300 rooms in five adjoining hotels, from the three-star Barceló Bávaro Caribe Beach to the upscale Barceló Palace. The Barceló Casino and Barceló Golf hotels are inland of the beach. It has 14 restaurants and 16 bars, a casino, plus plenty of water sports. A shuttle connects the hotels.

🛈 2,300 🅿 ⬆ 🌀 🌀 🏊
🏋 🆑 AE, MC, V

🍴 BALICANA
$$$

LA PISCINA DE LOS CORALES, BÁVARO

TEL 829/455-7432

balicana.com

A gorgeous poolside setting at this romantic thatched hotel restaurant is almost as tantalizing as its pan-Asian menu. Try the chicken satay in peanut sauce, or the Malaysian coconut curry, or Thai pineapple fried rice. Large portions..

🍽 60 🅿 🆑 MC, V

SOMETHING SPECIAL

🍴 JELLYFISH
$$$

PLAYA BÁVARO

TEL 809/840-7684

jellyfishrestaurant.com

A long-term favorite of jet-setters with its curving coralstone walls and stylish shade canopies, this atmospheric beachfront restaurant, open to the breezes, serves Italian/Mediterranean fare, such as Greek salads and *langostina* in brandy. Try the delicious sea bass filet and shrimp with passion fruit and ginger sauce, or the steam-cooked lobster with tail with herb butter sauce. It has a cigar lounge, plus an airy mezzanine alfresco lounge with deep-cushion sofas. Free hotel transfers.

🍽 100 🅿 🕐 Closed B
🆑 Most credit cards

SOMETHING SPECIAL

🍴 RISTORANTE BACCO
$$$

AVE. REAL, BÁVARO

TEL 809/330-5353

thegolfsuites.com

This Italian restaurant, at The Golf Suites, serves a predictable menu of well-executed dishes, from pork scaloppine to lasagna and spinach ravioli—all for delivery to your hotel or apartment.

🍽 60 🕐 Closed B, L
🆑 All major cards

🍴 CAPITÁN COOK
$$

PLAYA EL CORTECITO

TEL 809/552-0645

This thatched seafood restaurant sits over the sands. Favorite dishes include charbroiled fresh fish and lobster thermidor, but hungry patrons opt for the all-you-can-eat *parrillada mixta* platter. Complimentary appetizers.

🍽 60 🅿 🕐 Closed B
🆑 MC, V

BAYAHIBE

🏨 IBEROSTAR HACIENDA DOMINICUS
$$$$$

PLAYA DOMINICUS,

3 MILES (5 KM) S OF BAYAHIBE

TEL 809/688-3600 OR

888/923-2722

iberostar.com

A gracious Spanish-villa-themed, all-inclusive resort with eccentric yet exquisite decor (antique Cuban armoires, plump sofas, and oversize chandeliers). Top-quality restaurants, three pools, plus scuba diving.

🛈 504 🅿 ⬆ 🌀 🌀 🏊
🏋 🆑 All major cards

🏨 **VIVA WYNDHAM DOMINICUS PALACE/ BEACH**
$$$$
PLAYA DOMINICUS
TEL 809/686-5658 OR
800/996-3426
wyndham.com
A two-wing hotel with lively entertainment for the party crowd, especially in the beach wing. Bargain-priced, with excellent food. Full amenities, including eight restaurants, full-service spa, kids' club, nightclub, tennis, a climbing wall, and complete water sports.
🛈 613 🅿 🔁 🚫 🎿 ☠ 🍸
🃏 All major cards

🍴 **BAMBOO BEACH**
$
PLAYA BAYAHIBE
TEL 829/410-1326
Charming thatched, open-air French-run restaurant overlooking the fishermen's beach. Menu ranges from crêpes to spaghetti and curry chicken, but we recommend the grilled lobster or calamari.
🪑 30 🅿 🕐 Closed Wed.
🃏 No credit cards

BOCA CHICA

🏨 **HOTEL BE LIVE HAMACA BEACH**
$$$$
CALLE DUARTE 26
TEL 809/523-4611
www.belivehamaca.com
Six-story, all-inclusive hotel stair-stepping up from a private beach. Large free-form pool. Tasteful classical decor and subdued color schemes. A spa, mini-golf, tennis, and plentiful activities, including a casino and a kids' club.
🛈 670 🅿 🔁 🚫 🎿 ☠ 🍸
🃏 All major cards

🏨 **DON JUAN BEACH RESORT**
$$$
AVE. ABRAHAM NUÑEZ 8
TEL 809/687-9157
donjuanbeachresort.com
The modestly appointed yet spacious accommodations and lively entertainment offered at this mid-range all-inclusive resort appeal to a domestic clientele. Several water sports take place on the gorgeous beach. It has an adults-only section.
🛈 224 🅿 🔁 🚫 🎿 ☠
🃏 MC, V

🏨 **REFUGIO NEPTUNO'S**
$$
CALLE DUARTE 17
TEL 809/523-9934
EMAIL **neptunosrefugio@ hotmail.com**
Five-story hotel with spacious, modestly appointed rooms and apartments in a quiet section of Boca Chica. Firm mattresses, but flimsy door locks; beware of your valuables. Small plunge pool.
🛈 6 rooms & 10 apartments
🅿 🚫 ☠ 🃏 MC, V

SOMETHING SPECIAL

🍴 **RESTAURANT BOCA MARINA**
$$$$
CALLE DUARTE 12-A
TEL 809/688-6810
bocamarina.com.do
A class act, this hip, upscale restaurant overhangs the waters at the west end of town. Its travertine floor, soaring palenque roof, glossy hardwood furnishings, and candlelit tables create a sophisticated mood, while the turquoise ocean is floodlit from below The broad seafood menu includes salads, spaghetti, Thai shrimp, and lobster with garlic and white wine.
🪑 300 🅿 🚫
🃏 All major cards

PRICES

HOTELS
An indication of the cost of a double room in the high season is given by **$** signs.

$$$$$	Over $200
$$$$	$100–$200
$$$	$50–$100
$$	$25–$50
$	Under $25

RESTAURANTS
An indication of the cost of a three-course meal without drinks is given by **$** signs.

$$$$$	Over $35
$$$$	$20–$35
$$$	$10–$20
$$	$5–$10
$	Under $5

🍴 **NEPTUNO'S CLUB**
$$$
CALLE DUARTE 12
TEL 809/523-4703
Jutting over the water, this flavorful seafood restaurant replicates the interior of a galleon with waiters in pirate costume. Lobster ravioli and the seafood plate are recommended.
🪑 120 🅿 🚫 🃏 AE, MC, V

BOCA DE YUMA

🏨 **HOTEL RESTAURANTE EL VIEJO PIRATA**
$$
0.5 MILE
(1 KM) W OF BOCA DE YUMA
TEL 809/471-1706
Crenellated, canary-yellow cliff-top hotel with ocean views. Smallish rooms are nicely decorated with rattan and have ceiling fans and sofa beds. Patio restaurant is shaded beneath an arbor.
🛈 10 🚫 ☠
🃏 No credit cards

JUAN DOLIO

🏨 COSTA CARIBE CORAL
$$$
BLVD. JUAN DOLIO
TEL 809/562-6725
coralhotels.com
Pleasant family-focused, all-inclusive resort splashed with lively tropical pastels. Complete water sports, mini-golf, plus three pools, live entertainment and spacious rooms in seven-story units.

ⓘ 400 🅿 ⬦ ⓢ ⓢ ⛵ 🏋
ⓢ MC, V

LA ROMANA

SOMETHING SPECIAL

🏨 CASA DE CAMPO
$$$$$
1 MILE (1.6 KM) E OF LA ROMANA
TEL 809/523-3333 OR
855/877-3643
casadecampo.com.do
Favored by international celebrities, this massive and exclusive deluxe resort exudes sophistication and flair. Sprawling villas and suites exquisitely furnished to designer Oscar de la Renta's sensibilities combine with pampering service and upscale activities that include polo, a shooting complex, horseback riding, and boating at the chic Marina & Yacht Club. The world-famous Teeth of the Dog Golf Course is one of three Pete Dye–designed courses in this country-club-style playground. All guests get their own golf cart. A choice of exceptional restaurants.

ⓘ 350 rooms & 150 villas
🅿 ⓢ ⓢ ⛵ 🏋
ⓢ All major cards

SOMETHING SPECIAL

🍴 LA PIAZZETTA
$$$$
ALTOS DE CHAVÓN
TEL 809/523-3333 EXT. 5339

Classic Italian menu and ambience in this re-creation of a Tuscan restaurant, with rustic country decor. Chef Manuel Sánchez does a superb job with such recommended dishes as *caprese* salad with mozzarella, linguini with pesto sauce, a divine risotto with porcini mushrooms, and profiteroles and chocolate tarts with ice cream. Huge wine list. Top-notch service from staff in crisp formal wear.

🍴 140 🅿 🕐 Closed B & L, Sat. & Sun. ⓢ ⓢ
ⓢ All major cards

🍴 RESTAURANTE LUCAS
$$
CALLE LOS ROBLES 9, BUENA VISTA NORTE
TEL 809/550-3401
An unpretentious family-run Italian restaurant beloved of locals. The menu features delicious calamari and other seafood, plus pizza and gnocchi, raviolis, etc. using home-made pastas. Indoor and outdoor dining. Occasional live music.

🍴 40 🅿 🕐 Closed B
ⓢ ⓢ MC, V

MACAO

SOMETHING SPECIAL

🏨 HARD ROCK HOTEL & CASINO
$$$$$
BLVD. TURÍSTICO DEL ESTE KM 28
TEL 809/731-0015
hardrockhotelpuntacana.com
Opened in January 2010, this sumptuous hotel is the largest luxury all-inclusive resort in the Dominican Republic. Grounds feature Venetian-style canals behind 2,400 feet (750 m) of beach, plus 13 pools and a lazy river. Renovated in 2011, when it became the Hard Rock Hotel & Casino, guest rooms cause a "Wow!" response for their

sensational chic styling. Nine restaurants, 23 bars, a mega-spa, the country's largest casino, plus access to the Jack Nicklaus–designed Cana Bay Golf Club.

ⓘ 1,791 🅿 ⬦ ⓢ ⛵ 🏋
ⓢ All major cards

SOMETHING SPECIAL

🍴 SIMON MANSION & SUPPER CLUB
$$$$$
BLVD. TURÍSTICO DEL ESTE KM 28
TEL 809/754-0094
simonmansion.com
Don your best clothes to dine at this suave restaurant with outrageously avant-garde décor, in the Hard Rock Hotel & Casino. Chef Kerry Simon oversees a bold, haute cuisine menu that includes sushi and sashimi, plus such divine treats as spicy corn cream soup; shrimp chicharron in black beer marinade; and marinated Chilean sea bass with fennel beurre blanc with cauliflower and roast garlic puree.

🍴 80 🅿 🕐 Closed B & L
ⓢ ⓢ All major cards

MICHES

🏨 COCO LOCO BEACH
🍴 CLUB
$$
PLAYA MICHES
TEL 809/886-8276 OR
809/974-8182
abatrex.com/cocoloco
Simply appointed beach cabins amid lawns; cold water only. A thatched restaurant of stone and timber serves excellent breakfasts and seafood meals and has an upstairs lounge.

ⓘ 10 🅿 ⓢ ⓢ No credit cards

🏨 HOTEL LA LOMA
$$
800 YARDS (0.7 KM) S OF MICHES
TEL 809/553-5562
michesnow.com

Due to its superb hilltop position, this Swiss-owned hotel has staggering views. Simple decor, but an airy ambience. Ceiling fans. Hard to find!

🛏 8 rooms ⅋ 1 suite 🅿 🔲
🌊 🔲 No credit cards

PLAYA LIMÓN

🏨 **HOTEL RANCHO LA CUEVA**
$$
PLAYA LIMÓN
TEL 809/519-5271
rancholacueva.com
No-frills three-story hotel 400 yards (0.4 km) inland of the beach. Large rooms are simply furnished. The seafood restaurant specializes in lobster and roast suckling pig and caters primarily to tour groups. Offers horseback rides and excursions to Laguna Limón.

🛏 8 🅿 🔲 🔲 MC, V

PUNTA CANA

SOMETHING SPECIAL

🏨 **PUNTACANA RESORT**
🍴 **⅋ CLUB**
$$$$$
2 MILES (3 KM) S OF THE AIRPORT
TEL 809/959-2222 OR
888/442-2262
puntacana.com
The original Punta Cana resort boasts two signature oceanfront golf courses and the area's nicest restaurant. The project includes the elegant Westin Puntacana Resort ⅋ Club, on Playa Blanca, making handsome use of a surfeit of coralstone; Four Points by Sheraton Puntacana Village, near the airport; plus the superdeluxe Tortuga Bay, which offers full-service villas furnished in colonial fashion to designs by fashion designer Oscar de la Renta, who was a major shareholder. This top-of-the-line deluxe resort boasts

its own marina, stables, full-service Six Senses Spa, water sports, and even a petting zoo. Guests travel via golf cart. The nine restaurants include **La Yola,** a chic eatery serving nouvelle cuisine; and **Bamboo,** serving mouthwatering Asian fusion dishes.

🛏 400 rooms ⅋ several villas
🅿 🔲 🔲 🔲 🌊 🔲
🔲 All major cards

SABANA DE LA MAR

🏨 **PARAÍSO CAÑO HONDO**
$$
LOS HAÏTISES, 8 MILES (13 KM) W OF SABANA DE LA MAR
TEL 829/259-8549
paraisocanohondo.com
Native-themed eco-oriented hotel constructed of river stone and wood on the edge of Parque Nacional Los Haitises. River-fed waterfalls tumble through the lush grounds. Choice of standards, junior suites, or villas, all tastefully appointed and with ceiling fans. Day visitors have access; the place can be noisy.

🛏 28 🅿 🌊 🔲 MC, V

UVERO ALTO

SOMETHING SPECIAL

🏨 **SIVORY PUNTA CANA**
🍴 **$$$$$**
PLAYA UVERO ALTO
TEL 809/333-0500
sivorypuntacana.com
This sublime all-suite boutique resort hotel—a member of the Small Luxury Hotels of the World—is decorated in minimalist fashion combining Polynesian-style thatched architecture, an Asian motif, and 21st-century amenities. It enjoys a private beach setting and features a spectacular pool complex. Guest rooms have elegant bathrooms with

Jacuzzi tubs and vast walk-in showers. Butler and beach valet service are 24/7. Three gourmet restaurants serve Asian fusion, Mediterranean, and international fare; the **Gourmand Restaurant** is a member of the Chaine de Rotisseurs. Sommelier Juan Pierre presides over a huge wine cellar. Cigar lounge. One-hour drive from Punta Cana.

🛏 55 🅿 🔲 🔲 🌊 🔲
🔲 AE, MC, V

🏨 **ZOËTRY AGUA PUNTA CANA**
$$$$$
PLAYA UVERO ALTO
TEL 809/468-0000
zoetryresorts.com
This resort draws its architectural inspiration from the Taíno. Spacious, beautifully appointed suites have comfy king beds in bi-level units (upper rooms accessed by a rustic, uneven boardwalk are preferable). Full-service spa;

jeep and driver for exploring; butler service.

ⓘ 96 🅿 🚭 🅰 🏊 🔲
🅢 All major cards

▪ LA PENÍNSULA DE SAMANÁ

CAYO LEVANTADO

🏨 GRAN BAHÍA PRINCIPE CAYO LEVANTADO
$$$$
CAYO LEVANTADO
TEL 809/538-3232
bahia-principe.com
Opened in 2007, this splendid all-inclusive resort enjoys an enviable island location, with lovely beaches and ocean waters. State-of-the-art amenities include marble-clad bathrooms with Jacuzzi tubs, plus six restaurants, four bars (including cigar bar), tennis, and jogging trail.

ⓘ 268 🚭 🅰 🏊 🔲
🅢 AE, MC, V

EL LIMÓN

🏨 SANTI RANCHO
🍴 **$$**
EL LIMÓN, 8 MILES (13 KM)
E OF LAS TERRENAS
TEL (829) 342-9976
cascadalimonsamana.com
Rustic thatched restaurant on the main junction in El Limón village. Camp tables and bench seats. Sandwiches, plus filling and tasty *criollo* dishes, including fish in coconut. Spanish-Dominican couple, Santi and Suni, recently added four simple cabins, and excursions are offered.

🛏 40 🅿 🅢 No credit cards

LAS GALERAS

SOMETHING SPECIAL

🏨 VILLA SERENA
$$$$

400 YARDS (366 M) E OF PLAZA
LUSITANIA
TEL 809/538-0000
villaserena.com
A magnificent plantation-style mansion set in lush gardens atop a limestone platform that slopes to its own tiny beach. A gourmet restaurant offers garden and ocean views. Each guest room is individually themed; all have terra-cotta terraces. Most rooms have king beds, several being four-posters with drapes. A nightly three-course menu is offered in the garden restaurant. Yoga and Zumba classes.

ⓘ 21 🅿 🚭 🅰 🏊 🅢 MC, V

LAS TERRENAS

🏨 BALCONES DE ATLÁNTICO
$$$$$
PLAYA LAS TERRENAS
TEL (809) 732-6543
balconesdelatlantico.com.do
A stunning newcomer for 2010, this deluxe Rockresort offers lavish two- and three-bedroom suites in three-story units facing stunning white sands. Each villa-suite has hand-carved furnishings, plus a private veranda and plunge pool.

ⓘ 86 🅿 🚭 🅰 🏊
🅢 All major cards

SOMETHING SPECIAL

🏨 VILLA EVA LUNA
🍴 **$$$$$**
CALLE MARICA
TEL 809/978-5611
villa-evaluna.com
A three-minute stroll from the beach, this complex of five lovely, albeit pricey, villas in Mexican adobe style offers a delightful haven enhanced by color schemes in tropical pastels. Each simply appointed villa has a kitchen and interior and outside lounges, plus a

bar area, private patio, and king-size beds with quality linens and gauzy netting (but lumpy pillows). Chic **Le Table de l'Oly** restaurant offers sushi and gourmet fusion fare in an exquisite thatched setting.

ⓘ 5 🅿 🚭 🅢 MC, V

🏨 SUBLIME SAMANA
🍴 **HOTEL & RESIDENCES**
$$$$
BAHÍA DE COSÓN
TEL 809/240-5050
sublimesamana.com
A member of the Small Luxury Hotels of the World, this well-named and romantic beachfront resort offers one-, two-, and three-bedroom suites and casitas—all gorgeously furnished in soft pastels and gleaming white decor. Twice-weekly complimentary spa. Chef Cristian Báez delivers sublime fusion cuisine in the hotel bistro restaurant.

ⓘ 26 🅿 🚭 🚭 🅰 🏊 🔲
🅢 All major cards

SOMETHING SPECIAL

🏨 ALISEI BEACHFRONT
🍴 **HOTEL, RESTAURANT & SPA**
$$$
CALLE FRANCISCO CAMAAÑO
DEÑO
TEL 809/240-5555
aliseihotelspa.com
With an attractive contemporary look and an inviting beachfront setting, this Italian-run hotel a short walk from the heart of affairs is bargain priced. Arrayed around a delightful free-form pool complex set amid lawns, guest quarters feature colorful fabrics and mahogany furniture, Wi-Fi connectivity, and balconies with poured-concrete sofas with cushions. The stylish bar and glass-walled **Baraonda** restaurant is

the trendiest spot in town to eat and imbibe.

[i] 48 apartments, 6 suites, & 1 penthouse **P 🔁 📶 🏊** **🍽 📶 ⛲** AE, MC, V

🏨 GRAN BAHÍA PRINCIPE EL PORTILLO
$$$
CARRETERA LAS TERRENAS–EL LIMÓN KM 4
TEL 809/240-6100
bahia-principe.com
This sprawling low-rise all-inclusive resort fronts onto an exquisite shore. The rooms and suites in two-story units lack ocean views. Plenty of water sports and activities are available.

[i] 606 **P 📶 📶 🏊** **⛲** AE, MC, V

🏨 HOTEL RESIDENCE PLAYA COLIBRI
$$$
CALLE FRANCISCO CAMAAÑO DEÑO, PLAYA BONITA
TEL 809/240-6434
hotelplayacolibri.com
Exquisite Caribbean-style interiors in these self-catering units with high-speed Internet access. Some have ceiling fans only. Simple thatched restaurant serves seafood and Italian fare.

[i] 45 apartments, studios, & suites **P 📶 🏊 📶 ⛲** MC, V

🍽 LA DOLCE VITA
$$$
CALLE 27 DE FEBRERO
TEL 809/989-5766
With its redbrick walls and country furnishings, this cozy oceanfront restaurant boasts an inventive Italian menu wedding Dominican ingredients, such as pasta with gorgonzola and pumpkin cream sauce. Go for the divine passion fruit and chocolate dessert. Relaxed service.

⚡ 100 **P 🕐** Closed B **⛲** MC, V

SAMANÁ

🏨 GRAN BAHÍA PRINCIPE CAYACOA
$$$$
LOMA PUERTO ESCONDIDO
TEL 809/538-3131
bahia-principe.com
Deluxe all-inclusive hotel with fantastic hilltop position offering magnificent views over Samaná and the bay. Highlights include a cliff-top pool and circular restaurant with stunning vistas. The private beach with water sports is accessed by a panoramic elevator.

[i] 295 **P 🔁 📶 📶 🏊 🍽** **⛲** AE, MC, V

SOMETHING SPECIAL

🍽 CAFÉ DE PARIS
$$$$
AVE. MALECÓN 6
TEL 829/925-8384
Overlooking the harbor, this laid-back French-run café-bar specializes in crêpes, such as chicken and mushroom. It also has panini and pizzas, best washed down with an ice-cold beer. Leave room for a crêpe with chocolate ice cream and sauce for dessert. Occasional live music.

⚡ 30 **P ⛲** MC, V

🍽 CLUB DE PLAYA CAYENAS DEL MAR
$$$
PLAYA ANADEL,
2 MILES (3 KM) E OF SAMANÁ
TEL 809/538-3114
cayenasdelmar-anadel.com
Tucked into a cove, this open-air, thatch-roofed restaurant invokes a Mediterranean mood. It overlooks a wooden deck and its own beach with lounge chairs. Secure parking available. Serves sandwiches, eggplant rolls, Mediterranean salad, grilled sea bass, and coconut shrimp. Independent travelers

---

need to purchase a day pass.
⚡ 130 **P ⛲** No credit cards

■ NORTH COAST

CABARETE

🏨 HOTEL BANNISTER
$$$$
PUERTO BAHÍA, CARRETERA SÁNCHEZ-SAMANÁ KM 5
TEL 809/503-6363
thebannisterhotel.com
Opened in 2014, this modestly sumptuous resort overlooks the Puerto Bahía marina west of Samaná. Its minimalist suites have fully equipped kitchens and west-facing bay-view verandas—perfect for sunset. Choice of four stylish restaurants.

[i] 28 **P 🔁 🏊 🍽** **⛲** Most major cards

🏨 MILLENNIUM RESORT & SPA
$$$$

CALLE PRINCIPAL

TEL 809/571-0504

cabaretemillennium.com

Inspired by Miami's South Beach, this hotel takes Cabarete upscale. Blazing whites blend with dynamic colors that highlight the ultra-modern one-, two- and three-bedroom suites. Flat-screen TVs, Wi-Fi, and iPod docks are included. Three restaurants, water sports, and spa.

ⓘ 53 suites 🅿 🔁 🅢 🌊 🛗 🛜 Free 🅢 All major cards

🏨 VIVA WYNDHAM TANGERINE
$$$$

PLAYA ENCUENTRO

TEL 809/571-0402 OR

877-999-3223

vivawyndhamresorts.com

Three restaurants, a full-service spa, an excellent kids' camp, nonstop entertainment, plus convention facilities are found at this small-scale (by Dominican Republic standards), family-focused, all-inclusive resort.

ⓘ 273 🅿 🅢 🔁 🅢 🌊 🛗 🅢 All major cards

SOMETHING SPECIAL

🏨 AGUALINA
$$$

CARRETERA PRINCIPAL, KITE BEACH

TEL 809/571-0805

agualina.com

A class operation at a fair price, this modern, small-scale hotel makes good use of coral-stone. Heaps of hot water in large walk-in showers. Meals are served in a small breeze-swept beachfront restaurant. A half-moon pool studs the lawn by the beach, and there's a kiteboarding school on-site. Free Internet. The service is courteous and efficient.

ⓘ 22 🅿 🅢 🌊 🅢 MC, V

🏨 HOTEL VILLA TAINA
$$$

PLAYA ENCUENTRO

TEL 809/571-0722

villataina.com

In the heart of Cabarete, this peaceful, contemporary, European-style *pensióne* caters to independent travelers. Eight room types, all clean and spacious. Beachfront restaurant and bar, plus windsurfing school on-site.

ⓘ 61 🅿 🔁 🅢 🅢 🌊 🅢 MC, V

🏨 VELERO BEACH RESORT
$$$

CALLE LA PUNTA 1

TEL 809/571-9727

velerobeach.com

A handsome beachfront hotel with oceanfront junior suites and suites in three-story buildings. Lively tropical decor includes rattan furnishings.

ⓘ 22 condos and 7 penthouse suites 🅿 🅢 🌊 🅢 MC, V

🏨 KITE BEACH HOTEL
$$–$$$$$

KITE BEACH

TEL 809/571-0878

kitebeachhotel.com

Pricey contemporary hotel catering primarily to kiteboarders. Handsome look to these one- and two-bedroom apartments with cable TV.

ⓘ 38 🅿 🅢 🅢 🌊 🅢 No credit cards

🏨 HOTEL MAGNIFICO CONDOMINIUMS
$$–$$$$

LA PUNTA, CARRETERA 5

TEL 809/571-0868

hotelmagnifico.com

Six separate buildings of condominiums, each uniquely themed, from art deco to contemporary units handsomely furnished with clinical white and chocolate brown

decor and blazingly colorful Caribbean art. Room configurations range from studios to penthouse suites. Lush and lovely grounds with half-moon Jacuzzi.

ⓘ 30 🅿 🅢 🌊 🅢 MC, V

🏨🍽 CABARETE SURF CAMP
$–$$$

KITE BEACH

TEL 829/548-6655

cabaretesurfcamp.com

Delightfully furnished thatched studios, bungalows, and apartments at bargain rates. All have fans and Internet connection. Popular with kiteboarders—the kiteboard camp Kite Club Cabarete is here. **Chichiguas Surf Side Grill** serves tuna burgers, teriyaki chicken burgers, and pastas of the day.

ⓘ 20 🅿 🌊 🅢 No credit cards

🍽 LAX
$$$

PLAYA ENCUENTRO

TEL 829/745--8811

laxojo.com

A bohemian vibe enlivens this German-run, log-and-bamboo beachfront bar serving pastas, pizzas, seafood, and sushi. Killer cocktails. Live music at night makes this the most popular spot on the beach. Every night is themed: Thursday is "Latin Night" and Saturday is "Crazy Outfit Party."

🍴 120 🅢 V (25 percent surcharge)

🍽 FRIENDS
$$

CALLE PRINCIPAL

TEL 809/571-9733

This colorful, French-run, open-air bar-restaurant on the main street is a great place to start the day with muesli and yogurt or bacon and egg croissant. The lunch menu ranges from burgers and pizzas to

---

🅢 Nonsmoking 🅐 Air-conditioning 🅢 Indoor pool 🌊 Outdoor pool 🛗 Health club 🛜 Wi-Fi 🅢 Credit cards

curry chicken. Great cappuccinos and smoothies.

⊞ 40 P ⊕ Closed D 📶 Free
🚫 No credit cards

CABRERA

⊞ HOTEL LA CATALINA
$$$

3 MILES (5 KM) W OF CABRERA
TEL 809/589-7700
lacatalina.com
This inviting French Canadian–run hillside hotel in lush grounds catches the breezes and offers grand coastal views. Colorful tropical furnishings are a plus. There's a tennis court and billiard room. Horseback excursions are also offered. A French chef prepares meals.

🛈 30 rooms & apartments
P 🏖 🚫 All major cards

LUPERÓN

⊞ CASA DEL SOL
$$

AVE. 27 DE FEBRERO
TEL 829/973-4215
casa-del-sol-luperon.com
Clean, comfortable albeit simply furnished rooms are the hallmark of this small German-run property, two blocks from the beach. Ceiling fans. Thatched restaurant serves American-style breakfasts and daily special dinners.

🛈 5 P ⓢ
🚫 No credit cards

PUERTO PLATA

SOMETHING SPECIAL

⊞ BLUEBAY VILLAS
🍽 DORADAS
$$$$$

PLAYA DORADA
TEL 809/320-3000
bluebayresorts.com
This stylishly hip hotel is

an architectural stunner. A gorgeous open-walled lobby furnished with rattan sofas sets the tone. White-washed guest rooms and villas feature tastefully simple decor. Gourmet cuisine is on the menu in four restaurants. One of the five bars offers live shows. Volleyball, tennis, windsurfing are among the activities. Top-notch service. No children allowed.

🛈 245 P ⓢ ⓢ 🏖 🍽
🚫 AE, MC, V

SOMETHING SPECIAL

⊞ CASA COLONIAL BEACH & SPA
$$$$$

PLAYA DORADO
TEL 809/320-3232
casacolonialhotel.com
A superb spa highlights this elegant all-suite boutique hotel, with hallways filled with a museum's worth of eclectic displays. Walls and floors of coral-stone, custom-designed Caribbean furniture, sheer cotton drapes, and a combination of historical prints and contemporary Dominican art grace guest rooms. A rooftop infinity pool has four Jacuzzis and a teak sundeck. Two superb restaurants under the care of Dominican-born chef Rafael Vásquez offer a choice of casual and elegant dining. Cigar and lounge bars guarantee postprandial pleasure. World-class gym.

🛈 50 ⓢ ⓢ 🏖 🍽
🚫 All major cards

⊞ IBEROSTAR COSTA
🍽 DORADA
$$$$$

CARRETERA LUPERÓN KM 4,
1 MILE (1.6 KM) W OF
PLAYA DORADA COMPLEX
TEL 809/320-1000

PRICES

HOTELS

An indication of the cost of a double room in the high season is given by **$** signs.

$$$$$	Over $200
$$$$	$100–$200
$$$	$50–$100
$$	$25–$50
$	Under $25

RESTAURANTS

An indication of the cost of a three-course meal without drinks is given by **$** signs.

$$$$$	Over $35
$$$$	$20–$35
$$$	$10–$20
$$	$5–$10
$	Under $5

---

iberostar.com
Dramatic primary colors highlight this neocolonial-themed all-inclusive resort. Three restaurants specialize in Brazilian, Mexican, and Caribbean fare. Adult and children's pools.

🛈 498 rooms & 18 suites
P ⓢ ⓢ ⓢ 🏖 🍽
🚫 All major cards

⊞ VICTORIA GOLF & BEACH RESORT
$$$$$

PLAYA DORADO
TEL 809/320-1200 OR
866/376-7831
vhhr.com
Exotic use of coralstone and travertine lends to the graciousness of this contemporary deluxe resort with guest rooms at ground level zigzagging along the golf course. Minimalist decor in soothing pastels.

🛈 190 P ⓢ ⓢ 🏖 🍽
🚫 AE, MC, V

🏨 LÓASE RETREAT
$$

PLAYA REAL 21, COSTÁMBAR
TEL 809/837-6845
loase.com

A lovely home away from home and a far cry from the nearby all-inclusive resorts, this delightful B&B is run by a friendly U.S.-Dominican couple, Joe and Vasthi. Simply yet colorfully furnished rooms with ceiling fans. A private villa with its own pool can be rented. It has a racquetball court and world-famous **Sam's Bar & Grill**.

🛏 9 rooms + 7-room villa
P 📶 ⊗ No credit cards

🍴 VERANDA RESTAURANT
$$$$

CASA COLONIAL,
PLAYA DORADO
TEL 809/320-3232
casacolonialhotel.com
/dining-en.html

A classy air-conditioned indoor restaurant with a wall of glass opening to a tree-shaded wooden deck overhanging the beach. The fusion menu highlights chop suey shrimp, pasta of the day, plus burgers, sandwiches, and salads.

🍴 72 P 🕐 Closed B ⊗ ⊗
⊗ AE, MC, V

🍴 RISTORANTE STEFY & NATALE
$$$

LAS ROCAS, 1 MILE (1.6 KM)
E OF OCEAN WORLD, COFRESÍ
TEL 809/970-7764
stefyenatale.com

Thatched Italian-run restaurant with rock walls, fishnets, and Italian decor. Shrimp with porcini mushrooms, penne with vodka, and pizzas typify the menu. Homemade pastas. Open for breakfast and lunch on Sunday.

🍴 45 🕐 Closed Mon., B
P ⊗ ⊗ No credit cards

🍴 LE PAPILLON BAR
$$

VILLAS COFRESI
TEL 809/970-7640
lepapillon-puertoplata.com

Within the Villas Cofresi complex, this relaxed open-air restaurant offers elegantly rustic decor. The personable German owner-chef delivers deliciously unpretentious fare, such as goulash soup, escargot tartlets, and shrimp-stuffed chicken breast, and even vegetable curry.

🍴 36 P 🕐 Closed B & L
⊗ All major cards

🍴 SAM'S BAR & GRILL
$$

LÓASE RETREAT, PLAYA REAL 21,
COSTÁMBAR
samsbardr.com

The good-old-American fare (pancake breakfasts, Philly cheese steak, Mexican scramble, meatloaf, tuna salad, apple pie) at this popular bar and grill draws the expatriate U.S. crowd, despite recently relocating from downtown to the Lóase Retreat B&B. (see above).

🍴 36 🕐 Closed Mon., Sun. D, & Tue.-Sat. B
⊗ No credit cards

RÍO SAN JUAN

🏨 GRAND BAHÍA PRINCIPE SAN JUAN
$$$$

5 MILES (8 KM) W OF RÍO SAN JUAN
TEL 809/226-1590
bahia-principe.com

This mammoth, well-run all-inclusive resort is so large that golf cart shuttles are used to ferry guests around. Colorful decor in pleasing guest rooms. The pool complex is vast and the grounds lush. Complete facilities and amenities.

🛏 608 P ⊗ ⊗ ⊗ 🏊 📶
⊗ All major cards

SOMETHING SPECIAL

🍴 CAFÉ DE PARIS
$$

LAGUNA GRI-GRI
TEL 809/778-0687

Yet another French-run restaurant, this one overlooks the lagoon and serves a simple menu ranging from ceviche to burgers, but also more sophisticated fare such as beef medallions with mustard vinaigrette. Gets lively at night.

🍴 30 P 📶 Free
⊗ No credit cards

SOSÚA

SOMETHING SPECIAL

🏨 VICTORIAN HOUSE BOUTIQUE HOTEL
$$$$$

CALLE DR. ALEJO MARTÍNEZ 1
TEL 809/571-4650
victorianhousehotel.com

A converted Victorian mansion with an elegant plantation-style motif, this deluxe hotel offers stunning vistas across the bay. Many rooms boast four-poster mahogany beds; suites have king beds and en suite Jacuzzis. Adjoins the Sosúa Bay Resort, with which it shares facilities, including a choice of six restaurants plus a wide range of activities.

🛏 50 P ⊗ ⊗ 🏊 📶
⊗ All major cards

🏨 SOSÚA BAY RESORT
$$$$

CALLE DR. ALEJO MARTÍNEZ 1
TEL 809/571-4000
sosuabayclub.com

This elegant, Spanish-hacienda-themed, all-inclusive resort overlooks Playa Sosúa. The dramatic lobby features a mezzanine Internet lounge. The rooms are inviting and there's a pool complex

---

⊗ Nonsmoking 🏢 Air-conditioning 🏊 Indoor pool 🏊 Outdoor pool 📶 Health club 📶 Wi-Fi ⊗ Credit cards

and a choice of restaurants, plus a casino.

🛈 144 🅿 ⬌ ⬡ ⬡ ⬟ ⬛
🂠 All major cards

🏨 PIERGIORGIO PALACE HOTEL
$$$
CALLE LA PUNTILLA
TEL 809/571-2626
hotelpiergiorgio.com
Colonial gingerbread-style hotel atop the cliffs. Spacious rooms have white rattan furniture with pink fabrics. Romantic restaurant offers cliff-top patio dining.
🛈 56 rooms & 3 suites
🅿 ⬡ ⬡ ⬟ 🂠 AE, MC, V

🏨 CASA VALERIA
$$
CALLE DR. ROSEN 28
TEL 809/571-3565
hotelcasavaleria.com
Rustic yet quaint New Mexican–themed family-run hotel in the heart of the village. Rooms around a patio with small pool. Rough-hewn beds and colorful, simple furnishings.
🛈 9 🂠 No credit cards

🍴 CARPE DIEM VI
$$$
CALLE PEDRO CLISANTE 54
TEL 809/660-7492
enjoy-carpe-diem.com
The French owners know how to deliver artistic and divine fusion dishes at this splendid open-air restaurant with chic black-and-white decor. The inventive menu features such treats as veal stew, anise-flavored mussels, and leek and white fish risotto. Large wine list.
🪑 40 🅿 🕓 Closed B & L
🂠 Most major cards

🍴 MORUA MAI
$$
CALLE PEDRO CLISANTE
TEL 809/571-3682

Huge open-air restaurant with ceiling fans and rattan furniture. The wide-ranging menu includes superb burgers, club sandwiches, and seafood, including paella.
🪑 120 🂠 MC, V

◼ EL CIBAO

BONAO

🏨🍴 HOTEL AKUARIUS, BAR & RESTAURANT
$$$
CALLE DUARTE 104
TEL 809/296-0303
akuariushotel.com
Set in the city center, this modern hotel has pleasantly appointed rooms with Internet access. The lively bar accommodates dancing.
🛈 29 rooms & 5 suites
🅿 ⬡ 🂠 MC, V

MONTE CRISTI

🏨🍴 EL MORRO ECO-ADVENTURE HOTEL
$$$
CARRETERA AL MORRO KM 2
TEL 849/886-1605
elmorro.com.do
Surprisingly chic, this recently upgraded hotel offers ocean views from its sloping perch outside town. Flat-screen TVs and Wi-Fi are standard in all rooms. The curtain-draped open-air **Restaurant Bubí** is the region's finest, offering gourmet fusion dishes, plus pizzas, and the region's trademark oregano-flavored goat stew, all served on a wooden deck.
🛈 12 🅿 ⬡ 📶 Free 🂠 V

🏨 CHIC HOTEL
$$
AVE. BENITO MONCIÓN 44
TEL 809/579-2316
chichotel.net
Eclectic styling includes

PRICES

HOTELS
An indication of the cost of a double room in the high season is given by **$** signs.

$$$$$	Over $200
$$$$	$100–$200
$$$	$50–$100
$$	$25–$50
$	Under $25

RESTAURANTS
An indication of the cost of a three-course meal without drinks is given by **$** signs.

$$$$$	Over $35
$$$$	$20–$35
$$$	$10–$20
$$	$5–$10
$	Under $5

colonial columns, glazed tile floors, and rattan furnishings in modestly spacious rooms, each with refrigerator and TV. Restaurant serves traditional local fare.
🛈 20 🅿 ⬡ 🂠 V

SAN FRANCISCO DE MACORÍS

🏨 HOTEL LAS CAOBAS
$$$
CALLE LUIS ENRIQUE CARRÓN, 2 MILES (3 KM) W OF SAN FRANCISCO
TEL 809/290-5858
Modern hotel in the countryside on the edge of town. Modestly furnished; soft mattresses. Western-style restaurant plus a casino.
🛈 42 🅿 ⬡ ⬟ 🂠 MC, V

SANTIAGO DE LOS CABALLEROS

🏨 HODELPA GRAN ALMIRANTE
$$$$

AVE. SALVADOR ESTRELLA
SADHALA
TEL 809/580-1992
hodelpa.com
Stylish hotel on the northern
outskirts of town. Retro-
themed contemporary decor.
Choice of restaurants includes
a hip tapas bar.
① 155 P ⊖ ⊗ ⊗ ⊠
⊗ AE, MC, V

SOMETHING SPECIAL

⊞ HODELPA CENTRO PLAZA
$$$
CALLE MELLA 54
TEL 809/581-7000
hodelpa.com
This heart-of-the-city hotel
exudes a contemporary flair
that begins in the impressive
lobby. Guest rooms offer har-
monious beige, white, and
mahogany color schemes and
high-quality linens. Suites
have Jacuzzi tubs. There's a
ground-floor casino. The
hotel is a splendid steps-from-
everything base for exploring
the historic center.
① 85 ⊖ ⊗ ⊗ ⊡
⊗ AE, MC, V

⊞ HOTEL ALOHA SOL
$$
CALLE DEL SOL 50
TEL 809/583-0090
alohasol.com
Quality hotel in the city
center at reasonable rates.
Comfortable rooms with
classic decor. Has a pleasant
restaurant, Internet, and
plenty of services.
① 103 P ⊗ ⊗ ⊗ AE, MC, V

⊞ PEZ DORADO
$$$
CALLE DEL SOL 43
TEL 809/582-2518
Top-class, Spanish bodega
draws the business crowd for
lunch. Beamed ceilings. Gener-
ous portions and excellent ser-
vice. The wide-ranging menu

spans smoked salmon, duck in
orange sauce, and stuffed sea
bass, to Chinese cuisine.
⊞ 104 ⊕ Closed B ⊗
⊗ All major cards

⊞ KUKARAMACARA COUNTRY BAR & RESTAURANT
$$
AVE. FRANCIA 7
TEL 809/241-3143
kukaramacara.net
A Western-themed restaurant
adorned with John Wayne
posters and cow-hides; the
waitstaff is dressed in cowboy
duds. Buffalo wings, onion
soup, pork ribs, and filet
Roquefort typify the menu.
⊞ 100 ⊕ Closed B
⊗ All major cards

▦ CORDILLERA CENTRAL

CONSTANZA

SOMETHING SPECIAL

⊞ DILENIA HOTEL & RESTAURANT
$$
CALLE GASTON F. DELIGNE 7
TEL 809/539-2213
Simply furnished rooms
with cable TV and modern
bathrooms set around a gar-
den away from the city hub-
bub. The charming and
atmospheric country-style
restaurant offers tempting
dishes, at bargain prices, with
unusual ingredients, such as
guinea fowl, rabbit, and a
superb stewed goat in wine.
You can dine on a patio over-
looking a garden thronged
with hummingbirds and liz-
ards. The owner-chef, Dilenia
de la Rosa Durán, oversees the
excellent service.
① 24 ⊞ 60 ⊕ Closed B
⊗ DC, MC, V

⊞ HOTEL ALTO CERRO
$$
CALLE GUAROCUYA 461
TEL 809/539-1553 OR
809/530-6192
altocerro.com
This sprawling hillside hotel
overlooks the valley. You have
a choice of simply appointed
rooms, villas, or camping
(tents are provided) on spacious tree-shaded lawns.
Conscientious management.
The restaurant is known
for its turkey, geese, and
guinea fowl dishes. A spa is
being added.
① 10 rooms & 30 villas
P ⊗ ⊡ ⊗ MC, V

⊞ MI CABAÑA RESORT
$$
CARRETERA GENERAL
ANTONIO DUVERGÉ,
1 MILE (1.6 KM) S OF C
ONSTANZA
TEL 809/539-2930
An if-all-else-fails option, this
resort-style hotel offers mar-
velous views down the valley.
Rooms have balconies, but
thin walls and dim lighting
detract. Basketball court.
① 14 P ⊠ ⊗ MC, V

JARABACOA

⊞ HOTEL GRAN JIMENOA
$$$
AVE. LA CONFLUENCIA
TEL 809/574-6304
granjimenoahotel.com
Recently upgraded, this hotel
offers huge, modestly furnished rooms with cable TV
and comfy beds, but the bathrooms are unimpressive (hot
water is not guaranteed).
Riverside restaurant.
① 60 P ⊗ ⊗ ⊠ ⊗ MC, V

⊞ RANCHO LAS GUÁZARAS
$$$
CARRETERA Á MANABAO KM 9
TEL 829/630-4386

mijarabacoa.com
Set amid landscaped lawns surrounded by forest, this sprawling resort-style hotel has handsome two-story villas, some perched above the river. Horseback excursions, canyoning, and other activities.

🛈 60 🅿 🖼
🖼 Most major cards

🏨 HOTEL BRISAS DEL YAQUE
$$–$$$
CALLE LUPERÓN & CALLE PEREGRINA HERRERA
TEL 809/574-2100
An in-town hotel close to restaurants (the hotel has none). Wood-and-brick rooms are small yet clean. Many have mountain views.

🛈 12 🅿 🖼 MC, V

🏨 HOTEL PINAR DORADO
$$
CALLE DEL CARMEN,
1 MILE (1.6 KM) S OF JARABACOA
TEL 809/574-2820
grupobaiguate.com
Handsome motel-style option with faux-wood tile floors, redbrick walls, and pleasant furnishings. An appealing restaurant serves buffets.

🛈 37 🅿 🖼 🖼
🖼 AE, MC, V

🏨 RANCHO BAIGUATE
$$
BARRIO LA JOYA, 2 MILES (3 KM) SE OF JARABACOA
TEL 809/574-6890
ranchobaiguate.com
This adventure center known for river rafting has dorms, standard rooms, and suites on lovely grounds. There's an Olympic-size pool and natural lagoons for swimming. Thatched restaurant on-site, plus lots of activities. This makes the perfect base for adventure-oriented travelers.

🛈 8 rooms, 9 dorms, & 10 suites 🅿 🖼 🖼 AE, MC, V

🍴 LEÑA DE PARRILLADA RESTAURANT
$
CALLE HERMANAS MIRABAL 8
TEL 809/574-7656
This atmospheric thatched restaurant with rough-hewn timbers faces the central park. Serves Dominican fare such as *mofongo*, plus pork filet in pineapple sauce and barbecued chicken.

🪑 66 🕐 Closed B
🖼 No credit cards

PARQUE NACIONAL VALLE NUEVO

🏨 VILLA PAJON
$$$
2 MILES (3 KM) E OF LA SIBERIA
TEL 809/412-5210 OR 809/334-6935
villapajon.do
Mountain resort set amid pines and alpine meadows full of wild blackberries on the north side of the park, at a 7,500-foot (2,286 m) elevation. The simple yet cozy one- to three-bedroom log cabins of have hearths and kitchens. Horseback riding, mountain biking, and ATV tours are offered. Often closed; call ahead. Bring all your own supplies.

🛈 7 cabins 🅿
🖼 No credit cards

▦ THE SOUTHWEST

AZUA

🍴 FRANCIA
$$
AVE. FRANCISCO DEL ROSARIO SÁNCHEZ 104
TEL 809/521-2900
This simple restaurant specializes in creole dishes, including

---

creole snapper and garlic shrimp. Servings are ample and bargain priced.

🪑 30 🅿 🖼 No credit cards

BARAHONA

SOMETHING SPECIAL

🏨 CASA BONITA TROPICAL LODGE
$$$$$
CARRETERA DE LA COSTA KM 17
TEL 809/540-5908 OR 800/961-5133
casabonitadr.com
A true stand-out hotel, this supremely lovable place nestled on forested slopes high above the ocean deserves its Small Luxury Hotels of the World billing. Draped four-poster beds, ceiling fans, and wicker highlight the tropically themed, thatched rooms and suites, with their 21st-century amenities and chic marble-clad bathrooms. Organic produce is used in the health-conscious menu at the alfresco Pat's Organic Garden restaurant,

---

where dinner delights include coconut-crusted shrimp, beef tenderloin with mustard and red wine sauce, and Caribbean *asopao* (rice soup with rum) with lobster medallions.

🏨 13 P 🏊 🏖
🏧 AE, MC, V

🏨 CASA DEL MAR LODGE
$$$
CARRETERA BARAHONA-PARAÍSO KM 16
TEL 829/330-3395
casadelmarlodgebarahona
.com
With its gorgeous and understated aesthetic, this charming palm-shaded, thatched, beachfront villa offers breakfast delivered to your deck. Some units have kitchens and wraparound sofas on private verandas with lounge chairs, Beds have mosquito-net drapes. It even has a hot tub, and massage is offered.

🏨 3 P 🏖 📶 Free 🏧 V

SOMETHING SPECIAL

🏨 PLAYAZUL HOTEL-RESTAURANT
$$$
CARRETERA BARAHONA-PARAÍSO KM 7
PUNTA PRIETA
TEL 809/204-8010
playazulbarahona.com
This French-owned seafood hotel boasts a magnificent setting above its own cove and beach. Modestly appointed rooms feature pleasant decor and ceiling fans plus cable TV and balconies with rockers. The landscaped grounds sweep down to rich blue waters, and a restaurant serves seafood and classic local dishes. Massage is offered.

🏨 120 P 🏖
🏧 No credit cards

🏨 HOTEL COSTA LARIMAR
$$
AVE. ENRIQUILLO 6
TEL 809/524-5111
hotelcostalarimar.com
This dated five-story beach-front hotel with spacious but dowdy rooms is the best in the town itself. The beach here is lackluster. Friendly staff.

🏨 108 P 🔁 🏊 🏖 🏧 MC, V

🍴 BRISAS DEL CARIBE
$$
AVE. ENRIQUILLO 73
TEL 809/524-2794
A thatched, open-air restaurant with ocean views. Excellent seafood dishes make this a popular lunchtime stop for locals, who consider it the best restaurant in town.

🍴 84 P 🏧 MC, V

LAS SALINAS

🏨 HOTEL SALINAS
$$
CALLE PUERTO HERMOSO 7
TEL 809/310-8141
A favorite of yachters, this informally run, vaguely New Mexican–style hotel has simply appointed rooms and a vast suite with varied decor—all rooms are the same price. The bayfront open-air restaurant serves U.S. favorites, from burgers to pastas and seafood.

🏨 16 rooms & 6 villas
P 🏊 🏖 🏧 MC, V

PEDERNALES

🏨 HOTEL VILLA DEL MAR
$$
CALLE CACIQUE ENRIQUILLO 2
TEL 809/524-0448
Despite being overpriced, the cubicle-size rooms at this villa-style, family-run hotel are the best in town. Small restaurant with minimal fare. Cold water only. Noisy!

🏨 14 P 🏊 🏖
🏧 No credit cards

PARAÍSO

🏨 RANCHO PLATÓN
$$$
PARAÍSO, 38 KM S OF BARAHONA
TEL 809/383-1836
ranchoplaton.com
An eco-resort in the forested hills off the road that leads to Polo. Delightfully furnished wooden cottages (some with bunks) are your base for horseback excursions, hikes, and tubing or kayaking. Or choose one of the two Tree House cabins. Hearty creole meals served overlooking a small lagoon with rope swings. Perfect for families.

🏨 9 P 🏖 🏧 AE, MC, V

SAN CRISTÓBAL

🍴 FELA'S PLACE
$
CALLE GENERAL LEGER 55
TEL 809/288-2124
A simple restaurant serving down-home Dominican staples, including *pastelito en hoja* (pastry in paper, an empanada stuffed with meat and veggies), the town's culinary claim to fame.

🍴 40 P 🏧 AE, MC, V

SAN JUAN DE LA MAGUANA

🏨 HOTEL MAGUANA
$$
AVE. INDEPENDENCIA 72
TEL 809/557-2244
Most rooms of this state-owned and recently remodeled historic hotel (built to house Trujillo during his visits) cluster around an atrium courtyard. Dark but well-appointed guest rooms are the nicest in town. The wood-paneled restaurant serves local and international fare, from fettuccine to guinea fowl.

🏨 41 P 🏊 🏧 MC, V

Shopping

The Dominican Republic's tourist boom has spawned a great deal of kitsch but also an outpouring of quality crafts, from wooden carvings, papier-mâché figurines, leatherwork, and wicker baskets to linen blouses with larimar buttons. Most upscale hotels have gift stores selling quality crafts. However, artisans' markets have by far the widest choice, and you will have more fun bargaining with the vendors or even the artists themselves. All the major tourist resorts have plenty of craft markets and stores, usually spilling onto the beach. Santo Domingo is also blessed with crafts stores and galleries selling Haitian art. Large malls in the capital city and Santiago offer a complete selection of well-known clothing brands and accessories.

The robust art scene includes works from faux-primitive Haitian paintings to sophisticated Dominican contemporary art. Haitian art is everywhere, although much is mediocre and mass produced. Carvings include quality sculptures hewn from *guayacán*—a beautiful hardwood.

Typically, jewelry sold in crafts markets and the ubiquitous Museo de Ámbar chain stores makes use of local amber and larimar—the country's prize gems. Look for necklaces, bracelets, and rings. Watch for fake amber (real amber changes color under ultraviolet light, and also sinks in saltwater). Unfortunately, much jewelry uses black coral—refrain from buying this endangered species. Likewise, avoid products made of turtle shells and other creatures protected by international conventions, such as sharks. Harrison's Fine Caribbean Jewelers is the leading outlet for high-end quality jewelry and has shops throughout the country.

Many people today consider the Dominican Republic's cigars to be better than Cuban cigars. They're also cheaper, and, unlike Cuban cigars, they can be imported into the United States. The nation's rum is also renowned.

When buying rums, stick with the quality—albeit more expensive—brands, such as Brugal and Bermúdez, and with aged *añejos*. (Liquor and other liquids should be packed in checked luggage for flights to the United States.) And the nation's aromatic highland-grown coffee is a great bargain; stick with export-quality labels.

Music CDs and DVDs of *bachata* and merengue are sold at roadside stalls, but the quality is often questionable. Buy recordings at more established outlets.

Bargaining is the norm at markets, but prices are usually already discounted due to competition.

Every settlement has its *colmados,* little corner grocery stores that sometimes double as informal bars. Many towns located near the Haitian border also have bustling Haitian markets.

■ SANTO DOMINGO

The capital city is blessed with shopping opportunities. In the Zona Colonial, the pedestrian-only Calle El Conde is a cornucopia of stores selling cheap T-shirts, plus CDs, cigars, and jewelry. Art galleries selling both Haitian and contemporary works by leading Dominican artists abound, as do shops selling amber and larimar jewelry. The modern shopping district of Naco is chock-full of designer stores and malls. Downtown, Calle del Sol is lined with department stores, banks, and street stalls.

Arts & Antiques

Arte Berri Calle Hostos 105, tel 829/343-4514, arteberri.com.

Contemporary art by leading artists.

Galería Bidó Calle Dr. Báez 5, Gazcue, tel 809/685-5310. The gallery of the world-renowned painter Cándido Bidó; also represents other contemporary artists.

Lyle O. Reitzel Gallery Calle Torre Piantini 1A, tel 809/227-8361, lyleoreitzel.com. Works by avant-garde Latin American artists.

Mesa Fine Art Ave. Roberto Pastorizo 356, tel 809/565-6060, www.facebook.com/mesafineart. Works by Dominican and international artists.

Books & Maps

Librería Cruz Ferbore Ave. Juan Pablo Duarte 275, tel 809/245-1847. Specializes in academic books.

Mapas Gaar Calle Arzobispo Nouel 355 & Calle Espaillat, tel 809/688-8004, mapasgaar.com.do. Large selection of maps.

Clothes & Accessories

Maison Marie Ave. Tiradentes cnr. Gustavo Mejia Ricart, tel 809/732-9068, www.maison marie.do. Latest designer fashions and accessories.

Plaza Central Ave. Winston Churchill & Ave. 27 de Febrero, tel 809/549-3181. Four-story mall with numerous clothing stores, shoe stores, and high-end boutiques.

Crafts & Jewelry

Casa de los Dulces Calle Emiliano Tejera 106, tel 809/685-0785.

Tourist shop, popular with cruise ship passengers, with wide range of crafts.

Columbus Plaza Calle Arzobispo Meriño 204, tel 809/689-0565. Three floors crammed with crafts, including the handmade porcelain faceless dolls from La Vega Real.

Museo de Ámbar Calle El Conde 107, tel 809/221-1333, closed Sun. Excellent selection of amber and larimar jewelry, plus gold and silver items.

Museo Larimar Calle Isabel la Católica 54 & Calle Padre Bellini, tel 809/686-5700. Largest selection of larimar jewelry in Santo Domingo.

Gifts & Miscellaneous

Boutique del Fumador Calle El Conde 109, tel 809/685-6425. A wide choice of quality Dominican cigars.

Cigar King Calle Conde 208, tel 809/686-4987. The best choice of cigars in town.

Malls

Acrópolis Ave. Winston Churchill & Calle Julio A. Aybar, tel 809/955-2020, acropolisdr.com. More than a hundred stores on five levels.

Blue Mall Ave. Winston Churchill 93, tel 809/955-3000, bluemall.com.do. High-end mall with fashion and jewelry stores, plus banks and a food court.

Plaza Central Ave. 27 de Febrero & Ave. Winston Churchill, tel 809/549-3181, closed Sun. Large uptown complex with boutiques, jewelry stores, restaurants, a bank, and a movie theater.

Markets

Mercado de las Pulgas Centro de los Héroes, Ave. Luperón, Sun. Flea market selling household bric-a-brac, clothing, and food.

Mercado Modelo Ave. Mella 505, bet. Calle Tomás de la Concha & Calle Del Monte. Bustling and cavernous covered market with a warren of stalls selling souvenirs, including Haitian art and *vodu* items; plus *botánicas* (herbalists) to the rear.

■ THE SOUTHEAST

As the center of the tourism boom of the past decade, the southeast boasts plenty of options for shopping, from cigars and rums to arts, crafts, and trendy boutiques. The airport departure lounge at Puerto Plata has several boutiques selling duty-free items and quality crafts, plus rum and cigars. Most upscale all-inclusive resorts also have boutiques and gift stores, and handicraft vendors visit many of them on set days, when they are permitted to display their wares.

Arts & Antiques

Most tourist centers, such as Boca Chica and Bávaro, have no shortage of vendors selling Haitian art. Although the best quality is usually associated with formal galleries, informal street and beachfront stalls offer the largest selection.

Art' Arena Calle Barlovento 21, Marina Casa de Campo, La Romana, tel 809/523-2271. Quality artwork.

Clothes & Accessories

Bibi León Jenny Polanco Atos de Chavón, La Romana, tel 809/523-3333. High fashion for women.

Rubilana Collection Portico de Sopravento 35, Marina Casa de Campo, La Romana, tel 809/523-2265. High-end fashions and accessories.

Crafts & Jewelry

Everett Designs Altos de Chavón, La Romana, tel 809/877-3643.

Harrison's Fine Caribbean Jewelers Palma Real Shopping Village, Bávaro, tel 809/552-8721. Fine-quality jewelry.

Museo de Ámbar Playa Bávaro, tel 809/552-8710. Fine collection of quality amber and larimar jewelry, plus a museum. Directly atop the sands.

Plaza Artesanal Bibijagua Playa Bávaro. An enclave of beachside shacks selling Haitian paintings and the like.

Tienda Batey Altos de Chavón, La Romana, tel 809/877-3643. Linens handcrafted by local women.

Veronica & Alessandro Joyería Calle Barlovento, Marina Casa de Campo, La Romana, tel 809/523-8646. Designer watches and jewelry, plus amber and larimar pieces.

Gifts & Miscellaneous

Cabinet Tobacco Boutique, Altos de Chavón, La Romana, tel 809/877-3643.

Club del Cigarro Pórtico de Sotavento 1, Marina Casa de Campo, La Romana, tel 809/523-2275. Quality Dominican and Cuban cigars from a well-stocked humidor.

Domenico Premium Cigar Manufactory Ave. Estados Unidos, Bávaro, tel 809/772-6873, domenicocigars.com. Free factory tour.

Malls

Palma Real Shopping Village Carretera El Cortecito 57, Bávaro, tel 809/852-8725. Two dozen boutiques and stores, plus banks, a cinema, and restaurants. Fashion highlights include Carmen Sol New York (for Gucci, Fendi, Prada, etc.), plus Planeta Fashion and Bruga Boutique.

Markets

Mercado Artesanal Bibijagua Playa Bávaro, Bávaro. Everything from T-shirts to cigars and jewelry.

Mercado El Cortecito Playa El Cortecito. Various stalls selling shell jewelry, wooden statues, Haitian paintings, and miscellaneous crafts.

Mercado Municipal Calle Teófilo Ferry & Fray Juan de Utera, La Romana. Colorful street market selling fresh produce and flowers.

■ LA PENÍNSULA DE SAMANÁ

Las Terrenas has about a dozen small stores selling beachwear, crafts, and Haitian art. The large all-inclusive resorts also have boutiques and gift shops.

Arts & Antiques

Haitian Caraibes Art Gallery Calle Principal 159, Las Terrenas, tel 809/240-6250. One of the best art galleries in the country. Naive works plus other art by recognized names, and batiks, jewelry, and high-end crafts.

Crafts & Jewelry

Blue Corazón Plaza El Paseo, Las Terrenas, tel 809/240-6284. Fine jewelry, including amber and larimar.

Harrison's Fine Caribbean Jewelers Pueblo Principe Shopping Center, Carrereta Samaná–El Valle 1, Samaná, tel 809/538-3933. High-end jewelry, including amber and larimar.

Gifts & Miscellaneous

Mundo Puro Calle Principal, Las Terrenas, tel 829/886-7353. Hand-rolled cigars made on-site.

Malls

Plaza Comercial El Paseo Calle Juan Pablo Duarte, Las

Terrenas, tel 849/763-3281. Various stores, including jewelry.

Pueblito Caribeño Ave. La Marina & Ave. Francisco de Rosario, Samaná. Various boutiques and gift shops.

Markets

Mercado Nocturno Barrio Dominicano, Las Terrenas. Weekend night market for locals, complete with drumming and dancing.

■ NORTH COAST

With its well-established resort hotels, local amber mines, and boutiques catering to independent travelers, the north coast is blessed with shopping options. Its strong suit is amber jewelry, centered on Puerto Plata. The main street of Cabarete is lined with shops selling beachwear, artwork, crafts, cigars, and items for the kitesurfing and windsurfing crowd.

Arts & Antiques

571 Art Gallery El Batey, Sosúa, tel 809/712-3632. Art by talented local Leo Díaz.

Clothes & Accessories

Carib Wind Center Calle Principal, Cabarete, tel 809/571-0640, caribwind.com. Huge selection of hip duds for surfers and kiteboarders.

Crafts & Jewelry

Amber Museum Calle Duarte 61, Puerto Plata, tel 809/586-2848 or 809/320-2215, ambermuseum .com, closed Sun. A large collection of amber and larimar jewelry for sale.

Calle Gregorio Luperón Sosúa. An end-to-end row of Haitian art galleries and beachwear boutiques. Extends along Playa Sosúa.

Harrison's Fine Caribbean Jewelers Ave. Luperón km 3.5, Puerto Plata, tel 809/586-3933, and Centro Comercial, Playa Dorada, tel 809/320-2219. Fine jewelry.

Joyería y Artesanía La Canoa Calle Beller 18, Puerto Plata, tel 809/586-3604. Particularly large selection of fine jewelry, plus amber and larimar. Also a good place to sample and buy *mamajuana*.

Joyería Las Américas Plaza Las Américas, Calle José Kunhardt 1, Puerto Plata, tel 809/244-4885. Large selection of jewelry.

Patrick's Silversmithy Calle Pedro Clisante 3, Sosúa, tel 809/571-2121. Avant-garde silver, amber, and larimar jewelry by Patrick Fagg.

Gifts & Miscellaneous

Brugal Rum Bottling Plant Ave. Louis Ginebra, tel 809/541-9438 or 809/261-1888, closed Sat.–Sun. Brugal rums at the source.

Fifi Jewelry & Cigar Store Calle Separación 41, Puerto Plata, tel 809/261-3278. Hand-rolled Monseñor de Puerto Plata cigars.

Vivonte Cigars Calle José del Carmen Arizo 5, Puerto Plata, tel 809/586-5257. Small artisanal hand-rolled cigar factory with lounge.

Malls

Playa Dorado Plaza Playa Dorado, tel 809/320-6645. Big shopping mall with boutiques, cigar stores, and jewelry and cosmetic stores.

Plaza Turisol Ave. Luperón km 2.5. Largest shopping center on the north coast, with more than 80 outlets.

Markets

Cabarete Night Market Cabarete beach. Every Sunday evening, with eclectic arts and crafts.

Mercado Nuevo Calle Isabel de Torres & Calle Villanueva, Puerto

Plata, closed Sun. Small covered crafts market selling everything from T-shirts to rums and cigars.

Mercado Viejo Calle Ureña & Calle Separación, Puerto Plata. Utilitarian market for locals. The *botánicos* sell herbal remedies, folk religion icons, and *mamajuana*.

■ EL CIBAO

The Cibao region is renowned for its gaily colored papier-mâché devil masks made in La Vega (but available island-wide), and for the faceless dolls known as *muñecas sin rostro*, representing typical country women. The region is also the center for cigar manufacture. Many factories are open to visitors—a chance to buy some of the world's best cigars at their source. In the far west, Haitian markets sell cheap clothing (including designer counterfeits) and household goods. Dajabón has the largest such market, taking up eight square blocks.

Crafts & Jewelry
Centro León Ave. 27 de Febrero 146, Santiago, tel 809/582-2315, centroleon.org.do, closed Mon. Superb quality art and crafts, plus books.

Hermanos Guillén Cerámica Taína Calle Duarte 9 & Calle Ramón Guillén, Yamasá, tel 809/454-7665. Traditional hand-made Taíno artwork.

Jesús Caretas Art Calle Ocho 15, Santiago, tel 809/576-5400. Fantastical Carnaval masks and costumes.

Gifts & Miscellaneous
Fábrica de Cigarros La Aurora Ave. 27 de Febrero 1, Santiago, tel 809/575-1903, laaurora.com .do, closed Sat.–Sun. Some of the finest of Dominican cigars are made here.

Tabacalera La Caya Calle Real 169, Santiago, tel 809/570-9930, closed Sun., visits by appt. Superb hand-rolled cigars.

Markets
Fería Artesanal Salcedo. Artisans' fair held the first week of August. Everything from hammocks to wooden religious icons.

Mercado Haitiano Eight square blocks bordering the Puente de Amistad (Friendship Bridge), Dajabón. Haitian market held Monday & Friday.

Mercado Modelo Calle Sánchez & Calle Castillo, San Francisco de Macorís. Produce and cacao market enlivened by pack animals bearing goods.

Mercado Modelo Turístico Calle del Sol & Ave. España, Santiago. Especially known for its ceramics.

■ CORDILLERA CENTRAL

The mountain valleys are the nation's breadbasket and the center for production of flowers and food crops, including strawberries. The few shopping opportunities are associated with farm produce.

Gifts & Miscellaneous
Floristería Aves del Paraíso Calle Gastón F. Deligne & Calle Sánchez, Jarabacoa, tel 809/574-4608. Fresh-cut flowers and floral displays.

Jardín Constanza, Calle Del Monte y Tejada 21, Constanza, tel 809/688-7072, jardinconstanza .com. Roses, sunflowers, and other fresh-cut flowers.

Markets
Mercado Agropecuario Calle Luperón, Constanza. Daily farmers market.

Mercado Público Calle Mario Nelson Galán & Calle Mella,

Jarabacoa. Public market selling everything from produce to T-shirts and wicker baskets.

■ THE SOUTHWEST

Receiving few tourists, the southwest has few crafts markets or other stores of interest to visitors. Its strong suit is the Haitian markets held in several major towns close to the Haitian border. The main items sold are clothing (including counterfeit designer jeans, sports clothes, and sneakers) and household goods at rock-bottom prices. The main patrons are Dominican wholesalers.

Gifts & Miscellaneous
Abordage Zona Franca La Armería, San Cristóbal, tel 809/528-1992, abordage.com. Hand-made wooden model ships crafted by skilled artisans.

Artesania Puello Peatonal Uno 7A, San Cristóbal, tel 809/528-8303. Quality wooden carvings and art in naive style by Juan Puello.

Factoria de Café Américo Melo Calle Anacaona 12, Barahona, tel 809/524-2440, closed Sun. Sells home-roasted coffee beans and ground coffee (*café molinado*).

Plaza de los Pilones Carretera 2, 2 miles (3 km) W of Baní. Wooden mortars and pestles of every size, including decorative Haitian models. Perfect for making *mofongo* (mashed plantains with garlic).

Haitian Markets
Mercado Haitiano Bánica, Thurs. & Sun.

Mercado Haitiano Parque Central, Comendador, Mon. & Fri.

Mercado Haitiano Mal Paso, 1 mile (1.6 km) W of Jimaní, Mon. & Fri.

Mercado Haitiano Pedernales, Mon. & Fri. Held just beyond the border post.

Activities

Activities in the Dominican Republic make the most of the country's natural diversity. The companies listed may cover additional activities and areas. Activity-oriented tour operators are based in all the key beach resort towns: Jeep safaris are popular, as are horseback rides and ATV excursions. The Cordillera Central is a venue for white-water rafting and for hikes up Pico Duarte, and the national parks of the southwest offer exceptional birding. Water sports are well developed. Most all-inclusive resorts offer a selection of watercraft, plus scuba diving and snorkeling. Boat excursions are popular, as is whale-watching during winter months.

The following companies specialize in a range of outdoor activities:

Colonial Tours Calle Arzobispo Meriño 209, Santo Domingo, tel 809/688-5285, colonialtours .com.do. Retails a wide range of tours.

Iguana Mama Calle Principal 74, Cabarete, tel 809/654-2325, iguanamama.com. Dependable adventure outfitter offering canyoning, mountain biking, trekking, and cascading trips.

Outback Safari Transporte Tureca S.A., km 2.1, Carretera Veron-Bávaro, Bávaro, tel 809/455-1573 & Plaza Turisol, Local 7, Ave. Luperón km 2.5, Puerto Plata, tel 809/320-2525, outbacksafari.com .do. Offers cultural and ecological encounters, plus activities.

Tours Trips Treks & Travel Calle Principal, Cabarete, tel 809/867-8884, 4tdomrep.com. Specializes in customized educational and cultural tours.

Birding

Birds of the Dominican Republic and Haiti by Steven Latta et al. is a good birding primer.

Two U.S. companies offering organized birding tours from the United States to the Dominican Republic are:

Victor Emmanuel Nature Tours 2525 Wallingwood Dr., Ste. 1003, Austin, TX 78746, tel 512/328-5221 or 800/328-8368, ventbird.com.

Wings Birding Tours 1643 N. Alverton, Ste. 109, Tucson, AZ 85712, tel 520/320-9868 or 866/547-9868, wingsbirds.com.

Within the republic, **Tody Tours** *(Calle José Gabriel García 105, Santo Domingo, tel 809/686-0882, tody tours.com)* offers birding trips.

Ornithologist-guide **Miguel Angel Landestoy** *(tel 809/705-2430, email mango_land@yahoo .com)* offers personalized tours.

Caving & Canyoning

The country is pocked with cave systems, many containing ancient Taíno pictographs and petroglyphs. Domingo Abréu Collado, of **Espeleogrupo de Santo Domingo** *(Independencia 518, Santo Domingo, tel 809/682-1577, e-mail domingo@ espeleo.redid.org.do)* is the nation's leading tour guide specializing in caves.

The **Fundación Espeleobuceo Hispaniola** *(Ave. Winston Churchill & Paseo de los Locutores, Santo Domingo, fax 809/472-2248, e-mail info@ espeleobuceo.org, espeleobuceo.org)* specializes in underwater caving.

Tours Trips Treks & Travel *(tel 809/867-8884, 4tdomrep.com)* offers cave tours to view Taíno art.

Canyoning involves hiking, climbing, and rappelling to the bottom of river canyons.

Iguana Mama *(Calle Principal 74, Cabarete, tel 809/654-2325, iguanamama.com)* and **Rancho Baiguate** *(Jarabacoa, tel 809/574-6890, ranchobaiguate.com)* offer canyoning trips.

Cruising & Sailing

Marinas on both Atlantic and Caribbean shores cater to private yachters. Several companies offer daylong to ten-day boating adventures. Sunset cruises are available at some locales.

An annual international regatta is hosted by **Marina Casa de Campo** *(Casa de Campo, La Romana, tel 809/523-8646, marinacasade campo.com)*.

Fishing

The Mona Passage, separating Hispaniola from Puerto Rico, is flush with feisty billfish and tuna that give anglers rod-bending fights to remember. The Punta Cana region is home to a well-equipped fleet of charter sport-fishing boats. Charter boats also operate out of La Romana's Marina Casa de Campo, as well as from Samaná and Puerto Plata. Boat charters cost about RD$450 a half day (up to four people). Local fishermen also offer trips for negotiable rates.

Inland lakes offer good fishing for bass, carp, and tilapia, but you will need to bring your own tackle. No license is required.

Golfing

The Dominican Republic has more than three dozen 18-hole courses, with many others under construction. Premier golf courses are concentrated around Punta Cana and the north coast beach resorts.

The **Federación Dominicana de Golf** *(tel 809/338-1004, fedogolf.org.do)* can provide information on tournaments, as can golfdominicano.com.

Horseback Riding

Horseback riding is available nationwide, including at all the major beach resorts.

Kayaking & Rafting

See entries for the Río Yaque del Norte (see p. 230), in the Cordillera Central, the setting for kayaking and white-water rafting.

Miscellaneous

Flying Tony *(tel 809/848-3479, flyindr.com)* offers paragliding and tandem trike flights out of Jarabacoa.

Helidosa *(tel 809/552-6066, helidosa.com)* offers helicopter tours from Punta Cana, Puerto Plata, La Romana, Bávaro, Bayahibe, and Samaná.

Motorcycle Tours

MotoCaribe Motorcycle Tours Calle Las Palmas 3, Jarabacoa, tel 809/574-6507. Six- to 12-day tours nationwide.

Mountain Biking

The **Federación Dominicana de Ciclismo** *(Centro Olímpico Juan Pablo Duarte, Santo Domingo, tel 809/565-5209, fedoci.com)* is a good resource for biking options throughout the country, but the Cordillera Central is perhaps the best venue for mountain biking. **Rancho Baiguete** *(Jarabacoa, tel 809/574-6890, ranchobaiguate .com)* offers mountain-bike trips, as does **Iguana Mama** *(Calle Principal 74, Cabarete, tel 809/654-2325, iguanamama.com).*

Scuba Diving

The seas off the republic offer spectacular diving. Atlantic diving focuses on coral reefs. Spanish galleons and coral formations highlight the dives off Isla Catalina, Monte Cristi, Boca Chica, and Bayahibe's bay on the Caribbean.

ScubaCaribe *(tel 809/552-1435, scubacaribe.com)* has outlets at more than 20 hotels in Punta Cana, Puerto Plata, and Río San Juan.

Decompression chambers for divers are located at the **Centro de Medicina Hiperbárica** *(Garcia Godoy 11 & Ave. Bolivar, tel 809/689-8775)* in Santo Domingo and at **Hospital Ricardo Limardo** *(Ave. Justo 22, tel 809/586-2210)* in Puerto Plata.

Whale-watching

Whale-watching occurs from January through April in Samaná Bay and the remote Silver Bank.

Windsurfing & Kiteboarding

Strong winds along the Atlantic coast whip up big waves along the Dominican Republic's north coast. Cabarete is acclaimed as one of the world's best places to windsurf and kiteboard.

■ SANTO DOMINGO

For Children

Agua Splash Caribe Ave. España 50, tel 809/766-1928, aguasplashrd.com. Aquatic theme park.

Museo Infantil Trampolín Calle Las Damas, tel 809/685-5551, trampolin.org.do, closed Mon. Fun, educational museum on life and social sciences.

Water Sports

Golden Arrow Technical Diving Center Calle Mustafa Kemal Ataturk 10, tel 809/566-7780, cavediving.com.do. Advanced dive school.

■ THE SOUTHEAST

Caving & Canyoning

Rancho Capote Calle Sánchez 5, Hato Mayor, tel 809/553-2656, cuevafunfun.net. Horseback riding and caving at Cueva Fun-Fún.

Ecotours

Outback Safari Carretera Veron Bávaro km 2.1, Bávaro, tel 809/455-1573, outbacksafaris .com.do. Offers daylong cultural tours of the countryside by open-air truck.

Paraíso Caño Hondo Sabana, tel 829/259-8549, paraisocano hondo.com. Guided tours of Parque Nacional Los Haitises.

Runners Adventures Punta Cana, tel 829/599-7444, runners adventures.com. Country safari combines visits to local farms and a school with zip line adventure.

Golf

Casa de Campo La Romana, tel 809/523-3333, casadecampo .com.do. Several courses, including three designed by Peter Dye. The Dye Fore course has a river gorge. The Links is reminiscent of Scottish links. The 30-year-old Teeth of the Dog Golf Course was recently redesigned.

Catalonia de Toro Golf Club Catalonia Bávaro, Cabeza del Toro, Punta Cana, tel 809/412-0000. Designed by Alberto Sola.

Cocotal Golf & Country Club Playa Bávaro, tel 809/687-4653, cocotalgolf.com. Designed by Spanish golf champion Jose "Pepe" Gancedo.

Guavaberry Golf & Country Club Carretera del Este, Juan Dolio, tel 809/333-4653, guava berrygolf.com.do. Designed by Gary Player, with a waterfall on the 13th hole.

La Cana Golf Course Punta-cana Resort & Club, Punta Cana, tel 809/959-4653, puntacana.com. Pete Dye–designed championship course.

Punta Blanca Golf Course Bávaro, Punta Cana, tel 829/468-4734, punta-blanca.com. Nick Price–designed championship golf course.

Punta Espada Golf Course Cap Cana, Punta Cana, tel 809/227-2262, capcana.com. Jack Nicklaus–designed championship course.

Horseback Rides & Polo
Casa de Campo Equestrian Center Casa de Campo, La Romana, tel 809/523-3333, casadecampo.com.do.

Hotel Rancho La Cueva Playa Limón, Las Lisas, tel 809/519-5271. Horseback trips to Laguna Limón.

Rancho Comatillo Bayaguana, tel 809/547-9004, comatillo.com.do. Horseback rides to Parque Nacional Los Haitises.

Miscellaneous
Zipline Eco Adventure Punta Cana, tel 809/523-3333, capcana.com/vive-cap-cana. Casa de Campo hosts this adrenaline-charged clifftop experience.

Racquet Sports
Casa de Campo Casa de Campo, La Romana, tel 809/523-3333, casadecampo.com.do. Twenty-four-hour tennis courts.

Scuba Diving
Coral Point Diving Bayahibe, tel 829/574-9655, coralpointdiving.com. Offers dives and snorkeling.

Scubafun Calle Principal 28, Bayahibe, tel 809/833-0003, scubafun.info. Scuba trips and certification.

Sportfishing
Marina Casa de Campo Casa de Campo, La Romana, tel 809/523-8646, marinacasadecampo.com.

Mike's Marina Fishing Charters Bávaro, tel 809/729-5164, mikesmarina.info.

Punta Cana Fishing Charters Punta Cana, tel 809/552-1124, fishingpuntacana.com.

Water Sports
All the all-inclusive resort hotels offer water sports. Concession stands at Boca Chica, Juan Dolio, and Playa Bávaro offer speedboat trips, glass-bottom boat rides, and parasailing. Also check out the following:

Bayahibe Fishing Center Bayahibe, tel 809/833-0009, bayahibefishingcentre.com. Boat trips and charters, including to Isla Saona.

Ocean Adventures Punta Cana Playa Bávaro, Bávaro, tel 809/390-6734, oceanadventures-puntacana.com. Speedboat excursions with snorkeling.

◼ LA PENÍNSULA DE SAMANÁ

ATVs
The following offer ATV tours:

IndrinaTour Quad Las Terrenas, tel 829/348-7245, facebook.com/indrinatoursquad. Also catamaran excursions and trips to El Saltón.

Tauro Tours Santa Barbara de Samaná, tel 849/658-8997, taurotours-excursionsamana.com.

Ecotours
Centro para la Conservación y Ecodesarollo de la Bahía de Samaná Ave. La Marina 1, Samaná, tel 809/538-2042. Promotes environmental awareness.

Salto Limón Excursiones El Limón, Las Terrenas, tel 829/342-9976, cascadalimonsamana.com. Hiking, horseback trips, and tours to farms and conservation projects.

Horseback Riding
Salto Limón Excursiones El Limón, Las Terrenas, tel 829/342-9976, cascadalimonsamana.com. Horseback treks to Salto del Limón waterfall.

Kiteboarding
Kite World Las Terrenas, tel 809/769-4978, kiteworldlasterrenas.com.

LT'Kite Las Terrenas, tel 809/801-5671, lasterrenas-kitesurf.com. Kiteboarding lessons.

Miscellaneous
Samaná Zipline El Valle, tel 829/542-3005, samanazipline.com. Twelve lines rush through mountain terrain.

Mountain Biking
Tour Samana With Terry Samaná, tel 809/538-3179, tour samanawithterry.com. Mountain-biking excursions and rental.

Scuba Diving
Grand Paradise Samaná Dive Center Las Galeras, tel 809/571-3690, amhsamarina.com. Scuba diving and PADI certification.

Samaná Diving Calle Francisco Caamaño, Las Terrenas, tel 809/786-1043, samanadiving.com. Scuba diving, snorkeling, and kayak rentals.

Whale-watching
Moto Marina Tours Samaná, tel 809/538-2302, motomarina tours-excursionsamana.com. Whale-watching plus other excursions.

Whale Samaná Calle Mella & Ave. La Marina, Samaná, tel 809/539-2494, whalesamana.com, Jan.–March.

NORTH COAST

Cabarete is the extreme sports center of the Caribbean. Inland, the Cordillera Septentrional offers adventure activities.

Adventure Tours

Alf's Tours Calle Pedro Clisante 12, Sosúa, tel/fax 809/571-9904, alftour.com. Nature excursions as far afield as Salto de Limón and Las Terrenas.

Colonial Tours Tel 809/688-5285, colonialtours.com.do/cayo_arena_puerto_plata.htm. Speedboat and catamaran excursions to Punta Rucia and Cayo Paraíso.

Outback Safari Calle Aldo Moro 6, Puerto Plata, tel 809/320-2525, outbacksafari.com.do. Community visits, hiking, and swimming.

Canyoning

Iguana Mama Calle Principal 74, Cabarete, tel 809/654-2325, iguanamama.com. Five different canyoning experiences are offered, including advanced trips for more experienced canyoneers.

Golf

Playa Dorado Golf Club Playa Dorado, tel 809/320-3472, playadoradagolf.com. Famous Robert Trent Jones Jr.–designed course.

Playa Grande Golf Course Playa Grande, Río San Juan, tel 809/582-0860 ext. 21, playa grande.com. Another Robert Trent Jones Jr. course, considered the Pebble Beach of the Caribbean.

Horseback Riding

Wise Mountain Gaspar Hernández, tel 829/769-5055, wisemountain.org. Rides in the mountains.

Mountain Biking

Iguana Mama Calle Principal 74, Cabarete, tel 809/654-2325, iguanamama.com. Mountain-bike tours, from 7 to 12 days.

Sailing Excursions

Freestyle Catamarans Puerto Plata, tel 892/894-4636, free stylecatamarans.com. Day excursions including snorkeling.

Scuba Diving

Aqua Adventures Sosúa, tel 829/662-8588, scubadivesosua .com.

Merlin Dive Center Playa Sosúa, tel 809/545-0538, dive centermerlin.com. PADI certification and dive trips.

Northern Coast Aquasports Calle Pedro Clisante 8, Sosúa, tel 809/571-1028, northerncoast diving.com.

Sportfishing

Ocean World Marina Cofresí, Puerto Plata, tel 809/970-3373, oceanworldmarina.com. Sportfishing charters.

Surfing

Lessons and board rentals:

Cabarete Surf Camp Calle B, Cabarete, tel 829/548-6655, cabaretesurfcamp.com.

No Work Team Calle Principal, Cabarete, tel 809/571-0825, noworkteamcabarete.com.

Take Off Surfing Playa Encuentro, Cabarete, tel 809/963-7873, 321takeoff.com.

Whale-watching

Aquatic Adventures *(tel 954/382-0024 in the U.S., aquatic adventures.com)* and **Conscious Breath Adventures** *tel 305/753-1732 in the U.S., consciousbreathadventures.com)* offer trips to the Silver Bank from Puerto Plata.

Windsurfing & Kiteboarding

Cabarete is a kiteboarding and windsurfing mecca. The kiteboarding and windsurfing schools at Playa Encuentro and Kite Beach include:

Carib Wind Center Calle Principal, Cabarete, tel 809/571-0640, caribwind.com. Specializes in Laser boats.

Kite Excite Kitebeach Hotel, Cabarete, tel 809/981-0778, kitexcite.com

Laurel Eastman Kiteboarding Aparthotel Caracol, Cabarete, tel 809/571-0564, laureleastman .co.

EL CIBAO

Fishing

One of the best locations is Lago Hatillo, near Cotuí. Bring your own tackle.

Golf

Bella Vista Bonao Golf Club Club Falcondo, Bonao, tel 809/525-3575. Nine-hole course open to the public.

Scuba Diving

Scuba diving is exceptional off Monte Cristi April through November. **Montecristi Diving Center** *(Calle Duarte, Montecristi, tel 849/855-3978, email marcoando68@hotmail.com)* arranges scuba diving.

CORDILLERA CENTRAL

Adventure Tours

Constanza Extreme Constanza, tel 809/480-4837, email constanzaextremeadventure@gmail.com. Activities from ATV quad adventures to paragliding.

Flying Tony Calle Medina 2, Jarabacoa, tel 809/854-5880, flyindr.com. Wide range of adventure excursions, from hiking to tandem trike flights.

Rancho Baiguate Jarabacoa, tel 809/574-6890, rancho baiguate.com. Horseback rides, canyoning, white-water rafting, and four-wheel-drive adventures, plus hikes up Pico Duarte.

Rancho Jarabacoa Jarabacoa, tel 809/222-3202, ranchojarabacoa .com. From canyoning to trekking and Jeep safaris.

Rancho Las Guazaras, Carretera Manabao km 9, Jarabacoa, tel 829/630-4386, mijarabacoa.com. Rafting, horseback trips, and canyoning.

Rancho Macajo 6 miles (10 km) SE of Constanza, tel 809/539-3947 or 809/707-3805, facebook.com/ranchomacajo123. Hiking, horseback rides, and ATV rentals.

Fishing

Several reservoirs in the foothills are stocked with bass, carp, and tilapia. One of the best is Presa de Monción, near Monción. No license is required. Bring your own tackle.

Golf

Jarabacoa Golf Club Quintas de Primavera, tel 809/782-9883, jarabacoagolf.com. Nine-hole course.

Motorcycle Tours

MotoCaribe Motorcycle Tours Calle Las Palmas 3, Jarabacoa, tel 809/574-6507. Tours of the Cordillera Central and further afield.

Paragliding

Flying Tony Calle Medina 2, Jarabacoa, tel 809/854-5880, flyindr.com

Hawk Paragliding School Calle Venecia 1, Jarabacoa, tel 809/878-7366, hawkparagliding.com

Rafting

The following offer organized trips down the Río Yaque del Norte:

Iguana Mama Calle Principal 74, Cabarete, tel 809/654-2325, iguanamama.com

Rancho Baiguate Jarabacoa, tel 809/574-6890, ranchobaiguate .com

Rancho Jarabacoa Jarabacoa, tel 809/222-3202, ranchojarabacoa .com.

▨ THE SOUTHWEST

Ecotours

Colonial Tours Santo Domingo, tel 809/688-5285, colonialtours .com.do/bahiadelasaguilas.htm. Excursions to Bahía de las Águilas.

Ecotour Barahona Calle Enriqillo, Edif. 7, Paraíso, tel 809/682-2454 or 809/243-1190, ecotourbarahona.com. Various ecologically focused excursions.

Ecoviajes La Perla del Mar Tours Pedernales, tel 809/545-0382, bahiadelasaguilas.net/eco viajes.html. Land programs, including birding and caving; plus sea excursions, including to Isla Beata.

Grupo Jaragua Calle Paseo Mondesí 4, Oviedo, tel 809/472-1036, grupojaragua.org.do.

Rancho Platon Paraíso, tel 809/383-1836, ranchoplaton.com. Wide range of excursions, from Bahía de las Águilas and Laguna de Oviedo to Parque Eólico Juancho–Los Cocos wind farm.

Rafting & Tubing

Rancho Platon Paraíso, tel 809/683-1836, email rancho .platon@gmail.com. Rafting and tubing adventure in the Sierra de Baoruco.

Entertainment

Santo Domingo has a thriving art scene, and it and most towns throughout the country have plenty of bars and discos, as do the tourist resorts. However, the scene in Boca Chica and Sosúa can be seamy at night. Most discos and nightclubs don't open their doors until 10 p.m. All-inclusive beach resorts provide nightly entertainment, theater style. Vegas-style revues—many quite risqué—are standard fare, even at highbrow hotels. Larger resort hotels usually have discos plus several bars. Local youth typically meet for dancing at their local "car wash," a mixture of a real car wash and a bar-disco. Events are listed in the daily newspapers as well as *Diario Libre,* available free in shops.

■ SANTO DOMINGO

Santo Domingo takes its role as capital city seriously with everything from theater and classical concerts to casinos and hip discos. Many casinos are associated with the high-rise hotels, while some of the most atmospheric bars are found in the Zona Colonial.

The Arts

Casa de Teatro Calle Arzobispo Meriño 110, tel 809/689-3430, casadeteatro.org. Theater, art gallery, and performance space with weekly events.

Centro Cultural Español Calle Arzobispo Meriño & Calle Arzobispo Portes, tel 809/686-8212, ccesd.org. Musical, film, and theatrical events.

Orquesta Sinfónica Nacional Ave. Eduardo Vicisoso 1, tel 809/535-8690, sinfonia.org.do. Classical concerts May through October.

Teatro Nacional Plaza de la Cultura, Ave. Máximo Gómez 35, tel 809/687-3191, teatro.com.do. Theater, exhibitions, dance, and music.

Baseball

Estadio Quisqueya 2nd fl. Ensanche La Fe, tel 809/567-6371 or 809/563-5085, lidom .com. A 14,000-seat stadium that hosts some of the best players outside the United States.

Casinos

Casino Diamante Meliá Santo Domingo Hotel, Ave. George Washington 365, tel 809/682-2102.

Occidental El Embajador Hotel & Casino Ave. Sarasota 65, tel 809/221-2131

Renaissance Jaragua Hotel & Casino del Caribe Ave. George Washington 367, tel 809/221-2222. The largest casino in town.

Cinemas

Broadway Cinema Plaza Central, Ave. 27 de Febrero & Calle Winston Churchill, tel 809/872-1000. Alternative films, as well as Hollywood hits.

Malecón Center Cinemas Ave. George Washington 457, tel 809/688-6665. Close to major hotels.

Horse Racing

Hipódromo V Centenario Ave. Las Américas km 11.5, tel 809/689-6076, hvc.com.do. Horse racing Tuesday, Thursday, and Saturday.

Nightlife

Nightclubs are concentrated in the Zona Colonial and Naco districts. Some don't get going until well past midnight; many bars and upscale restaurants also feature live music.

Cameroon Cigar Lounge Ave. George Washington 25, tel 809/686-2940. Classy and intimate lounge-bar with shop.

El Sartén Calle Hostos 153, Zona Colonial, tel 809/686-9621. Merengue, *guaracha*, and other traditional music forms.

La Guácara Taína Paseo de los Indios & Ave. Cayetano, tel 809/995-5853, guacarataina.net, closed Mon. The city's most atmospheric nightclub with cabaret, fashion shows, and live merengue bands inside a cave.

Mamma Club Gustavo Meija Ricart 75, tel 829/569-6785, facebook.com/MammaClubRD. High-energy party spot.

MINT Napolitano Ave. George Washington 51, tel 809/687-1131, napolitano.com.do. Popular hotel disco bar.

Special Events

Santo Domingo de Fiesta Plaza de España, Zona Colonial, May–Dec. The Ballet Folklórico Nacional performs free Friday and Saturday nights.

■ THE SOUTHEAST

The Arts

Altos de Chavón Amphitheater La Romana, tel 809/523-8011 or 800/336-5520, casadecampo .com.do. Greek-style amphitheater hosting concerts, from classical to rock.

School of Design Altos de Chavón, La Romana, tel 809/523-8011, casadecampo.com.do/altos-de-chavon. Courses in fine art and design.

Baseball

Campo Las Palmas Guerra, tel 809/526-5249. Spring training camp of the Los Angeles Dodgers.

Estadio de Béisbol Francisco **Micheli** Ave. Abreu *&* Calle Luperón, La Romana, tel 809/556-6188, lostorosdeleste.com. Hosts La Romana Azucareros, mid-November to February.

Estadio Tetelo Vargas Ave. Circunvalación *&* Carretera Mella, San Pedro de Macorís, tel 809/529-3618, estrellasorientales.com.do. Hosts the Estrellas Orientales, mid-November to February.

Casinos
Barceló Bávaro Casino, Barceló Bávaro, Bávaro, tel 809/686-5797, barcelo.com

Hard Rock Hotel *&* Casino Macao, tel 809/687-0000, hardrockhotelpuntacana.com

Nightlife
In the Bayahibe and Costa del Coco area, nightlife centers on the all-inclusive resorts. Most sell night passes for nonguests.

Bávaro Beach Resort Barceló Bávaro, Palace Deluxe, Bávaro, tel 809/686-5797. Upscale disco open to the public. Opens 11 p.m.

Disco Club Mangu Occidental Gran Flamenco Hotel, Bávaro, tel 809/221-8787. Dressy disco for serious dancers.

Kviar Disco Carretera Cabeza del Toro, Punta Cana, tel 809/769-3036, kviar.do. The wildest nightspot for miles.

Oro Nightclub Hard Rock Hotel *&* Casino, Macao, tel 809/687-0000, hardrockhotelpuntacana.com. Late-night dancing at its best.

Strikers Sports Bar *&* Bowling Center Barceló Bávaro Beach, Bávaro, tel 809/686-5797.

▨ LA PENÍNSULA DE SAMANÁ

Casinos
Hotel Casino Niza Las Terrenas, tel 809/204-6154, hotelcasinoniza.com

Nightlife
The Malecón in Santa Bárbara de Samaná becomes an informal alfresco venue for music and dance on weekends.

Gaia Nightclub Pueblo de los Pescadores, Las Terrenas, tel 809/914-1023

Lazy Dog Beach Bar *&* Grill Pueblo de los Pescadores, Las Terrenas, tel 809/853-4721. A great place for postprandial drinks and hookah pipes.

▨ NORTH COAST

Casinos
Casino El Millón Hotel Riu Bachata, Bahía de Maimón, Puerto Plata, tel 809/320-1010

Nightlife
Sosúa has German beer halls and open-air bars; most are seamy. Cabarete is far more pleasant, with delightful bar-restaurants spilling onto the beach.

José O'Shay's Irish Beach Pub Calle Principal, Cabarete, tel 809/571-0775. Popular beach bar known for Russell White's live acoustic guitar.

Kviar Show Disco *&* Casino Carretera Luperón km 4.5, Puerto Plata, tel 809/964-3575, kviar.com.do. Sensual shows at this high-octane nightclub.

Lax Calle Principal, Cabarete, tel 829/915-4842, laxojo.com. The hottest nightclub for miles. Special theme nights.

Show Bravíssimo Ocean World, Puerto Plata, tel. 809/291-1000, oceanworld.net. High-octane cabaret.

Theme Parks
Ocean World Adventure Park Cofresí, Puerto Plata, tel 809/291-1000, oceanworld.net. Marine theme park where visitors can swim with dolphins.

▨ EL CIBAO

The Arts
Centro de la Cultura de Santiago Calle del Sol *&* Antonio Guzmán, Santiago, tel 809/856-7326. Cultural events.

Centro León Ave. 27 de Febrero, Santiago, tel 809/582-2315, centroleon.org.do, closed Mon. Exhibitions, lectures, concerts, and films.

Gran Teatro del Cibao Ave. Las Carreras 1, Santiago, tel 809/583-1150. Concerts, exhibitions, and dance.

Museo Cultural Fortaleza San Luís, Ave. Emiliano Tardiff *&* Calle San Luis, Santiago de los Caballeros. Exhibitions, lectures, and musical events.

Casinos
Casino Gran Almirante Ave. Estrella Sadhalá *&* Calle Santiago de los Caballeros, Santiago, tel 809/580-1992, hodelpa.com

Nightlife
Santiago is a hot spot for discos and lively bars.

Cosmopolitan Bar Gran Almirante Hotel *&* Casino, Ave. Estrella Sadhalá *&* Calle Santiago de los Caballeros, Santiago, tel 809/580-1992. Chic contemporary decor for the martini crowd.

Kukaramacara Country Bar *&* Restaurant Ave. Francia 7, Santiago, tel 809/241-3143. Western-themed bar with cold beer and live music.

▨ THE SOUTHWEST

Nightlife
Tupinamba Ave. Independencia 12, San Juan de la Maguana, tel 809/557-2166. Popular disco.

Festivals

Almost every town in the country celebrates Carnaval, usually held in the last week of February, coinciding with Día de la Independencia on February 27. Dates vary town to town. During Easter celebrations, *vodu* (voodoo) ceremonies are often held in towns near the Haitian border and in Haitian communities in the sugar plantations. Similar ceremonies are also held on November 1 for All Souls' Day. Festivals are listed in the daily newspapers plus *Diario Libre,* available free in stores and other outlets.

■ SANTO DOMINGO

Carnaval (Feb.) carnaval.com.do. Colorful, lively parade along Avenida George Washington.
Día de la Independencia (Feb. 27) The culmination of the Carnaval period with streets floats, a parade, and music.
Music Festival (mid-March) Ten days of classical music concerts. Biannual.
Merengue Festival (late July–Aug.) Concerts along the seafront Malecón.
Restoration Day (Aug. 16) Plaza de España and Plaza Independencia host parties to celebrate the country's "second independence."

■ THE SOUTHEAST

Virgen de Altagracia pilgrimage (Jan. 21) Higüey
Carnaval (1st week of March) Punta Cana. Colorful floats and costume parades, plus street parties.
Fiesta Patronal de San Pedro Apóstol (June 29) San Pedro de Macorís. Patron saint festival.
Festival of the Bulls (Aug.) Higüey. Cowboy passions hit fever pitch.
Fiesta Patronal San André (Nov.) Boca Chica. Patron saint's festival.

■ LA PENÍNSULA DE SAMANÁ

Día de Santa Bárbara (Dec. 4) Santa Bárbara de Samaná.

Processions featuring *bamboula* music.

■ NORTH COAST

Master of the Ocean (Feb.) Cabarete, masteroftheocean .com. Kiteboarding, windsurfing, and surfing triathlon competition.
Fiesta Patronal de San Felipe Apóstol (May 3) Puerto Plata. Party to celebrate the town's patron saint.
Puerto Plata Cultural Festival (June) Puerto Plata. Week-long festivities.
Merengue Festival (Sept.–Oct.) Puerto Plata. Weeklong street parties along the Malecón.
Dominican Jazz Festival (Oct. or Nov.) Puerto Plata & Sosúa, tel 809/571-0882 or 809/706-9883, drjazzfestival .com. International and local celebrities.
Festival de Cine Global (Nov.) Puerto Plata and other cities, tel 809/685-9966, festival decineglobal.org. International movies.

■ EL CIBAO

Carnaval (Feb.) La Vega, carnaval vegano.do. The most colorful Carnaval in the country, with a fantastic display of the devil masks for which this town is known.
Carnaval (Feb.) Monte Cristi. Rival factions of town battle it out with fireworks and water bombs.

Carnaval (Feb.) Santiago, carnaval desantiago.org. The largest of the country's Carnavales, with floats, parades, beauty contests, and dramatic devil masks on display.
Fiesta Patronal de Fernando Rey (May 30) Monte Cristi. Honors the 16th-century Spanish monarch and town patron saint.
Fiesta Patronal de Santiago Apóstol (July 22) Santiago. Patron saint festival.

■ THE SOUTHWEST

Fiesta Patriótica de la Batalla de Azua del 19 de Marzo (March 19) Azua. Celebration of the Dominican Republic's victory over Haiti in 1844.
Expo Mango (June) Baní, expomango.org. Mango festival in Plazoleta Ayuntamiento.
Fiesta Patronal (June) San Juan de la Maguana. Folkloric religious festival.
Fiesta Patronal (mid-June) Baní. Musicians perform *sarandunga,* an Afro-Latin dance form unique to the town.
Procession of Nuestra Señora de Regla (Nov. 21) Baní. Images of the town's patron saint are paraded.
Fiesta Patronal (Dec. 13) Las Matas de Farfán. Procession honoring Santa Lucía.

INDEX

ILLUSTRATIONS CREDITS

All photographs by Gilles Mingasson/Reportage by Getty Images unless otherwise noted below:

Cover, Ian Cumming/Getty Images; spine, espiegle/Getty Images; 8, Radovan/Shutterstock; 26-27, The Art Gallery Collection/Alamy Stock Photo; 33, Leonard McCombe/Time Life Pictures/Getty Images; 34, Courtesy Carnival Cruise Line; 41, Bystrova M.B./Shutterstock; 45, World Pictures/Alamy Stock Photo; 60, Grete Howard; 94, Jonathan Blair/National Geographic Creative; 95, Jonathan Blair/Getty Images; 109, Raul Touzon/National Geographic Creative; 123, Westend61/Getty Images; 155, Tom Bean; 170, M. Timothy O'Keefe/Alamy Stock Photo; 171, Irène Alastruey/age fotostock; 190, Miguel A. Landestoy.

National Geographic

TRAVELER

Dominican Republic

THIRD EDITION

Since 1888, the National Geographic Society has funded more than 12,000 research, exploration, and preservation projects around the world. National Geographic Partners distributes a portion of the funds it receives from your purchase to National Geographic Society to support programs including the conservation of animals and their habitats.

National Geographic Partners
1145 17th Street NW
Washington, DC 20036-4688 USA

Become a member of National Geographic and activate your benefits today at natgeo.com/jointoday.

For information about special discounts for bulk purchases, please contact National Geographic Books Special Sales: specialsales@natgeo.com

For rights or permissions inquiries, please contact National Geographic Books Subsidiary Rights: bookrights@natgeo.com

Cutaway illustrations drawn by Maltings Partnership, Derby, England

ISBN: 978-1-4262-1768-5

Printed in Hong Kong

16/THK/1

THE COMPLETE TRAVEL EXPERIENCE

With more than 75 destinations around the globe; available wherever

books are sold and at www.shopng.com/travelerguides

TRIPS
natgeoexpeditions.com

MAGAZINE

for iPhone®,
iPod touch®,
and iPad®

APPS